A FEW QUESTIONS TO ASK YOURSELF

—Are you a victim? A prosecutor? A rescuer?

—Whose lifescript are you following?

—What part of you is a child? A parent? An adult?

—How much of your relationships with others is superficial? How much truly intimate?

—Do you stroke people positively to give them a feeling of OKness, or do you discount them with negative stroking?

—Are you a winner or a loser?

When you understand these questions, and begin to find their answers, you will be well on the way to becoming what you were always meant to be—

BORN TO WIN

"Enriching, stimulating, rewarding . . . for anyone interested in understanding himself, his relationships with others and his goals."   —KANSAS CITY TIMES

"The most exciting contribution to self-understanding."
      —PROGRESSIVE WOMAN

DR. MURIEL JAMES is a licensed marriage and family counselor, an international consultant in human relations to government agencies, school systems, and business, and an adviser to the California Commission on The Status of Women. Dr. James received her doctorate from the University of California at Berkeley. She is the author of TRANS-ACTIONAL ANALYSIS FOR MOMS AND DADS, BORN TO LOVE, and THE OK BOSS, and is the co-author of WINNING WITH PEOPLE and A NEW SELF.

DR. DOROTHY JONGEWARD earned her Ph.D. at California Western University, and is a Teaching Member of the International Transactional Analysis Association, a Professor of Human Behavior and Transactional Analysis at California American University, and a life member of the California Association of Marriage and Family Counselors. Dr. Jongeward is the author of EVERYBODY WINS: Transactional Analysis Applied to Organizations, and is the co-author of AFFIRMATIVE ACTION FOR WOMEN, WINNING WITH PEOPLE, and WOMEN AS WINNERS

P9-DGU-564

BORN TO WIN

Transactional Analysis with Gestalt Experiments

Muriel James
Dorothy Jongeward

Human Relations and
Communications Consultants

A SIGNET BOOK

SIGNET
Published by the Penguin Group
Penguin Books USA Inc., 375 Hudson Street,
New York, New York 10014, U.S.A.
Penguin Books Ltd, 27 Wrights Lane,
London W8 5TZ, England
Penguin Books Australia Ltd, Ringwood,
Victoria, Australia
Penguin Books Canada Ltd, 2801 John Street,
Markham, Ontario, Canada L3R 1B4
Penguin Books (N.Z.) Ltd, 182–190 Wairau Road,
Auckland 10, New Zealand

Penguin Books Ltd, Registered Offices:
Harmondsworth, Middlesex, England

Published by Signet, an imprint of New American Library,
a division of Penguin Books USA Inc.

This is an authorized reprint of an edition published by Addison-Wesley Publishing
Company, Inc. The Addison-Wesley edition was published simultaneously in Canada.

First Signet Printing, July, 1978
25 24 23 22 21 20 19 18 17

 REGISTERED TRADEMARK—MARCA REGISTRADA

Printed in the United States of America

*Dedicated in fond memory
to our friend and teacher: Eric Berne, M.D.*

Foreword

It has been said that the psychotherapist's job is to put himself out of business. Research and writing efforts in the field are directed toward curing patients faster, in a way that is fun, economical, and long lasting. The ideal in therapy is the one-session cure, the ideal in writing is the one-book cure. So much of the writing in psychology is written like hieroglyphics on the Rosetta Stone that a Jean-François Champollion therapist or writer is invariably needed for the deciphering and application.

Born To Win bypasses this middle-man system and presents psychological insights in an immediately recognizable way. It is in line with the '70's trend of making all information more readily available to people, and the "Aquarian Age" of bringing together information from both worlds. Humanistic Man, interested in personal growth and higher levels of awareness, can now handle information intelligently that before he could handle only intellectually.

Born to Win seems free of the codifying "games writers play." In the writing style there is a patience, thoroughness, clarity, and "giving" that is unique in the field. Here the needs of the reader are met, not discounted. The numerous examples should be meaningful to reader and student alike, even to those programmed for minimal insight. It has the clearest use of examples I have seen in any book, and I see it as a landmark book in the field of psychological writing.

(Assistant Clinical Professor of Psychiatry, University of California Medical Center San Francisco, California)

Stephen B. Karpman, M.D.
San Francisco
July 1971

"I think

    one must finally take one's life

        in one's arms."

—————————————————————

from *After the Fall*

Arthur Miller

Preface

Currently we find a resurgence of interest in the "why" and "how" of human behavior and in the search for meaning in human existence. Bosses study how to work with subordinates, parents take courses on rearing children, husbands and wives learn to talk to each other and how to "fight fair," teachers study how to cope with emotional disturbances in their students and how to reverse the effects of deprivation.

Along with their interest in material goods and technology, many people are concerning themselves with what it means to be human. As one young male executive with a large firm put it, "I have a Master's degree in accounting. When I went to work with this firm, I thought my problems were going to be accounting problems. But they're not. They're 'people' problems."

Two new approaches to understanding people are transactional analysis as developed by Dr. Eric Berne and gestalt therapy as interpreted by Dr. Frederick Perls. This book is primarily concerned with our interpretation of transactional analysis and its application to the daily life of the average person. Gestalt-oriented experiments are used to supplement the transactional analysis theory. Case illustrations are drawn from our experiences as teachers and counselors.

Transactional analysis gives people a rational method for analyzing and understanding behavior; gestalt therapy gives people a useful method for discovering the fragmented parts of their personality, integrating them, and developing a core of self-confidence. Both methods are concerned with discovering and fostering awareness, self-responsibility, and genuineness. Both methods are concerned with what is happening *now*.

We believe this book can be used as a text or as a study guide for those interested in personality theory and interpersonal relationships. It is intended to be of value to professionals in the mental health fields, to those in management and education, and to lay persons who are interested in new ways of understanding themselves. It is definitely not meant to take the place of professional psychotherapy. Seriously disturbed people need outside help as well as their own total commitment to get well.

We are convinced that people are not totally at the mercy of either their heredity or their environment. They can modify both. Our hope is that this book will increase your awareness of the real power you have to direct your own life, to make decisions, to develop your own ethical system, to enhance the lives of others, and to understand that you were born to win.

We extend our sincere appreciation to the many who have influenced and assisted us. It would be impossible to list them all by name. We wish to give special recognition to Dr. Eric Berne and Dr. Frederick Perls for their teaching and writings, and to the International Transactional Analysis Association* and Dr. Kenneth Everts, its former president.

We want to express our appreciation to our students and counselees for their trust in us and for what we have learned from each other.

And we thank our husbands and children for their patience, love, and encouragement.

Muriel James   **Dorothy Jongeward**
Lafayette, California   *May 1971*   Orinda, California

---

*Information concerning training in TA may be directed to the International Transactional Analysis Association, 1772 Vallejo Street, San Francisco, CA 94123. This Association publishes a directory of affiliates and geographical list of *accredited* members and also has many TA publications available for sale.

Contents

Contents

Photo Credits

Cover photo: John Pearson

Plate I, pages 20-21: All three photos by Sherry Morgan

Plate II, pages 24-25: All three photos by Sherry Morgan

Plate III, pages 40-41: page 40, Dorothy Jongeward; page 41, top, John Pearson; bottom, Sherry Morgan

Plate IV, pages 62 and 63: page 62, top, John James; bottom, John Pearson; page 63, top, John Pearson; bottom, Dorothy Jongeward

Plate V, pages 67-69: page 67, top, John Pearson; bottom, Dorothy Jongeward; page 68, top, Eric W. Cheney; bottom, John Pearson; page 69, top, John Pearson; bottom, Eric W. Cheney

Plate VI, pages 100-101: page 100, top, Eric W. Cheney; bottom, Dorothy Jongeward; page 101, top, Dorothy Jongeward; center, John Pearson; bottom, Sherry Morgan

Plate VII, pages 124-125: page 124, Muriel James; page 125, top, Eric W. Cheney; bottom, Daniel Buop

Plate VIII, pages 128-129: page 128, top, Daniel Buop; bottom, Sherry Morgan; page 129, top, Sherry Morgan; bottom, Sherry Morgan

Plate IX, pages 142-144: page 142, top, Wayne Miller; bottom, Muriel James; page 143, top, John James; bottom, John Pearson; page 144, top, Wayne Miller; bottom, Wayne Miller

Plate X, pages 146-147: All four photos by John Pearson

Plate XI, pages 150-151: page 150, top, Dorothy Jongeward; bottom, John Pearson; page 151, top, Eric W. Cheney; bottom, John Pearson

Plate XII, pages 154-155: All four photos by John Pearson

Plate XIII, page 160: Left, Wayne Miller; upper right, John Pearson; lower right, Wayne Miller

Plate XIV, pages 164-165: page 164, top, Dorothy Jongeward; bottom, John Pearson; page 165, top, Wayne Miller; bottom, Daniel Buop

Plate XV, pages 184-185: page 184, top, Dorothy Jongeward; cen-

ter, John James; bottom, Daniel Buop; page 185, top, Dorothy
Jongeward; bottom, Dorothy Jongeward

Plate XVI, pages 224-225: All three photos by Sherry Morgan

Plate XVII, pages 228-229: All four photos by Sherry Morgan

Plate XVIII, pages 270-271: page 270, top, John Pearson; bottom,
Sherry Morgan; page 271, top, John Pearson; bottom, Eric W.
Cheney

Plate XIX, pages 276-277: page 276, John Pearson; page 277, top,
Daniel Buop; bottom, Sherry Morgan

Plate XX, pages 294-295: page 294, top, Daniel Buop; bottom,
John Pearson; page 295, top, Sherry Morgan; bottom, John James

Plate XXI, page 303: Photo by John James

1

Winners and Losers

You cannot teach a man anything.
You can only help him discover it within himself.
  Galileo

Each human being is born as something new, something that never existed before. Each is born with the capacity to win at life. Each person has a unique way of seeing, hearing, touching, tasting, and thinking. Each has his or her own unique potentials— capabilities and limitations. Each can be a significant, thinking, aware, and creative being—a productive person, a winner.

The words "winner" and "loser" have many meanings. When we refer to a person as a winner, we do not mean one who makes someone else lose. To us, a winner is one who responds authentically by being credible, trustworthy, responsive, and genuine, both as an individual and as a member of a society. A loser is one who fails to respond authentically. Martin Buber makes this distinction as he retells the old story of the rabbi who, on his deathbed, is asked if he is ready for the world to come. The rabbi says yes. After all, he will not be asked, "Why were you not Moses?" He will only be asked, "Why were you not yourself?" [1]

Few people are one hundred percent winners or one hundred percent losers. It's a matter of degree. However, once a person is on the road to being a winner, his or her chances are greater for becoming even more so. This book is intended to facilitate the journey.

WINNERS

Winners have different potentials. Achievement is not the most important thing. Authenticity is. The authentic person experiences self-reality by knowing, being, and becoming a credible, responsive person. Authentic people actualize their own unprecedented uniqueness and appreciate the uniqueness of others.

Authentic persons—winners—do not dedicate their lives to a concept of what they imagine they *should* be; rather, they are themselves and as such do not use their energy putting on a performance, maintaining pretence, and manipulating others. Winners can reveal themselves instead of projecting images that please, provoke, or entice others. They are aware that there is a difference between being loving and acting loving, between being stupid and acting stupid, between being knowledgeable and acting knowledgeable. Winners do not need to hide behind a mask. They throw off unrealistic self-images of inferiority or superiority. Autonomy does not frighten winners.

All people have moments of autonomy, if only fleeting. However, winners are able to sustain their autonomy over ever-increasing periods of time. Winners may lose ground occasionally and may even fail. Yet, in spite of setbacks winners maintain a basic self-confidence.

Winners are not afraid to do their own thinking and to use their own knowledge. They can separate facts from opinion and don't pretend to have all the answers. They listen to others, evaluate what they say, but come to their own conclusions. Although winners can admire and respect other people, they are not totally defined, demolished, bound, or awed by them.

Winners do not play "helpless," nor do they play the blaming game. Instead, they assume responsibility for their own lives. They do not give others a false authority over them. Winners are their own bosses and know it.

A winner's timing is right. Winners respond appropriately to the situation. Their responses are related to the message sent and preserve the significance, worth, well-being, and dignity of the people involved. Winners know that for everything there is a season and for every activity a time.

A time to be aggressive and a time to be passive,
A time to be together and a time to be alone,

A time to fight and a time to love,
A time to work and a time to play,
A time to cry and a time to laugh,
A time to confront and a time to withdraw,
A time to speak and a time to be silent,
A time to hurry and a time to wait.

To winners, time is precious. Winners don't kill it, but live it here and now. Living in the now does not mean that winners foolishly ignore their own past history or fail to prepare for the future. Rather, winners know their past, are aware and alive in the present, and look forward to the future.

Winners learn to know their feelings and limitations and to be unafraid of them. Winners are not stopped by their own contradictions and ambivalences. Being authentic, they know when they are angry and can listen when others are angry with them. Winners can give and receive affection. Winners are able to love and be loved.

Winners can be spontaneous. They do not have to respond in predetermined, rigid ways, but can change their plans when the situation calls for it. Winners have a zest for life, enjoying work, play, food, other people, sex, and the world of nature. Without guilt they enjoy their own accomplishments. Without envy they enjoy the accomplishments of others.

Although winners can freely enjoy themselves, they can also postpone enjoyment, can discipline themselves in the present to enhance their enjoyment in the future. Winners are not afraid to go after what they want, but they do so in appropriate ways. Winners do not get their security by controlling others. They do not set themselves up to lose.

A winner cares about the world and its peoples. A winner is not isolated from the general problems of society, but is concerned, compassionate, and committed to improving the quality of life. Even in the face of national and international adversity, a winner's self-image is not one of a powerless individual. A winner works to make the world a better place.

LOSERS

Although people are born to win, they are also born helpless and totally dependent on their environment. Winners successfully make the transition from total helplessness to independence, and then to interdependence. Losers do not. Somewhere along the line they begin to avoid becoming responsible for their own lives.

As we have noted, few people are total winners or losers. Most of them are winners in some areas of their lives and losers in others. Their winning or losing is influenced by what happens to them in childhood.

A lack of response to dependency needs, poor nutrition, brutality, unhappy relationships, disease, continuing disappointments, inadequate physical care, and traumatic events are among the many experiences that contribute to making people losers. Such experiences interrupt, deter, or prevent the normal progress toward autonomy and self-actualization. To cope with negative experiences, children learn to manipulate themselves and others. These manipulative techniques are hard to give up later in life and often become set patterns. Winners work to shed them. Losers hang on to them.

Some losers speak of themselves as successful but anxious, successful but trapped, or successful but unhappy. Others speak of themselves as totally beaten, without purpose, unable to move, half dead, or bored to death. Losers may not recognize that, for the most part, they have been building their own cages, digging their own graves, and boring themselves.

A loser seldom lives in the present, but instead destroys the present by focusing on past memories or future expectations. The loser who lives in the past dwells on the good old days or on past personal misfortunes. Nostalgically, the loser either clings to the way things "used to be" or bemoans his or her bad luck. The loser is self-pitying and shifts the responsibility for an unsatisfactory life onto others. Blaming others and excusing oneself are often part of the loser's games. A loser who lives in the past may lament *if only*:

"If only I had married someone else . . ."
"If only I had a different job . . ."
"If only I had finished school . . ."
"If only I had been handsome (beautiful) . . ."
"If only my spouse had stopped drinking . . ."
"If only I had been born rich . . ."
"If only I had had better parents . . ."

People who live in the future may dream of some miracle after which they can "live happily ever after." Rather than pursuing their own lives, losers wait—wait for the magical rescue. How wonderful life will be *when:*

"When Prince Charming or the ideal woman finally comes . . ."
"When school is over . . ."
"When the kids grow up . . ."
"When that new job opens . . ."
"When the boss dies . . ."
"When my ship comes in . . ."

In contrast to those who live with the delusion of a magical rescue, some losers live constantly under the dread of future catastrophe. They conjure up expectations of *what if:*

"What if I lose my job . . ."
"What if I lose my mind . . ."
"What if something falls on me . . ."
"What if I break my leg . . ."
"What if they don't like me . . ."
"What if I make a mistake . . ."

By continually focusing on the future, these losers experience anxiety in the present. They are anxious over what they anticipate —either real or imagined—tests, bill paying, a love affair, crisis, illness, retirement, the weather, and so forth. Persons overly involved with imaginings let the actual possibilities of the moment pass them by. They occupy their minds with material that is irrelevant to the current situation. Anxiety tunes out current reality. Consequently, these people are unable to see for themselves, hear for themselves, feel for themselves, or taste, touch, or think for themselves.

Unable to bring the full potential of their senses into the immediate situation, losers' perceptions are incorrect or incomplete. They see themselves and others through a prismlike distortion. Their ability to deal effectively with the real world is hampered.

Losers spend much of their time play-acting, pretending, manipulating, and perpetuating old roles from childhood. Losers invest their energy in maintaining masks, often projecting a phony front. Karen Horney writes, "The fostering of the phony self is always at the expense of the real self, the latter being treated with disdain, at best like a poor relative" [2]. To the play-acting loser, performance is often more important than reality.

Losers repress their capacities to express spontaneously and appropriately the full range of possible behavior. They may be unaware of other options for a more productive, self-fulfilling life path. Losers are afraid to try new things and instead maintain their own status quo. Losers are repeaters, repeating not only their own mistakes, but often those of their families and culture as well.

A loser has difficulty giving and receiving affection and does not enter into intimate, honest, direct relationships with others. Instead, a loser tries to manipulate them into living up to his or her expectations. Losers' energies are often channeled into living up to the expectations of others [3].

People who are losers are not using their intellect appropriately, but instead are misusing it to rationalize and intellectualize. When rationalizing, losers give excuses to make their actions seem plausible. When intellectualizing, they try to snow others with verbiage. Consequently, much of their potential remains dormant, unrealized, and unrecognized. Like the frog-prince in the fairy tale, losers are spellbound and live their lives being something they aren't meant to be.

TOOLS FOR CHANGE

A person who wants to discover and change a "losing streak," who wants to become more like the winner he or she was born to be, can use gestalt-type experiments and transactional analysis to make change happen. These are two new and exciting psychological approaches to human problems. The first was given new life by Dr. Frederick Perls; the second was developed by Dr. Eric Berne.

Perls was born in Germany in 1893 and left the country when Hitler came into power. Berne was born in Montreal in 1910. Both men were trained as Freudian psychoanalysts; both broke away from the use of orthodox psychoanalysis; both found their greatest popularity and acceptance in the United States. We have studied with both Berne and Perls, and we like their methods because their methods work.

In this book we hope to show how the theory of transactional analysis, *supplemented* by experiments we have personally designed and others which were derived from gestalt therapy, can be used to develop and extend a person's "winning streak." We believe that everyone—at least in some phase of his or her humanness—has the potential to be a winner: to be a real person, an alive person, an aware person.

FREDERICK PERLS AND GESTALT THERAPY

Gestalt psychology is not new. Gestalt therapy is new. Dr. Frederick Perls, a Freudian analyst of many years, used some of the principles and discoveries of gestalt psychology to invent and develop gestalt therapy. "Gestalt" is a German word for which there is no exact English equivalent; it means, roughly, an organized whole.

Perls perceives many personalities as lacking wholeness, as being fragmented. He claims people are often aware of only parts of themselves rather than of the whole self. For example, a woman may not know or want to admit that sometimes she acts like her mother; a man may not know or want to admit that sometimes he wants to cry like a baby.

The aim of gestalt therapy is to help people become whole—to help them become aware of, admit to, reclaim, and integrate their fragmented parts. Integration helps a person make the transition from dependency to self-sufficiency; from authoritarian outer support to authentic inner support [4]. Concretely, having inner support means that a person is self-reliant. Such a person is no longer compelled to depend on a spouse, academic degrees, job title, therapist, bank account, and so forth for support. Instead, he or she discovers that the needed capacities are internal and that they can be depended on. According to Perls, a person who refuses to do this is neurotic:

I call neurotic any man
Who uses his potential to
Manipulate the others
Instead of growing up himself.
He takes control, gets power-mad,
And mobilizes friends and kin
In places where he's impotent
To use his own resources.
He does so 'cause he cannot stand
Such tensions and frustrations
That go along with growing up.

And: taking risks is risky too
Too fearful to consider. [5]

Some of the methods common in gestalt therapy are role-playing, exaggeration of symptoms or behavior, use of fantasy, the principle of staying with the immediate moment, which is the experience of "being in the now," the use of the word "I" rather than "it" as a way to assume responsibility for behavior, learning how to talk *to* rather than *at* someone, becoming aware of bodily senses, and learning to "stay with feelings" until they are understood and integrated [6].

The most difficult method for many people to understand is Perls' specialized form of role-playing. Role-playing is not new to psychological practice. As early as 1908 Dr. Jacob Moreno was working on this method from which have emerged many forms of group encounter and treatment. He coined the word "psycho-drama" in 1919 to describe how he directed people to take on the identities of others and to act out their problems from different points of view [7].

In contrast to Moreno, Perls rarely uses other people to role-play with his patient. He claims these others would "bring in *their own* fantasies, *their own* interpretations" [8]. Therefore, Perls requires the patient to imagine and act out all the parts. He focuses on *how* the patient is acting *now*, not on the *why* of the patient's behavior.

Although many arrangements can be used for this kind of role-playing, the chair technique is uniquely Perls'. His props are (1) the "hot-seat," a chair for the patient who chooses to "work," (2) an empty chair facing the patient onto which the patient projects his or her many selves, and (3) a box of tissues for runny noses and tearful eyes.

The "hot-seat" method was used with a teacher who described herself as friendly and helpful yet couldn't understand why she had no close friends. Although she denied any angry feelings, common expressions she used were "you'll be sorry for that" and "I feel sorry for anyone like you." Others heard this as threatening and hostile.

When this woman role-played her fragmented parts, she acted her "friendly self" from the hot-seat and imagined her "angry self" on the opposite chair. She switched chairs when she switched roles and slowly began a dialogue:

Hot-seat: I don't know why I'm here. I'm always friendly and helpful.

Opposite chair: You do too know why you're here. You don't have any friends.

Hot-seat: I can't understand it. I'm always doing things for people.

Opposite chair: That's the trouble with you. Always being "helpful Hannah." You have everybody obligated to you.

In a short time the teacher's voice grew shrill and loud. When she was in the hot-seat, she struck out against the "helpful Hannah" comment. Amazed at her own aggressiveness, she commented in disbelief, "I never knew I could feel so angry." Although other people had seen this aspect of her personality quite often, this was the first time she admitted to her opposites of anger and helpfulness—her polarities.

Sometimes people are aware of only *one* of their poles, as in the case of the teacher above. Sometimes they may be aware of both and say, "I'm either as high as a kite or weighted down with depression," or "I'm either angry and aggressive, or afraid and full of doubt."

A person whose personality is fragmented by polarization operates in an either/or manner—either arrogant or worthless, helpless or tyrannical, wicked or righteous. A person who is stuck at the impasse of such opposing forces is fighting an internalized war. By using Perls' role-playing technique these opposing forces can have it out with each other, forgive each other, compromise, or at least come to know each other.

Using the double-chair technique, people can develop an awareness of their fragmented parts by starting a dialogue and by acting out various roles, switching chairs with each switch in role. The role players may be people—as they are now, or as children, or as a mother, father, spouse, or boss. The role played may also be physical symptoms—ulcers, headaches, backaches, sweaty palms, palpitating hearts. They may even be objects encountered in a dream, such as a piece of furniture, an animal, a window.

Role-playing, with the use of the hot-seat, can also be used to clarify any relationship between people. To do this, one person imagines another person in the opposite chair. The person speaks to this other, saying what's really on his or her mind. The person then becomes the other and responds. In this process unspoken resentments and affection often come to the surface, where they can be understood and resolved.

Various parts of a dream can also be role-played to gain self-awareness. According to Perls, the dream is "the royal road to integration" [9].

. . . all the different parts of the dream are fragments of our personalities. Since our aim is to make every one of us a wholesome person, which means a unified person, without conflicts, what we have to do is put the different fragments of the dream together. We have to *re-own* these projected, fragmented parts of our personality, and *re-own* the hidden potential that appears in the dream [10].

Or, put another way, all the dream is the dreamer. Each person and each thing in the dream is some aspect of the dreamer. By role-playing the people in the dream, the objects in the dream, or even a dream fragment, the existential message that the dream holds can be unlocked, not by analyzing it, but by reliving it.

For example, one man had a recurring dream in which there was always a desk. When asked to imagine himself as this piece of furniture he muttered, "How silly, I'm not a desk." With a bit of encouragement he got over his stage fright and started his performance. "I am a big desk. I'm stuffed full of other peoples' things. People pile things on me, write on me, poke me with pens. They just use me and I can't move. . . ." Later he said, "That's me, all right! Just like a desk I let everybody use me, and I just sit there!"

In gestalt therapy people gain both emotional and intellectual insight, but the methods focus on the former. Emotional awareness is that moment of self-discovery when a person says "ahah." Perls describes the "ahah" experience as ". . . what happens whenever something clicks, falls into place; each time a gestalt closes, there is this 'ahah!' click, the shock of recognition" [11]. Intellectual insight comes with the gathering of data.

ERIC BERNE AND TRANSACTIONAL ANALYSIS

In transactional analysis people gain both emotional and intellectual insight, but the method focuses on the latter. It is a thinking process, often analytical, in which the person frequently concludes, "So *that's* the way it is!"

According to Dr. Berne, his theories evolved as he observed behavioral changes occurring in a patient when a new stimulus, such as a word, gesture, or sound, entered his focus. These changes involved facial expressions, word intonations, sentence structure, body movements, gestures, tics, posture, and carriage. It was as though there were several different people inside the individual. At times one or the other of these inner different people seemed to be in control of his patient's total personality.

He observed that these various "selves" transacted with other people in different ways and that these transactions could be analyzed. He saw that some of the transactions had ulterior motives; the individual used them as a means of manipulating others into psychological games and rackets.* He also observed that people performed in predetermined ways—acting as if they were on stage and reading from a theatrical script. These observations led Berne to develop his unique theory called Transactional Analysis, abbreviated to TA.

Originally, TA was developed as a method of psychotherapy. Transactional analysis is preferably used in groups (as is gestalt therapy). The group serves as a setting in which people can become more aware of themselves, the structure of their individual personality, how they transact with others, the games they play, and the scripts they act out. Such awareness enables persons to see themselves more clearly so that they can change what they want to change and strengthen what they want to strengthen.

Change begins with a bilateral contract between the therapist and client. A contract may be about the alleviation of symptoms such as blushing, frigidity, or headaches. It may be about gaining control over behavior such as excessive drinking, mistreating children, failing in school. It may focus on childhood experiences which underlie current specific symptoms and behavior, experiences in which the child was belittled, abandoned, overindulged, ignored, or brutalized [13]. The contractual approach preserves the self-determination of a client. It also allows a client to know when the terms of the contract have been met.

TA is not only a useful tool for those in psychotherapy, it also provides a thought-provoking perspective of human behavior that

---

* The analysis of games has received wide popularity in Berne's bestseller, *Games People Play* [12].

most people can understand and put to use. It encourages the use of words that are simple, direct, and often colloquial instead of psychological, scientific words, or jargon. For example, the major parts of the personality are called the *Parent, Adult,* and *Child* ego states.

Transactional analysis is a rational approach to understanding behavior and is based on the assumption that all individuals can learn to trust themselves, think for themselves, make their own decisions, and express their feelings. Its principles can be applied on the job, in the home, in the classroom, in the neighborhood— wherever people deal with people.

Berne says an important goal of transactional analysis is "to establish the most open and authentic communication possible between the affective and intellectual components of the personality" [14]. When this happens, the person is able to use both emotions and intellect, not just one at the expense of the other. Gestalt techniques can accelerate the process, particularly at the feeling level.

In this book each chapter has exercises and experiments that are designed to assist you in personally applying the theory. We suggest that as you complete each chapter, you read through the experiments and exercises related to it. Do what seems possible and interesting immediately. Then at a later time, complete what is relevant to you.

SUMMARY

A person who is not aware of how she or he acts or feels is impoverished. Lacking a core of confidence, such a person fluctuates between conflicting inner forces. This person is less than whole, having alienated parts of the self—intellect, emotions, creativeness, body feelings, or some particular behavior. A person who becomes aware and moves toward becoming a whole person is enriched.

People who decide to become more of a winner than a loser allow such insights. Through them they discover that they can rely, more and more, on their own capacities for sensing and making judgments. They continue to discover and renew themselves. For them, life consists not in getting more but in being more. Winners are glad to be alive!

EXPERIMENTS AND EXERCISES

1. Trait Checklist

Move quickly through the following list of traits. Use a check mark (✔) beside those that fit your self-image. Use a cross (x) to mark those that do not fit. Use a question mark (?) to indicate the ones that you're unsure about.

—Like myself

—Afraid of or hurt by others

—People can trust me

—Put up a good front

—Usually say the right thing

—Feel bad about myself

—Fearful of the future

— Dependent on others for ideas

—Waste time

—Use my talents

—Think for myself

— Know my feelings

—Don't understand myself

—Feel hemmed in

—Use time well

—People avoid me

—Disinterested in community problems

—Enjoy work

—Enjoy nature

—Don't enjoy work

—Can't hold a job

—Trust myself

—Usually say the wrong thing

—Enjoy people

—Don't enjoy being the sex I am

—Discouraged about life

—Don't like to be around people

—Have not developed my talents

—Glad I'm the sex I am

—Often do the wrong thing

—Involved in solving community problems

—People like to be around me

—Competent on the job

—Control myself

—Enjoy life

—Trouble controlling myself

—Don't like myself

Now look at those traits you have marked.

• Is there a pattern?

• Are they winner traits, loser traits, a mixture?

• What traits would you like to change?

As you read through the book, come back to this checklist. Look over the traits you've marked and change what you decide to change.

2. Winner/Loser Continuum

Judging from how you feel about yourself, what you have accomplished in your life, and what your relationships are with others, rate yourself somewhere along the following continuum. Think of one end of the continuum as a tragic loser and the other end as a totally successful winner.

• How do you feel about yourself?

Loser _____ Winner

• How do you feel about what you have accomplished in your life?

Loser _____ Winner

• How do you feel about your relationships with others?

Loser _____ Winner

• Are you satisfied with where you placed yourself?

• If not, what would you like to change?

3. Role-Playing an Inner Dialogue

The next time you can't get to sleep, can't concentrate, can't listen to someone else because you have a dialogue going round and round in your head, become aware of the essence of the conversation.

• Listen to it. Who is talking in your head? Are you talking to a particular person?

• Now bring this conversation out in the open. Set two chairs facing each other. Using Perls' role-playing method, speak this conversation aloud. Switch from one chair to the other when it is appropriate.

• Try to bring this dialogue to some kind of conclusion.

2

An Overview of Transactional Analysis

The crazy person says, "I am Abraham Lincoln," and
the neurotic says, "I wish I were Abraham Lincoln,"
and the healthy person says, "I am I, and you are you."
  Frederick Perls [1]

Many people come to a time in their lives when they are provoked to define themselves. At such a time transactional analysis offers a frame of reference that most people can understand and put to use in their own lives. This chapter provides a brief overview of TA theory and its applications [2]. Subsequent chapters consider each phase in depth.

Transactional analysis is concerned with four kinds of analysis:

Structural Analysis:	the analysis of individual personality.
Transactional Analysis:	the analysis of what people do and say to one another.
Game Analysis:	the analysis of ulterior transactions leading to a payoff.
Script Analysis:	the analysis of specific life dramas that persons compulsively play out.

INTRODUCTION TO STRUCTURAL ANALYSIS

Structural analysis offers one way of answering the questions: Who am I? Why do I act the way I do? How did I get this way? It is a method of analyzing a person's thoughts, feelings, and behavior, based on the phenomena of ego states [3].

Imagine a mother loudly scolding her noisy, quarrelsome children. Her face wears a scowl. Her voice is shrill. Her arm is tense and held high in the air. Suddenly, the phone rings and she hears a friend's voice. The mother's posture, tone, and expression begin to change. Her voice becomes well modulated. Her once tense arm lies quietly in her lap.

Imagine two factory workers angrily arguing with each other about a work problem. Their argument is animated and fierce. They look like two children fighting over a piece of candy. Suddenly, they hear a crash of steel followed by an agonized scream. Their entire demeanor changes. Their argument is dropped. Their angry expressions give way to concern. One hurries to see what's wrong; the other calls an ambulance. According to the theory of structural analysis, the workers, as well as the mother, changed ego states.

Berne defines an ego state as "A consistent pattern of feeling and experience directly related to a corresponding consistent pattern of behavior" [4]. Berne writes:

. . . in this respect the brain functions like a tape recorder to preserve complete experiences in serial sequence, in a form recognizable as "ego states" —indicating that ego states comprise the natural way of experiencing and of recording experiences in their totality. Simultaneously, of course, experiences are recorded in fragmented forms . . . [5].

The implications are that a person's experiences are recorded in the brain and nervous tissue. This includes everything a person experienced in childhood and incorporated from parent figures, perceptions of events and feelings associated with these events, and the distortions brought to memories. These recordings are stored as though on videotape. They can be replayed, and the event recalled and even re-experienced.

Each person has three ego states which are separate and distinct sources of behavior: the Parent ego state, the Adult ego state, and the Child ego state. These are not abstract concepts but realities. "Parent, Adult, and Child represent real people who now exist or who once existed, who have legal names and civic identities" [6].

The structure of personality is diagrammed on the following page.

Ego states are colloquially termed Parent, Adult, and Child. When capitalized in this book they refer to ego states, not to actual parents, adults, or children.

The three ego states are defined as follows:

The *Parent ego state* contains the attitudes and behavior incorporated from external sources, primarily parents. Outwardly, it often is expressed toward others in prejudicial, critical, and nurturing behavior. Inwardly, it is experienced as old Parental messages which continue to influence the inner Child.

The *Adult ego state* is not related to a person's age. It is oriented to current reality and the objective gathering of information. It is organized, adaptable, intelligent, and functions by testing reality, estimating probabilities, and computing dispassionately.

The *Child ego state* contains all the impulses that come naturally to an infant. It also contains the recordings of the child's early experiences, responses, and the "positions" taken about self and others. It is expressed as "old" (archaic) behavior from childhood.

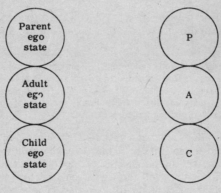

Ego State Structure   Simplified Diagram

When you are acting, thinking, feeling as you observed your parents to be doing, you are in your Parent ego state.

When you are dealing with current reality, gathering facts, and computing objectively, you are in your Adult ego state.

When you are feeling and acting as you did when you were a child, you are in your Child ego state.

Case Illustration

A client was advised to investigate a private school for his son. When he reported his findings about the school where the teaching was informal and creativity encouraged, three distinct reactions were easily observable. First, he scowled and said, "I can't see how anyone could learn anything at that school. There's dirt on the floor!" Leaning back in his chair, his forehead smoothed out as he reflected, "Before I decide, I think I should check on the school's scholastic rating and talk to some of the parents." The next minute, a broad grin crossed his face, and he said, "Gee, I'd love to have gone to a school like that!"

When queried about his responses, the client readily analyzed that his first was the way his father would have responded. His second was his Adult looking for more data. His third was his Child recalling his own unhappy school experience and imagining the fun he might have had at a school such as the one he visited.

Before making a final decision, he pursued his Adult questions. Subsequently, his son attended this school, is currently having a good time there, and is achieving well beyond his former level.

According to structural analysis, each person may respond to a specific stimulus in quite distinct ways from each of the ego states; sometimes these ego states are in concert, sometimes in conflict. Let's look at the following examples.

To a stimulus of a piece of modern art
Parent: Good grief! What's it supposed to be!

Adult: That costs $350 according to the price tag.

Child: Ooo, what pretty color!

To a request for an office report
Parent: Mr. Brown is not cut out to be a supervisor.

Adult: I know Mr. Brown needs these by five o'clock.

Child: No matter what I do, I can't please Mr. Brown.

To an act of violence on the street
Parent: It serves that girl right for being out so late.

Adult: I'd better call the police.

Child: Say, is this ever exciting!

To being offered a piece of chocolate cake when dieting

PLATE I

EVERYONE HAS THREE EGO STATES

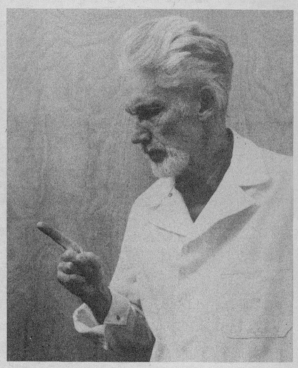

Critical behavior often comes
from the Parent ego state.

Problem-solving from the Adult ego state.

Joy and laughter
from the
Child ego state.

Parent: Go ahead, honey, it will keep up your energy.

Adult: That piece of cake must have at least 400 calories. I think I'll skip it.

Child: What yummy cake! I could eat the whole thing.

To a crash of rock music
Parent: That horrible stuff kids listen to today!

Adult: It's hard for me to think or talk when the music is so loud.

Child: That makes me want to dance.

To the late arrival of a young woman secretary
Parent: Poor thing looks as if she hasn't slept a wink.

Adult: If she doesn't make up her time, the other employees will be dissatisfied.

Child: I sure wish I could take time off for fun.

To a lecturer using four-letter words
Parent: Using such expletives only shows a weak vocabulary.

Adult: I wonder why he chooses those words to use and what their effect is on the audience.

Child: I wish I dared to talk like that.

To the smell of cabbage
Parent: Cabbage really keeps the family healthy.

Adult: Cabbage has high vitamin C content.

Child: Nobody's going to make me eat that stinky stuff.

To a new male acquaintance putting his arm around you
Parent: Never let a stranger touch you.

Adult: I wonder why he's doing it?

Child: He scares me.

People can feel, smell, touch, speak, listen, look, and act from each ego state. Each ego state has its own programming. Some people respond from one ego state more than from the others. People, for example, who tend to respond most often from their

Parent ego state view the world as they observed their parents viewing it. In this case their ability to sense the world for themselves is diminished or distorted.

DEVELOPMENT OF EGO STATES

When first born, the infant's awareness is centered on personal needs and comforts. The baby seeks to avoid painful experiences and responds at the feeling level. Almost immediately the infant's unique Child ego state emerges. (Prenatal influences on the Child ego state have not yet been determined.)

The Parent ego state develops next. It is often first observed when the young child plays at parenting, imitating parental behavior. Sometimes it's a shock for parents to see themselves being played back. Sometimes they are very pleased.

The Adult ego state develops as the child tries to make sense out of the world and figures out that other people can be manipulated. The child may ask, "Why do I have to eat when I'm not hungry?" and may try to manipulate others by faking a stomach ache in order to avoid eating.

Case Illustration

Sheri, aged twenty-two months, received a doll-stroller at Christmas. She tried to climb into it saying, "Me, baby." It was too small. She then tried putting her doll in. The doll fit. Sheri squealed, "Me, mommy," and started to push the stroller but soon grew tired of playing this part. Angrily she threw the doll out, pushed over the stroller, righted it, and tried to get in again. Still she could not fit. Frustrated, she put the doll in once more. She tried this switch four times. Then, apparently deciding she was too big, she settled for being mommy and acted toward her doll in ways her mother acted toward her.

Sheri's motherly behavior, an actual imitation of her mother, was from her Parent ego state. Although in her Child ego state Sheri wanted to be a baby, her emerging Adult ego state collected and processed objective data—that she couldn't fit into the stroller. Any situation may activate a specific ego state and sometimes,

PLATE II

EVEN CHILDREN HAVE THREE EGO STATES

Rational thinking from the
Adult ego state.

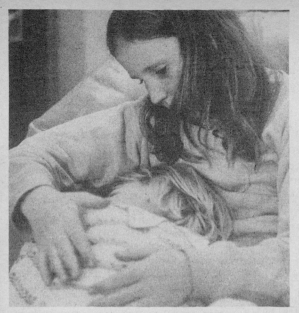

Nuturing behavior often comes from
the Parent ego state.

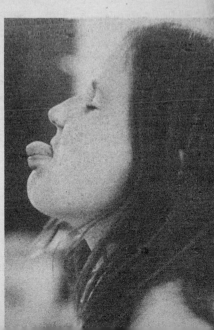

Rebellious behavior
from the
Child ego state.

as in the case of Sheri, different ego states within a person vie for control. Between two people, one "baby" confronted with another "baby" may try to be a parent or may try to be a "bigger" baby.

INTRODUCTION TO ANALYZING TRANSACTIONS

Any time one person recognizes another with a smile, a nod, a frown, a verbal greeting, etc., this recognition, in TA language, is called a *stroke*. Two or more strokes make a transaction. All transactions can be classified as complementary, crossed, or ulterior [7].

Complementary Transactions

A complementary transaction occurs when a message, sent from a specific ego state, gets the predicted response from a specific ego state in the other person. Berne describes a complementary transaction as one which is "appropriate and expected and follows the natural order of healthy human relationships" [8]. For example, if a wife who is grieving for her lost friend is comforted by a sympathetic husband, her momentary dependency need is answered appropriately (shown in the diagram below).

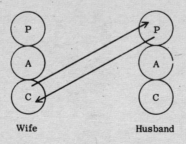

Wife   Husband

A complementary transaction can occur between any two ego states. For example, two people may transact Parent-Parent when lamenting their children's leaving home; Adult-Adult when solving a problem; Child-Child or Parent-Child when having fun together. A person can transact from his or her Parent with any of the ego states of another person and can also do this with the Adult and Child ego states. If the response is the expected one, the transaction is complementary. The lines of communication are *open*, and the people can continue transacting with one another.

Gestures, facial expressions, body posture, tone of voice, and so forth, all contribute to the meaning in every transaction. If a verbal message is to be completely understood, the receiver must take into consideration the nonverbal aspects as well as the spoken words.

To better understand the following illustrations, we must assume that the stimulus is straightforward and the verbal and nonverbal messages are congruent. Any illustration is, at best, an educated guess. To be totally accurate, the actual Parent, Adult, and Child ego states of each person would need to be known.

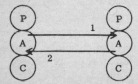

Data Exchange in Adult/Adult transaction (Fig. 2.2)

1. What is the yearly salary for this job?

2. It starts at $10,000.

Sympathetic Parent/Parent transaction (Fig. 2.3)

1. Those children really miss their father.

2. Yes, let's take them to the park for a little fun.

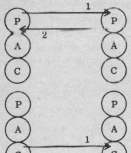

Playful Child/Child transaction (Fig. 2.4)

1. I really like you.

2. I like you, too.

Child/Nurturing Parent transaction (Fig. 2.5)

1. I'm so worried about my son I can't concentrate on this report.

2. You can leave work early to go by the hospital and see him.

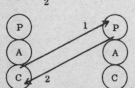

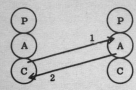

Angry Child/Listening Adult feed-back transaction (Fig. 2.6)

1. I'm so mad I could throw this darn typewriter out of the window.

2. Something made you so angry you'd like to throw the equipment around. Is that how it is?

In each of the above transactions communication is open because the responses given were expected responses and were appropriate to the stimulus. This does not always happen. Sometimes a stimulus receives an unexpected or inappropriate response, and the lines of communication become crossed.

Crossed Transactions

When two people stand glaring at each other, turn their backs on each other, are unwilling to continue transacting, or are puzzled by what has just occurred between them, it is likely that they have just experienced a *crossed transaction*. A crossed transaction occurs when an unexpected response is made to the stimulus. An inappropriate ego state is activated, and the lines of transacting between the people are crossed. At this point, people tend to withdraw, turn away from each other, or switch the conversation in another direction. If a husband responds unsympathetically to his grieving wife, "Well, how do you think I feel!" he is likely to cause her to turn away from him (Fig. 2.7).

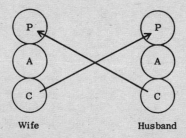

Wife   Husband

Crossed transactions are a frequent source of pain between people—parents and children, husband and wife, boss and employee, teacher and student, and so forth. The person who initiates a transaction, expecting a certain response, does not get it. The individual is crossed up and often feels discounted and misunderstood.

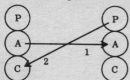

Figure 2.8

1. Boss: What time is it?

2. Secretary: You're always in such a hurry!

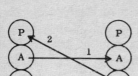

Figure 2.9

1. Husband: Can you take the car to be serviced this afternoon?

2. Wife: Today I iron. Johnny expects a birthday cake. The cat has to go to the vet, and now you want me to take the car in!

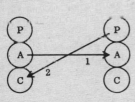

Figure 2.10

1. Boss: I need 25 copies of this report for the board meeting this afternoon. Can you get them for me?

2. Secretary: Aren't you lucky you've got me around to take care of you?

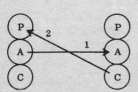

Figure 2.11

1. Scientist A: There may be some variables we haven't considered for this experiment.

2. Scientist B: So what, who cares around here?

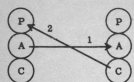

Figure 2.12

1. Wife: I'd like to use the car on Wednesday night and have a good visit with my sister.

2. Husband: Gee, you never want to talk to me.

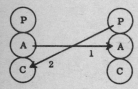

Figure 2.13

1. Supervisor: Have you seen the Willows contract, Miss Smith?

2. File clerk: If you ran this department the way you're supposed to, you wouldn't have to ask me where the Willows contract is.

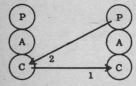

Figure 2.14

1. John: Let's have fun.

2. Marcia: Can't you ever be serious?

Transactions may be direct or indirect, straightforward or diluted, intense or weak. *Indirect transactions* are three-handed. One person speaks to another while hoping to influence the third who can overhear it. For example, a man may be too fearful to speak directly to his boss, so says something to a co-worker, hoping the boss will "get the message."

Diluted transactions are often half hostile, half affectionate. The message is buried in some form of kidding. For example, one student may say to another, "Hey genius, when are you going to finish that book? I want to read it." The other may toss the book, saying, "Here you are, butterfingers. Catch it if you can."

Weak transactions are those that are superficial, perfunctory, and lack feelings of intensity. Such is the case if a wife says to her husband, "I wonder if we should go out for dinner tonight," and he responds, "I don't care, dear. Whatever you say, dear."

In healthy relationships people transact directly, straightforwardly and, on occasion, intensely [9]. These transactions are complementary and free from ulterior motives.

Ulterior Transactions

Ulterior transactions are the most complex. They differ from complementary and crossed transactions in that they always involve more than two ego states. When an ulterior message is sent, it is disguised under a socially acceptable transaction. Such is the purpose of the old cliché: "Wouldn't you like to come up to see my etchings?" In this instance the Adult is verbalizing one thing while the Child, with the use of innuendo, is sending a different message (Fig. 2.15).

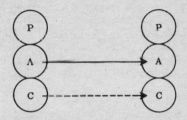

If a car salesman says with a leer to his customer, "This is our finest sports car, but it may be too racy for you," he is sending a message that can be heard by either the customer's Adult or Child ego state (see Fig. 2.16). If the customer's Adult hears, the response may be, "Yes, you're right, considering the requirements of my job." If the customer's Child hears, the response may be, "I'll take it. It's just what I want."

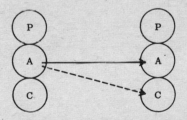

An ulterior message is also given when a secretary submits a letter with several typing errors to the boss. This invites the boss to give the secretary a Parental put-down (see Fig. 2.17). The same happens when a student is continually late with assignments, absent from class, writes illegibly, or in some way provokes the equivalent of parental criticism.

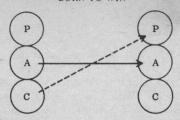

The same kind of ulterior transaction occurs if a man who has been a "reformed" alcoholic comes to work with a hangover, but a glimmer in his eye, and boasts to his co-worker, "Boy, I really blew it last night and drank myself under the table. What a head I've got today!" On the surface he is giving factual information. However, at the ulterior level, the alcoholic's Child ego state is looking for the Parent in the other to smile indulgently and thus condone his drinking.

Instead of a Parent response he may activate his co-worker's Child ego state, and he may respond by laughing at the tragedy. If the co-worker laughs, from either his Parent or his Child ego state, he reinforces the (parental) injunction, usually given nonverbally to the alcoholic (as a child), "Get lost, you bum." This inappropriate laugh or smile is described by Claude Steiner as the *gallows transaction* [10]. The smile serves to tighten the noose, and destructive behavior is reinforced.

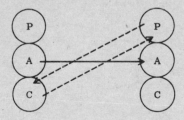

Any smiling response to a person's misfortunes may serve as a gallows transaction. Such is the case when

a teacher acts amused at a pupil's "stupid behavior,"

a mother laughs at her accident-prone three-year-old,

a father beams over the risks his son takes.

These gallows transactions, like other transactions with ulterior motives, are common among losers. Losers use them to promote their psychological games.

THE GAMES PEOPLE PLAY

People play psychological games with one another that are similar to games, like monopoly, bridge, or checkers, that people play at social gatherings. The players must know the game in order to play—after all, if one person enters a card party ready to play bridge, and everyone else is playing pinochle, that person can't very well play bridge.

All games have a beginning, a given set of rules, and a concluding payoff. Psychological games, however, have an ulterior purpose. They are not played for fun. Of course, neither are some poker games.

Berne defines a *psychological game* as "a recurring set of transactions, often repetitive, superficially rational, with a concealed motivation; or, more colloquially, as a series of transactions with a gimmick"[11]. Three specific elements must be present to define transactions as games:

1. an ongoing series of complementary transactions which are plausible on the social level,

2. an ulterior transaction which is the underlying message of the game, and

3. a predictable payoff which concludes the game and is the real purpose for playing.

Games prevent honest, intimate, and open relationships between the players. Yet people play them because they fill up time, provoke attention, reinforce early opinions about self and others, and fulfill a sense of destiny.

Psychological games are played to win, but a person who plays games as a way of life is not a winner. Sometimes, a person acts like a loser in order to win the game (Fig. 2.19). For example, in a game of *Kick Me* a player provokes someone else to a put-down response.

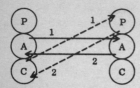

Student: I stayed up too late last night and don't have my assignment ready. (ulterior: I'm a bad boy, kick me.)

Instructor: You're out of luck. This is the last day I can give credit for that assignment. (ulterior: Yes, you are a bad boy and here is your kick.)

Though they may deny it, people who are used to this game tend to attract others who can play the complementary hand and are willing to "kick" in response.

Every game has a first move. Some first moves are nonverbal: turning a cold shoulder, batting a flirty eye, shaking an accusative finger, slamming a door, tracking mud in the house, reading someone's mail, looking woebegone, not speaking. Other first moves are verbal statements, such as:

"You look so lonesome over here by yourself . . ."
"How could you go to school wearing that get-up!"
"He criticized you. Are you going to take that?"
"I have this terrible problem . . ."
"Isn't it awful that . . ."

Barbara and Tom's favorite game was *Uproar*. They both knew the first move in the game, so either could start it. Once it was started, a predictable set of transactions occurred which climaxed with a loud fight. The outcome was always the same—hostile withdrawal to avoid closeness. This was their payoff for playing the game, the avoidance of intimacy.

To set up the game either Barbara or Tom provoked the other with nonverbal behavior such as sulking, chain-smoking, withdrawing, or acting irritated. When the partner was "hooked" into playing, the game was under way. As the game continued he/she got a put-off or a put-down. After exchanging many angry words, they finally withdrew from each other.

When Barbara starts the game, the transactions are:

Barbara: (Begins pouting and chain-smoking with exaggerated gestures)

Tom: "What's the matter? What's wrong?"

Barbara: "It's none of your business!"

Tom: (Goes out to the local bar)

Barbara: (Explodes in anger when he returns. A long battle ensues, filled with accusations and counteraccusations. The payoff comes when Barbara breaks into tears, runs into the bedroom, and slams the door. Tom retreats to the kitchen for another drink. They make no further contact that evening.)

When Tom initiates the game, the transactions are:

Tom: (Fixes a drink for himself, goes off to the den, and closes the door.)

Barbara: "Why didn't you fix a drink for me? Is something wrong?"

Tom: "Can't I even have a few minutes alone!"

Barbara: "If you want to be alone, I'll leave!" (Barbara goes shopping, buys things they can't afford, and returns carrying several packages.)

Tom: (Explodes in anger about the way she spends money. The game comes full circle when she stamps away mad, and he fixes his bed in the den.)

Games tend to be repetitive. People find themselves saying the same words in the same way, only the time and place may change. Perhaps the replay contributes to what is often described as "I feel as if I've done this before."

People play games with different degrees of intensity, from the socially accepted, relaxed level to the criminal homicide/suicide level. Berne writes:

a) A First-Degree Game is one which is socially acceptable in the agent's circle.

b) A Second-Degree Game is one from which no permanent, irremediable damage arises, but which the players would rather conceal from the public.

c) A Third-Degree Game is one which is played for keeps, and which ends in the surgery, the courtroom or the morgue [12].

Games are individually programmed. They are played from the Parent ego state if the parent's games are imitated. They are played from the Adult ego state if they are consciously calculated. They are played from the Child ego state if they are based on early life experiences, decisions, and the "positions" that a child takes about self and others.

DAYS OF DECISION

Before children are eight years old they develop a concept about their own worth. They also formulate ideas about the worth of others. They crystallize their experiences and decide what it all means to them, what parts they are going to play, and how they are going to play them. These are children's days of decision [13].

When decisions about self and others are made very early in life, they may be quite unrealistic. They are very likely to be somewhat distorted and irrational, because children perceive life through the small peekhole of their existence. These distortions can create some degree of pathology ranging from inconsequential to serious. However, they seem logical and make sense at the time the child makes them. The following story, reported by Betty, a woman of forty-three who had been married to an alcoholic for twenty years, illustrates the effect of early decisions.

Case Illustration

My father was a brutal alcoholic. When he was drunk he would hit me and scream at me. I would try to hide. One day when he came home, the door flew open and he was drunker than usual. He picked up a butcher knife and started running through the house. I hid in a coat closet. I was almost four years old. I was so scared in the closet. It was dark and spooky, and things kept hitting me in the face. That day I decided who men were—beasts, who would only try to hurt me. I was a large child and I remember thinking, "If I were smaller, he'd love me," or "If I were prettier, he'd love me." I always thought I wasn't worth anything.

The "days of decision" lead a person to take psychological positions [14]. In the above case the woman took the positions, "I'm unworthy (I am not-OK)" and "Men are beasts who will hurt me (men are not-OK)." On the basis of these positions she selected people who would play certain roles that fit into her life drama.

She married a "beast" who was also an alcoholic. In addition, she often played the game of *Rapo* at social gatherings. When playing her game, she would engage a man in conversation and lead him on seductively. If he responded to her message, she would turn away in righteous indignation, confident once more that "men are beasts who will hurt me."

PSYCHOLOGICAL POSITIONS

When taking positions about themselves, people may conclude:

I'm smart.　　I'm stupid.　　I'm powerful.　　I'm inadequate.

I'm nice.　　I'm nasty.　　I'm an angel.　　I'm a devil.

I can't do anything right.　　I can't do anything wrong.

I'm as good as anybody else.　　I don't deserve to live.

When taking positions about others, people may conclude:

People will give me anything I want.　　Nobody will give me anything.

People are wonderful.　　People are no damn good.

Someone will help me.　　People are out to get me.

Everybody likes me.　　Nobody likes me.

People are nice.　　Everybody's mean.

In general, the above positions are "I'm OK" or "I'm not-OK," and "You're OK" or "You're not-OK." The psychological positions taken about oneself and about others fit into four basic patterns [15]. The first is the winner's position, but even winners may occasionally have feelings that resemble the other three.

The First Position: I'm OK, You're OK

is potentially a mentally healthy position. If realistic, people with this position about themselves and others can solve their problems constructively. Their expectations are likely to be valid. They accept the significance of people.

The Second or Projective Position: I'm OK, You're not-OK

is the position of persons who feel victimized or persecuted, so victimize and persecute others. They blame others for their miseries. Delinquents and criminals often have this position and take on paranoid behavior which in extreme cases may lead to homicide.

The Third or Introjective Position: I'm not-OK, You're OK

is a common position of persons who feel powerless when they compare themselves to others. This position leads them to withdraw, to experience depression, and, in severe cases, to become suicidal.

The Fourth or Futility Position: I'm not-OK, You're not-OK

is the position of those who lose interest in living, who exhibit schizoid behavior, and who, in extreme cases, commit suicide or homicide.

People with the first position feel "Life is worth living." With the second they feel "Your life is not worth much." With the third they feel "My life is not worth much." With the fourth they feel "Life isn't worth anything at all."

SEXUALITY AND PSYCHOLOGICAL POSITIONS

Psychological positions are also sexualized. In the formation of self-identity, a person takes two positions, or appraisals, about his or her self; one is general and the other is sexual. Sometimes these positions are similar. Sometimes different. For example, some people take an OK position about themselves as students, workers, and so forth, but take a not-OK position about themselves as male or female. When this occurs, sexual games such as *Rapo* and *Kiss Off* may be played.

The ancient myth of Cadmus reflects this dual identity. Cadmus was highly competent at building the ancient city of Thebes but a failure in his sexual roles with his family. His offspring had many tragedies; the well-known Oedipus was one of his descendants.

In a counseling group a modern Cadmus, expressing the same problem, said, "I know I'm a capable architect, but I feel like a flop as a man—especially at home with my family." A woman responded, "I know how you feel. I made the highest grades of anyone in my senior class, but I really don't feel feminine." Many statements indicate a psychological position related to a particular sex [16].

I'll never *get* a man (woman).   I'll never *be* a man (woman).

I'm handsome (beautiful).   Women can't be trusted.

Women are tyrants.   Men are tyrants.

Women are sweet and tender.   Men will protect me

Some people take the position that one sex is OK and the other is not-OK:

Men are intelligent, but women are stupid.

Men are dirty, but women are pure.

Once a position is taken, the person seeks to keep his or her world predictable by reinforcing it. It becomes a life position from which games are played and scripts acted out. The more severe the pathology, the more the person feels pushed to reinforce it. This process can be diagrammed as follows:

			Script
Experiences→	Decisions→	Psychological→	Reinforcing
		Positions	Behavior

PLATE III

TRANSACTIONS CAN BE ANALYZED

All transactions can be
classified as complementary,
crossed, or ulterior.

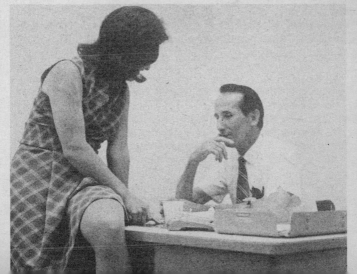

INTRODUCTION TO SCRIPT ANALYSIS

A script can be briefly defined as the life plan, very much like a dramatic stage production, that an individual feels compelled to play out.

A script is related to the early decisions and the positions taken by a child. It is in the Child ego state and is "written" through the transactions between parents and their child. The games that are played are part of the script. When the positions and games are identified, a person can become more aware of this life script.

Case Illustration

In counseling, Fred reported, "If I heard it once, I heard it a hundred times, 'What a stupid thing to do, Fred. Can't you do anything right?' I couldn't even talk fast enough for my folks, and I still stutter sometimes. When I went to school, I just couldn't seem to do anything right. I was always at the bottom of the class, and I can remember teachers saying, 'Fred, that was a stupid question.' Teachers were just like my mom. When they read the grades out loud, my name was last, and the kids laughed at me. Then I got to high school, and the counselor said I could do better. That I wasn't dumb, just lazy. I just don't get it."

In subsequent counseling sessions Fred learned that early in life he had taken the position, "I'm stupid. I'm not-OK." He thought of himself as a failure and acted out the role. Though he did poorly, Fred remained in school, played the game of *Stupid*, and evoked negative comments, low grades, and nagging from his teachers. This reinforced his basic psychological position.

Fred discovered his script was that of a loser. In his Child ego state he felt stupid and played the part of *Stupid*. He also discovered that his Parent ego state agreed with this position and thus encouraged him to fail. Fred's analysis of his ego states gave to his Adult the objective data about who he was, how he got that way, and where he was going with his life. It took Fred a while to decide which ego state would control his life. Finally, his Adult won out. He enrolled in college and maintained good grades.

After discovering his loser script, Fred decided that he didn't have to be a loser. He could become a winner if he chose to. Berne writes, "The ultimate goal of transactional analysis is the analysis of scripts, since the script determines the destiny and identity of the individual" [17].

SUMMARY

Modern people wear many masks and have many forms of armor that keep their reality confined and unknown, even to themselves. The possibility of encountering one's reality—learning about one's self—can be frightening and frustrating. Many people expect to discover the *worst*. A hidden fear lies in the fact that they may also discover the *best*.

To discover the worst is to face the decision of whether or not to continue in the same patterns. To learn the best is to face the decision of whether or not to live up to it. Either discovery may involve change and is therefore anxiety-provoking. However, this can be a creative anxiety which may be thought of as excitement—the excitement of enhancing one's possibilities for being a winner.

Transactional analysis is a tool you can use to know yourself, to know how you relate to others, and to discover the dramatic course your life is taking. The unit of personality structure is the ego state. By becoming aware of your ego states, you can distinguish between your various sources of thoughts, feelings, and behavior patterns. You can discover where there is discord and where there is agreement within your own personality. You can become more aware of the options available to you.

The unit of measure in interpersonal relationships is the transaction. By analyzing your transactions, you can gain a more conscious control of how you operate with other people and how they operate with you. You can determine when your transactions are complementary, crossed, or ulterior. You can also discover what "games" you play.

Transactional analysis is a practical frame of reference from which you can evaluate old decisions and behavior and change what you decide is desirable for you to change.

EXPERIMENTS AND EXERCISES

Find a place where you will not be interrupted. Taking enough time to imagine each fantasied situation in detail, consider the questions that follow.

1. Beginning to Know Your Ego States

Your Parent

- Think of one thing you now do which you copied from a parent figure and perhaps repeat to your spouse, children, friends, or co-workers.

- Think of one parental message you still hear in your head and obey, fight against, or feel confused about.

Your Adult

- Think of a recent situation in which you believe you gathered facts and on the basis of these facts, made a reasonable decision.

- Think of a recent situation in which you felt hostile and aggressive (or sulky, depressed, and so forth), yet were able to act reasonably and appropriately in spite of your feelings.

Your Child

- Think of one form of manipulation you used successfully as a child that you still use.

- Think of one thing you did for fun as a child that you still do.

2. Your Ego States and Feelings

Imagine you are at home alone on a stormy night. You've been asleep for several hours. The doorbell rings unexpectedly and by the sound of the clock's striking you know it is 3:00 a.m.

- What are your feelings and thoughts? What would you do?

- How would you have felt as a child? Do you feel this now?

- What would each of your parents have done? Would your behavior resemble that of one of your parent figures?

- What do you think is the "best" thing to do?

Imagine you've gone to work a usual. The boss, looking tense and angry, is there to meet you and immediately lights into you for something you forgot to do.

- What are your feelings and thoughts? What would you do?

- How would you have felt as a child if the boss was a parent or teacher? Do you feel this now?

- What would your parents have done? Would you be like either of them?

- What do you think is the "best" thing to do?

3. Analyzing a Transaction

Think back to a transaction you had today. Try to diagram it. Do you think there was an ulterior transaction that was concealed under another message? If so, include it in the diagram.

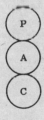 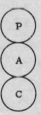

4. Your OKness

Imagine you are face-to-face with an important person who looks you directly in the eye and asks, "Do you feel OK or not-OK?"

- What would be your feelings and thoughts? How would you respond?

- Can you recall when you decided you were OK or not-OK?
- Imagine that scene. Who was there and what happened? Try to re-experience it.

5. Your Sexual OKness

Imagine yourself in a situation in which your sexual role is important. Picture yourself as a spouse, boyfriend/girlfriend, or parent. Do you feel like an OK or not-OK male or female?

- Think back to your parents' attitudes about your maleness or femaleness. Try to remember any words that were said.
- Try to re-experience one incident that you can remember that had to do with your sexuality.

3

The Human Hunger for Strokes and Time Structuring

If you touch me soft and gentle
If you look at me and smile at me
If you listen to me talk sometimes before you talk
I will grow, really grow.
   Bradley (age 9)

Every person has the need to be touched and to be recognized by other people, and every person has the need to do something with the time between birth and death. These are biological and psychological needs that Berne calls "hungers."

The hungers for touch and recognition can be appeased with *strokes*, which are "any act implying recognition of another's presence" [1]. Strokes can be given in the form of actual physical touch or by some symbolic form of recognition such as a look, a word, a gesture, or any act that says "I know you're there."

People's hunger for strokes often determines what they do with their time. They may, for example, spend minutes, hours, or a lifetime trying to get strokes in many ways, including playing psychological games. They may spend minutes, hours, or a lifetime trying to avoid strokes by withdrawing.

STROKING HUNGER

Infants will not grow normally without the touch of others [2]. This need is usually met in the everyday intimate transactions of diapering, feeding, burping, powdering, fondling, and caressing that nurturing parents give their babies. Something about being touched stimulates an infant's chemistry for mental and physical growth. Infants who are neglected, ignored, or for any reason do not experience enough touch, suffer mental and physical deterioration even to the point of death.

New-born infants, isolated from normal touching after birth, young children placed in detention facilities, and children reared under the theory that "picking up babies spoils them" may have a touch deprivation similar to serious nutritional deficiencies. Both impair growth.

Among transactional analysts there is a saying, "If the infant is not stroked, his spinal cord shrivels up" [3]. The documentary film *Second Chance* [4], which is summarized below, dramatically illustrates the need for touch.

Case Illustration

When Susan's father left her at a large children's hospital, she was 22 months old. However, she weighed only 15 pounds (the weight of a five-month-old baby) and was 28 inches tall (the average height of a ten-month-old). She had practically no motor skills, could not crawl, could not speak or even babble. If people approached her, she withdrew in tears.

After three weeks during which no one had come to see Susan, a social worker contacted the mother. Both mother and father were above average in education, yet the mother complained, "Babies are a poor excuse for human beings." She described Susan as not liking to be held and wanting to be left alone. She said she had given up trying to make contact with Susan and, in regard to taking care of her, admitted, "I don't want to do that anymore."

Examinations showed no physical reason for Susan's extreme mental and physical retardation, and her case was diagnosed as "maternal deprivation syndrome."

A volunteer substitute mother was called in to give Susan loving care for six hours a day, five days a week. The hospital staff also gave Susan much attention, and she was held, rocked, played with, and fed with an abundance of physical touching.

Two months later, although she was still markedly retarded, Susan had a highly developed affectional response. She had also gained six pounds and had grown two inches. Her motor ability was greatly improved. She could crawl and could walk if holding on. Without fear she could relate to relative strangers. Tender loving care had had a remarkable effect on Susan.

As a child grows older, the early primary hunger for actual physical touch is modified and becomes recognition hunger. A smile, a nod, a word, a frown, a gesture eventually replace some touch strokes. Like touch, these forms of recognition, whether positive or negative, stimulate the brain of the one receiving them and serve to verify for the child the fact that she or he is there and alive. Recognition strokes also keep the child's nervous system from "shriveling."

Some people need a great deal of recognition in order to feel secure. This hunger can be strongly felt anywhere—in the home, the classroom, even on the job. In an industrial situation a supervisor complained that one of his lab workers was spending too much time at the water cooler, leaving his isolated lab every hour looking for someone to talk to. The supervisor, after being trained in TA, made it a practice to poke his head in the lab at intervals for a brief, friendly conversation with this worker. The trips into the hallway diminished considerably. As this supervisor discovered, the varying human needs for recognition confront anyone who works with people. Effective managers are often those who are able to touch and recognize others appropriately.

POSITIVE STROKING

The lack of sufficient strokes always has a detrimental effect on people. Although either negative or positive strokes may stimulate an infant's body chemistry, it takes *positive strokes* to develop emotionally healthy persons with a sense of OKness. Positive strokes range in value from the minimal maintenance of a "hello" to the depth encounter of intimacy.

Some strokes are merely surface encounters. These are simple transactions which can be thought of as maintenance strokes. They usually lack meaningful content but at least give recognition, keep communication open, and maintain the person's sense of being alive. Greeting rituals such as bowing and shaking hands are structured ways for getting and giving strokes of this nature.

Positive strokes are usually complementary transactions that are direct, appropriate, and relevant to the situation. When strokes are positive, they leave the person feeling good, alive, alert, and significant. At a greater depth they enhance the individual's sense of well-being, endorse the person's intelligence, and are often pleasurable. The feelings beneath are feelings of goodwill and convey the I'm OK, You're OK position. If the stroking is authentic, honestly jibes with the facts, and is not overdone, it nourishes a person. The individual's winning streak is expanded.

A parent gives a positive stroke by swooping up his or her child spontaneously with "Gee, I love you!" A supervisor gives a positive stroke by answering a subordinate's question straight. A clerk gives a customer a positive stroke by greeting the customer with "Good morning."

Positive strokes are often an expression of affectionate or appreciative feelings:

"You're sure fun to dance with."

"I'm glad I've got you for a son."

"You really saved the day for me by finishing that report."

"It's a pleasure to work in the same office with you."

Positive strokes are sometimes compliments:

"You look good enough to be on a magazine cover."

"Having a girl around is great."

"Your flower arrangements really brighten up the office."

"You swim like a champion."

"That's a good-looking sport jacket you picked out."

"Your proposal is clear, concise, and just what we needed."

Positive strokes can also give people information about their competencies, can help them become more aware of their individual skills and resources. For example, if a father has his son mow the lawn and then says, "You mowed the lawn well. It really looks good and I appreciate it," he allows the son to infer positive things about himself and to know he has specific abilities. This helps him to maintain his I'm OK, winner position.

One woman student reported that her parents had constantly

evaluated her performance with "You're such a sweet, nice girl!" This stroking was not unpleasant but when, at forty, she sought employment and was asked what she could do, the parent tape was turned on again, "You can be such a sweet and nice girl."

The same is true of strokes given from one grown-up to another. For example, a new secretary who capably wards off an unwanted office visitor may be complimented with "You're an angel" instead of "I appreciate the tact you used in handling that person." Although many secretaries enjoy occasionally being called an angel, it doesn't give them much data on their job competencies, especially if they're new.

A child receives positive strokes when a parent, teacher, or a friend gives a warm "hello," uses the child's name (pronounced accurately), looks the child in the face attentively, and most importantly, listens without condemnation to what the child has to say about personal feelings and thoughts. All preserve a sense of dignity.

Listening is one of the finest strokes one person can give another. The most effective listening involves focusing all one's attention on the speaker, a discipline which can be learned. Many unaware or disinterested people never develop the skill, consequently:

Children complain, "My parents never listen to me."

Parents complain, "My kids never listen to me."

Husbands and wives complain, "He (she) never really hears me."

Bosses complain, "If I've told him once, I've told him a hundred times, and he still doesn't listen."

Subordinates complain, "Nobody up there ever listens to us."

A person who has been listened to leaves the encounter knowing that his or her feelings, ideas, and opinions have been really heard. This person has not been "turned off," but has been given active feedback. Active listening, sometimes called reflective listening, involves giving verbal feedback of the content of what was said or done along with a guess at the feeling underneath the spoken words or acts. These are verbalized. Real listening does not necessarily mean agreement. It simply means clarifying and understanding another person's feelings and point of view.

When a teen-age boy comes home, throws his books on the table, and groans, "School is sure lousy," the mother who listens will say something like, "School seemed lousy today, and you're feeling pretty mad about it. Is that right?"

When a secretary suddenly begins to make a number of typing mistakes, mutters inaudibly, and snaps at office visitors, a boss who really listens will say something like, "From what you just said, you sound upset. Are you?"

In the above cases the Adult feedback transaction is used. Without condemning or condoning, the Adult listens to both the content and feelings that the other person expresses from the Child ego state. The receiver does not engage in "I" talk, but emphasizes the "you" message. This transaction is appropriate when one person has had strong feelings activated and needs to be listened to rather than lectured to.

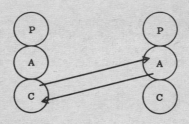

One teacher who had discipline problems in his class learned to use this transaction with a skill that improved the tone of his class. He confessed, "When I first tried this active listening, I really had to deal with my Parent and Child in my head. My first reaction to any behavior I didn't like was Parent, and I wanted to spank and scold the kid. My next reaction was Child. I felt very inadequate when kids misbehaved, and I thought, 'Boy, I'm a lousy teacher or this wouldn't happen.' Once I learned another way to respond, I didn't feel so inadequate or like scolding anymore. The kids seem to have a better feeling about the class, too."

Everyone needs strokes and if they do not get enough positive ones, they often provoke negative ones. Children can become bratty or delinquent, inviting parents to slap, scold, and degrade them. Spouses can whine, overspend, stay out late, flirt, drink, fight, or in some way provoke confrontation. The same applies to a working environment [5]. Workers can stall, make mistakes, hurt themselves. Studies show that if a job situation is sterile of feeling, the production goes down and conflict emerges. It appears that for children and grown-ups alike, negative attention is better than none.

DISCOUNTING AND NEGATIVE STROKING

If a parent discounts an infant's feelings and needs, healthy development is thwarted. A *discount* is either the lack of attention or negative attention that hurts emotionally or physically. A child who is ignored or given negative strokes receives the message, "You are not OK." A person who is ignored, teased, diminished, humiliated, physically degraded, laughed at, called names, or ridiculed is in some way being treated as insignificant. The individual is being discounted. Discounts always carry an ulterior put-down.

Many forms of discounting center on solving problems. A discount occurs if (1) the problem itself is not taken seriously (for example, if the mother watches TV while baby cries), (2) the significance of the problem is denied (a supervisor says, "You take it all too seriously. It's just not that important."), (3) the solution is denied ("There's nothing you can do about a wayward husband."), or (4) a person denies her or his own capacity to solve a problem ("I can't help it if I'm crabby. It's not my fault.") [6].

If a wife makes an honest inquiry of her husband, "Honey, when will you be home for dinner?" and he responds pompously, "I'll be home when you see me coming," she is discounted. Her significance is diminished by the ulterior message of "You're not important." From this toxic transaction she is likely to experience pain.

Being discounted is always painful. Between parents and children it leads to personality pathology—creating losers. Between grown-ups it leads to unhappy human relationships or feeds into destructive or "going nowhere" scripts.

As we saw in the Case Illustration about Susan, ignoring is a disastrous way of discounting a small child. Earl's case is somewhat similar. As a little boy he was rarely spoken to directly by his parents. One day, in desperation for some kind of direct encounter with them, he smashed a hole in the bedroom wall with his baseball bat and waited for their response. No response was forthcoming; his parents ignored his action. The next day he overheard his mother saying, "Earl must have fallen against the wall. There's a hole in it." Repeated incidents of being ignored so discounted the boy that he became psychotic.

The effects of insufficient touch can carry over into adult life.

Case Illustration

Howard was an only child. His mother was forty-one and his father fifty-eight when he was born. He was reared in a fourteen-room house on a two-acre plot of ground very isolated from neighbors. Howard described his parents as cool and aloof. Although they touched him if absolutely necessary, they never displayed a spontaneous burst of affection—a throwing of arms around him.

As a grown-up, Howard would not touch his wife and children. He rationalized his coolness by proclaiming, as his father had, "Public display of affection is in poor taste," and "Don't kiss me in front of the children, Alice. No telling what they might think!"

Howard was a teacher but found it uncomfortable to be with people and avoided them whenever he could. He refused to meet after class with students or parents, avoided faculty meetings, and described himself as "not able to get anywhere."

Howard's being insufficiently touched as a child contributed to his nonproductive script. He was indeed going nowhere until he discovered how to give and receive strokes. His learning to do this improved his home life and his career.

Parents ignore and fail to stroke their children for many reasons. Most often because in their own childhood they were themselves not touched enough and learned to "keep their distance."

Other parents, sensing their own intense anger, try to keep "hands off" as a deterrent for "knocking the kid's block off." As one father said, "If I ever touch her, I'm afraid I'll kill her. In fact, once when my father got mad, he threw my sister out of the window. Her skull was fractured and she never recovered."

Still other parents ignore their children because they resent them and the responsibility that accompanies them. Research indicates that as many as 700,000 unwanted American children are born each year [7]. Many of these children are never accepted by their parents and live in an emotional climate of hostility and rejection.

One mother describes the emotional climate she created because of her resentful reactions to her son, Dibs, a six-year-old schizophrenic who was considered mentally retarded although his intelligence quotient was 168:

He is a very difficult child to understand. I have tried. Really, I have tried. But I have failed. From the beginning, when he was an infant, I could not understand him. I had never really known any children before Dibs. I had no real experience as a woman with children or babies. I didn't have the slightest idea what they were like, really like as persons, that is. I knew all about them biologically, physically, and medically. But I could never understand Dibs. He was such a heartache—such a disappointment from the moment of his birth. We hadn't planned on having a child. His conception was an accident. He upset all our plans. I had my professional career, too. My husband was proud of my accomplishments. My husband and I were very happy before Dibs was born. And when he was born he was so different. So big and ugly. Such a big, shapeless chunk of a thing! Not responsive at all. In fact, he rejected me from the moment he was born. He would stiffen and cry everytime I picked him up! . . .

My pregnancy was very difficult, I was very ill most of the time. And my husband resented my pregnancy. He thought that I could have prevented it. Oh, I don't blame him. I resented it, too. We couldn't do any of the things we used to do together, couldn't go anyplace. I suppose I should say that we didn't, not couldn't. My husband stayed away more and more, buried himself in his work. He is a scientist, you know. A brilliant man! But remote. And very, very sensitive [8].

Ignoring and isolating people are well-known forms of punishment even for adults. Such punishment deprives persons of even minimal stroking and leads to intellectual, emotional, and physical deterioration.

If a discount is delivered through negative stroking, the not-OK message is sent either openly or by implication. To a little girl's request, "Can I wear my new dress?" direct discount could be "You're so sloppy you'll probably wreck it the first day." An implied discount could be "How can we be sure you won't be careless?" In either case, the girl infers "I can't be trusted."

Often, it is not the words but the intent which is expressed by tone of voice, facial expression, gesture, posture, and so forth, that makes a stroke ulterior and negative or straight and positive. A husband gives a positive stroke to his wife by saying, "Hi, honey," when he comes home from work. However, if a female clerk calls a customer "honey," she is likely to be discounting, implying that the customer is gullible.

Similar discounts are sometimes sent by people who facetiously say the opposite of what they mean. The following statements may, on paper, appear as compliments, but if said sarcastically or contemptuously, they are negative strokes. The real message is sent by an ulterior transaction through innuendo. Such is the case when

> "You look great in that sweater" is said with a disapproving look.

> "That's really good for the typewriter" is said sarcastically when someone is erasing directly over the working mechanism.

> "Your report is really something" is said with a sneer.

> "Well, good for you!" is said with a tone of disgust.

False flattery and false compliments delivered under the veil of sincerity are also forms of discounting:

> "Great idea!" says a committee chairman, although he may really think the idea is useless.

> "You're doing a great job" says a boss, although the sales volume has just dropped.

> "That hairdo is gorgeous" says a friend, when it's actually unbecoming.

Teasing remarks and gestures can be another form of discounting. A husband who says "No wonder the bumper's dragging, with you in the back seat" is likely to be expressing a real hostility toward his wife because she's overweight. Although adults can learn to say a straight "Lay off" when teasing really hurts them, this is very hard for children. Bach writes:

Parents fool themselves that children like to be teased. In truth, they put up with it, at best, to accommodate the parents' need for a hostility release.

When children allow themselves to be teased like "good sports," they are actually just hungry for parental attention. They are accepting the teasing or other hostilities as substitutes for genuine encouragement. To be teased is better than to be ignored [9].

Child battering is an extreme form of discounting usually carried out by parents who were themselves battered. The chain of battering can continue through several generations unless more adequate patterns for parent behavior are developed. In America it is estimated that 60,000 young children are killed or severely beaten each year at the hands of their parents. In San Francisco alone, 60 to 100 children who have been maimed by a parent come to the attention of authorities each year.

Parental violence toward children takes many forms. One father, who used pain as a training technique, burned his child's finger with a match while claiming he was teaching him to stay away from fire. Another father whipped his son and tied him to the bed for stealing a penny off the dresser. One mother beat her month-old infant, causing blood clots on his brain, and interpreted it, "No one loved me all my life, and then I had my baby and thought he would. When he cried I thought he didn't love me, so I hit him." He died.

Child-battering parents usually need professional treatment and often want it. Most of them have an inadequate Parent ego state as well as a hurt inner Child. By activating and informing their Adult ego states, these parents may learn what to realistically expect of a child and how to modify their own brutal behavior.

Case Illustration

Early in life Cynthia experienced physical cruelty. It was not uncommon for hot coffee to be "accidentally" spilled on her, and she suffered many scaldings. Cynthia was also deliberately cut with a knife by her mother "to teach her not to touch knives" and trained to avoid electrical sockets by having her finger stuck in one. Later, when Cynthia parented she was often cruel like her mother, brutalizing her own children. Furthermore, she was exceedingly suspicious if anyone was nice to her. She expected the "worst" to happen.

Through studying TA Cynthia became aware of what her mother had done to her and how she was repeating this behavior toward her children. She learned not to use the destructive behavior from her Parent ego state and instead parented by using Adult control. Eventually, she functioned as an adequate parent, stopped all display of brutality, and learned to give positive strokes.

Discounting in the work-a-day world usually is more subtle than physical violence. It takes either the form of crossed transactions or of ulterior put-downs, put-offs, and put-ons. Some put-offs at work resemble the "marshmallows" parents throw to their children to put them off. Berne writes:

Parental supportive statements (known colloquially as "throwing marshmallows" or "gumdrops") are fundamentally patronizing, and transactionally they are brush-offs. Functionally, they can be translated . . . as follows: (1) "I am glad to have an opportunity to patronize you; it makes me feel worthwhile," or (2) "Don't bother me with your troubles; take this marshmallow and keep quiet so I can talk about mine" [10].

One salesperson might toss a marshmallow to another with "That was terrible to have happen to you, but let me tell you about what happened to me that was even worse!" or "You think you've got troubles, just wait until you hear mine!"

The ways in which people are touched and recognized often affect their stroke patterns in Adult life. People who were brutalized or ignored tend to shrink from touch. People who were overstimulated may continue with an insatiable desire for physical contact; these people make very demanding spouses and may feel unloved unless they receive a great deal of physical touching. Many people develop peculiar touch patterns.

Case Illustration

One distressed husband complained that his wife wanted to have her back scratched whenever he felt amorous. He interpreted this as a rebuff and was further frustrated because she became negative when he wanted to fondle her breasts. In marriage counseling, his wife recalled that back-scratching was the only way her mother touched her affectionately as a child. To her, back-scratching meant love and affection. She also recalled that as a developing girl a farmhand grabbed her breasts unexpectedly and hurt her. She was adamant that she "didn't want to be hurt that way again."

This woman eventually learned not to confuse her husband with the farmhand. Every time the old, frightening tape was activated, she reminded herself, "This is my husband who loves me." She also gradually learned to cuddle in bed spoon fashion with her breasts touching her husband. Her husband in turn became more sensitive to her anxieties and realized that they were not negative reactions to his manhood.

THE HUNGER FOR STRUCTURED TIME

Being bored for a long time hastens emotional and physical deterioration in much the same way as inadequate stroking does. To avoid the pain of boredom, people seek something to do with their time. What parent has not heard a bored child whining, "Mama, what can I do now?" What married couple hasn't sat around musing, "What can we do this weekend?" What worker hasn't heard another one say, "I hate this job when there's not enough to do."

People structure their time in six possible ways. Sometimes, they withdraw from other people; sometimes, they engage in rituals or pastimes; sometimes, they play psychological games; sometimes, they work together; and occasionally, they experience a moment of intimacy.

Withdrawal

People themselves can withdraw from others either by removing themselves physically or by removing themselves psychologically, withdrawing into their fantasies. Withdrawal behavior can come from any of the three ego states.

Withdrawing is sometimes a rational Adult decision. People need time to be alone, to relax, to think their own thoughts, to take stock of themselves, and to be rejuvenated in their individual humanness. Even withdrawal into one's fantasies is often legitimate. A good fantasy may be a better use of time than listening to a bad lecture.

Withdrawing is sometimes based on copying parents. In this case, the person imitates parental behavior. For example, a man threatened by conflict with his wife may withdraw as his father did when his mother got mad. He may leave the house, retire to the shop, or go to his study. Or, instead of physically leaving, he may go to sleep or simply "tune out" his wife, not hearing what she says.

Withdrawing patterns also come from the Child ego state. These are often replays of a person's childhood adaptations out of the necessity for self-protection from pain or conflict. They may also be the result of training. A child trained to "Go to your room and shut the door and don't come out until you have a smile on your face" learns to withdraw either physically or psychologically behind a forced smile.

When a person withdraws psychologically, it is often into a fantasy world. These fantasies are likely to be of uncensored pleasure or violence, creative imaginings, or of learned fears and catastrophic expectations. Everyone withdraws into fantasy from time to time. Who hasn't imagined all those great things that "could have" been said? Who hasn't engaged in some fanciful, uncensored pleasure?

Rituals

Ritual transactions are simple and stereotyped complementary transactions, like everyday hellos and goodbyes. Someone who says, "Good morning, how are you?" is, in most instances, not actually inquiring into the other person's health and feelings, but instead is expecting to receive a ritualistic response, "Fine, how are you?" In this brief encounter both persons get maintenance strokes.

Many rituals of this nature grease the wheels of social interchange. They give strangers a way of coming together, they save time in figuring out who should go first or be served first, and so forth. Some cultures, church groups, political parties, secret orders, and social clubs structure a great deal of time with highly ritualistic patterns of behavior. Other groups are less structured, using their time in other ways. For many people, rituals become a way of life. After the ceremony is long past, the marriage may be only a series of ritualistic transactions consisting mainly of role-playing, of actions devoid of real meaning and intimacy, yet keeping the people alive with minimum strokes.

Pastimes

Pastime transactions are those in which people pass time with one another by talking about innocuous subjects, such as the weather. Who hasn't seen two old men sitting on a park bench avidly discussing politics? "The government ought to straighten out this mess . . .!" Who hasn't heard two parents passing time sharing common prejudices, "Aren't kids terrible today. The way they . . ." In both cases the persons may exchange opinion after opinion with total disregard for the facts and enjoy every minute of it.

Pastimes are relatively safe; these superficial exchanges are often used between people who don't know each other well. For example, at a dinner party it is not uncommon for the men to pass the time talking about occupations, cars, sports, or the stock market, while the women pass the time talking about recipes, children, or decorating.

Pastimes, as well as rituals, are ways people spend time together politely without getting involved at a deeper level. They provide the opportunity for people to "psych" each other out for the possibility of further involvement in games, activities, or intimacy.

Games

One "advantage" of playing psychological games is to structure time. Some games structure only five minutes of time. For example, a secretary who plays *Blemish* takes a few minutes to point out that the boss always forgets to put the "s" on the third-person singular verb or frequently misspells "absence."

Other games, such as *Debtor*, can structure a lifetime. For example, when a young married couple play *Debtor*, they go into heavy debt for furniture, appliances, cars, boats, and so on, and with each salary raise they go further into debt—a bigger house, two cars, and so forth. For a whole lifetime, no matter what they earn, they're always in debt. When *Debtors* play a "harder" game, they may end up filing for bankruptcy or going to jail.

Activities

Activities are ways of structuring time that deal with external reality and are commonly thought of as work, getting something done.

PLATE IV

THE NEED FOR TOUCH

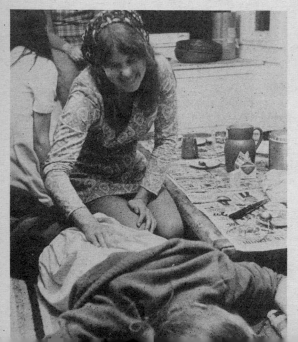

The hunger for touch is appeased with positive strokes.

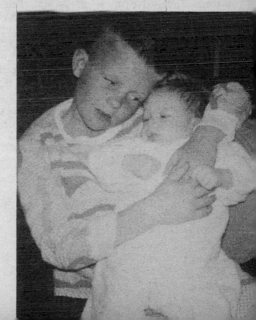

Activities are often what people want to do, need to do, or have to do—alone or with others.

serving on a committee	playing in a band
programming a missile	preparing a joint project
weeding the garden	answering the phone
organizing a precinct	cooking dinner
dictating a letter	unloading a ship
building a house	sewing a dress
drawing blueprints	building bridges

When some of the above and other time-honored activities come to an end, a person frequently feels empty, restless, or useless. This problem comes into sharp awareness when certain time-structuring activities, such as caring for children, going to school, or holding a job, come to an abrupt end.

Many mothers who completely fill their time with children and household chores are overwhelmed with a sense of boredom and inadequacy when the children grow up and leave home. Similarly, a father who devotes his life to being a breadwinner may suffer the same boredom and deteriorate rapidly after retirement.

In the midst of activities different ways for structuring time can emerge. Rituals, pastimes, games, and even intimacy may occur. For example, vice-presidents can play *Harried Executive* on the job, saying "Yes" to so many requests that they finally collapse. In the meantime, they harass and overwork their secretaries as well. When these Mr. or Ms. Harrieds leave the room, their secretaries may switch from their typing and filing activities to a common pastime of *Ain't it Awful*. "What a boss! saying 'Yes' to everybody, and we end up with a lot of extra work. Ain't it awful." When the boss re-enters the room, they may switch back to work activities or move to the ritual of a coffee break or withdraw into their own fantasies—perhaps angry ones—or initiate a game.

Intimacy

At a deeper level of human encounter than rituals, pastimes, games, and activities lies the potential that each person has for intimacy. Intimacy is free of games and free of exploitation. It occurs in those rare moments of human contact that arouse feelings of tenderness, empathy, and affection. Such affection is not just the warm sensation a person might get from a glimpse of shapely legs or broad shoulders. Intimacy involves genuine caring.

People can live or work together for many years but never really "see" or "hear" each other. Yet, a moment may come when one sees the other for the first time—sees the other's coloring, the other's expressions, the other's many shapes, movements, differences. The one may also hear the other for the first time—hear all the other's messages, verbal and nonverbal, emotional and factual.

The sense of intimacy can occur in the midst of a crowd or in a continuing friendship, at work or in a marriage relationship. Intimacy may happen if:

> A person at a concert briefly catches the eye of a stranger. For that moment they are aware of the bond of mutual enjoyment. They smile openly at each other in a moment of intimacy.

> A husband and wife at work weeding their garden experience a sense of closeness which spontaneously leads them to physical contact that validates their affection

> A father looks into the tear-soiled face of his son who has just buried his dog. He puts his arm around the boy and says, "It's tough to bury a good friend." The boy melts into his father's arms, releasing his grief. For that moment they are close.

> Two men work together for several weeks preparing an important proposal for the company. One presents it to management and the proposal is rejected. When he returns, his colleague looks into his face, and without words a feeling of understanding for their mutual disappointment passes between them.

Any activities such as going to a concert, digging in a garden, burying a dog, or working on a proposal serve as a context in which intimacy can occur. In modern life intimacy seems rare. People who feel crowded in one way or another often seek "psychological" space. They may withdraw or resort to ritualistic living and use "keeping your distance" techniques. Even when jammed into a crowded elevator or train they remain distant, pretending not to see one another.

Intimacy is often frightening because it involves risk. In an intimate relationship people are vulnerable, and many times it seems easier to pass time or to play games than to risk feelings either of affection or of rejection.

If the capacity for intimacy has been unnecessarily suppressed, it can be recovered. Through activating and strengthening the Adult ego state, people can change in spite of their early life experiences. Recovering the capacity for intimacy is a major goal of TA and is one of the marks of an autonomous person. Winners risk genuine intimacy [11].

SUMMARY

Every infant needs touch to grow. Positive stroking encourages infants to grow into the winners they were born to be. Discounting encourages losers. Infants who are ignored or stroked negatively are encouraged to become losers. Unless there is a strong intervention and a decision to fight against the loser's script, these people, in turn, tend to produce other losers.

Your own mental and physical health are likely to be related to the ways you were touched and recognized. If you have negative patterns about touch or recognition and wish to expand your capabilities, it is never too late to learn how.

Learning to change old habits of discounting is not always easy. However, people can become aware of how they discount themselves and others and develop new patterns of transacting. Instead of giving an ulterior put-down, they can deliberately activate their Adult to check destructive remarks and behavior. They can filter what they choose to use from their Parent and Child ego states through their Adult. Instead of discounting, they can give positive strokes to others and even to themselves. They take responsibility for their behavior.

Actual parents who are trying to make such changes usually need more Adult data. They need the skills taught in parent training courses [12]. They need to study child development. They need to watch more "successful" parents. And they need to work on transacting in nourishing ways.

When people decide to do this, their messages become more appropriate to the situation—clear, undiluted, direct, and relevant. They talk straight. When a little girl asks if she can wear her new dress, the parent states "Yes" or "No" with rational reasons. When a wife asks her husband when he'll be home, he answers her with available data.

PLATE V

STRUCTURING
TIME

Sometimes people engage in psychological games learned in childhood.

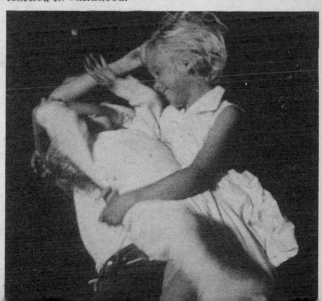

PLATE V
(continued)

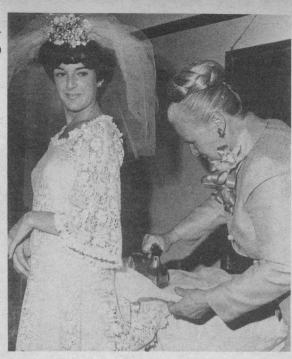

Sometimes they: engage in ritual or pastimes,
experience a moment of
intimacy, withdraw from one
another, work together.

Time is structured in the process of getting, giving, or avoiding strokes. Withdrawing is a way to avoid strokes. Rituals and pastimes provide minimal stroking at a superficial level. Games are also a source of strokes—often negative. Activities and intimacy allow for positive strokes that are befitting a winner.

EXPERIMENTS AND EXERCISES

1. You and Touch

To become more aware of your touch patterns, reflect on the last forty-eight hours. Evaluate your capacity to give and receive touch.

• Whom did you touch? How did you touch them? Positively? Negatively?

• Did you avoid touching someone? Why? Do you wish you had touched someone? Why?

• Who touched you? How did they touch you? Positively? Negatively?

• Did you avoid letting someone touch you? Why? Do you wish someone had touched you?

Now think of your hunger for touch as if it were on a continuum ranging from avoiding touch to seeking it incessantly. Where do you judge yourself to be on the continuum? Where would you like to be?

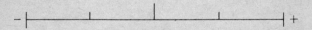

Now use a continuum to evaluate the frequency with which you touch others, the intensity you use, the authenticity of your touch.

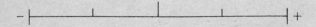

Can you relate your current touch patterns to your childhood experiences? If you can't remember how you were touched—and where—the following exercise will help.

• Draw an outline of your body, both front and back. Color the areas red where you were touched a great deal; color them pink where you were touched less frequently; green where you were seldom touched; blue where you were never touched. Where the touching was negative, draw black lines through the color. [13]

• Study your "touch portrait." Try to re-experience old feelings. Do you have current touch barriers that relate to these early experiences?

Now try one of Bernard Gunther's experiments in sensory awareness.

• ". . . Bend your fingers at the joints and begin tapping the top of your head; a lively half-inch bouncing vigorous tap like rain falling (15-20 seconds in each area). Next tap around the ears and the sides of the head. Then over the forehead. Now re-tap over your entire head, doing an especially good job over any place that feels it needs a little extra; gradually let the tapping subside. Put your hands down to your sides, close your eyes and become aware of how your head feels as a result of what you've just done and then slowly open your eyes." [14]

This experiment is for those fearful of touch:

• Think of one touch pattern you'd like to change. What is it you do now? What do you want to be able to do?

• Imagine yourself doing something different. Picture yourself in many situations touching the way you want to.

• Now filter through your imagining and ask yourself "What would be all right to do?"

• Imagine yourself doing this many times. See the other person. See yourself touching.

• When you feel confident enough, try it with an actual person.

2. You and Recognition

To become aware of your recognition patterns, return to Experiment 1. Substitute the word "recognition" for the word "touch."

Evaluate your hunger for recognition on the continuum below.

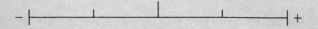

Now evaluate your ability to give recognition to others.

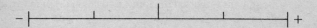

- Are you satisfied with your placement on the continuums? If not, what would you change?

Now recall the kind of recognition you received as a child. Do you believe your parents gave you enough? Was it positive or negative?

- How did they compliment or criticize you? What words did they use?

- What nonverbal messages of recognition were given to you? Were there any family signals such as winks of approval, hand signs indicating "O.K." or "crazy in the head," a finger shake of "no, no," a clenched fist in the face, or a threatening removal of a belt?

Consider your current recognition patterns:

- Do you now copy the recognition patterns of your parents with your children, friends, or work associates?

- What patterns have you successfully changed?

- Is there anyone in your life now—a spouse, boss, friend—who gives you the same kind of either negative or positive recognition as your parents did?

3. You and Time Structuring

- What did your parents say about time? Did they use phrases such as: "You only live once," "Enjoy it while you may," "Don't waste your time," "What are you going to do, sit around all day? Get going," or "Relax, honey, there's always another day."?

- How did they use their own time?

- Do any of their verbal or nonverbal messages on time influence you today? Do you feel driven, lazy, confused, stalled, fulfilled, empty, what?

- Are you fighting time? Killing it? Using it? Enjoying it?

- Now select an average weekday and try to determine what percentage of your time is structured with rituals, pastimes, withdrawing, activities, games, and intimacy.

- Do the same exercise considering a weekend.

- Are you satisfied with your attitudes and feelings about time?

- If not, what would you consider a better use of the time of your life? For example, if you stopped playing a game with your spouse or a friend, how could you structure your time in a more satisfying manner?

- When you are at work but not actually working, how do you structure your time?

4. Your Capacity for Intimacy

This experiment is for those who want to become more aware of their capacity for intimacy [15]. It should be conducted with a spouse or a trusted friend and with their agreement. The agreement should include a decision not to withdraw and not to indulge in rituals, pastimes, or games. Set a time limit of fifteen minutes.

Select a quiet place with few distractions. Sit facing each other, not more than five feet apart. Look directly into each other's eyes.

Take turns sharing something with each other that is a genuine concern—a worry, an interest, an incident. Share both thoughts and feelings.

When listening, try to give active feedback. When speaking, try to be clear. Be aware of your emotions and express them. Be aware of how your emotions change.

Share back and forth several times. What feelings do you have toward your partner after the experiment?

4

The Drama of Life Scripts

*All the world's a stage
And all the men and women merely players.
They have their exits and their entrances;
Each man in his time plays many parts.*
  Shakespeare

Most people are involved in some form of theatrics, performing on several stages for different audiences. At times, the audience exists only in the mind.

According to Frederick Perls, each person has two stages—the private stage where, in the hiddenness of secret thoughts, one continually rehearses for the future, and the public stage where a person's acting can be seen. Perls claims, "We live on two levels—the public level which is our *doing,* which is observable, verifiable; and the private stage, the thinking stage, the rehearsing stage, on which we prepare for the future roles we want to play" [1].

Rehearsing on the private stage in the mind may sometimes be appropriate, but too much of it leaves a person tuned out and preoccupied.

Case Illustration

At her first group counseling session, Doris avoided looking at anybody. She stared at the ceiling, the wall, the floor, or at her hands. When asked what was going on inside, she replied, "I was trying to figure out how I should act here. I thought and thought about it all the way over but still don't know what to do. I know I want everyone to like me. It may sound silly but I wondered, should I act shy or would I be liked better if I came on strong? Should I act smart or dumb? I was thinking so hard about it I almost didn't see a dog run in front of my car."

Doris had been so preoccupied with rehearsing on her private stage for the kind of performance she intended to act out on the public stage of the counseling group, that it was almost as though she didn't have eyes.

Public stages on which people act out their scripts can be home, place of worship, social gatherings, school, office, factory, etc. Some people prefer one stage over others. This is true of a person whose time is spent mostly at the office rather than at home, or of a person who is the perpetual student and whose only public stage is the campus. However, most people spread their energies to several stages and often play different parts on each. A man who is a tough boss on the job may, at home, become a mass of jelly at the hands of his three-year-old daughter.

SCRIPTS

In the life of every individual the dramatic life events, the roles that are learned, rehearsed, and acted out, are originally determined by a script.

A psychological script [2] bears a striking resemblance to a theatrical script. Each has a prescribed cast of characters, dialogue, acts and scenes, themes and plots, which move toward a climax and end with a final curtain. A psychological script is a person's ongoing program for a life drama which dictates where the person is going with his or her life and the path that will lead there. It is a drama an individual compulsively acts out, though one's awareness of it may be vague.

A person's script may resemble a soap opera, a wild adventure, a tragedy, a saga, a farce, a romance, a joyful comedy, or a dull play that bores the players and would put an audience to sleep. Different dramas contain varying degrees of constructiveness, destructiveness, or nonproductiveness—going nowhere.

The drama of life starts at birth. Script instructions are programmed into the Child ego state through transactions between parent figures and their children. As children grow they learn to play parts—heroes, heroines, villains, victims, and rescuers and—unknowingly—seek others to play complementary roles.

When grown up, people play out their scripts within the context of the society in which they live and which has its own dramatic patterns. As Shakespeare said, all the world *is* a stage. Individuals follow scripts; families follow scripts; nations follow scripts [3, 4]. Each individual's life is a unique drama which can include elements of both family and cultural scripts. The interplay of these scripts affects the drama of each person's life and thereby unfolds the history of a people.

CULTURAL SCRIPTS

Cultural scripts are the accepted and expected dramatic patterns that occur within a society. They are determined by the spoken and unspoken assumptions believed by the majority of the people within that group. Like theatrical scripts, cultural scripts have themes, characters, expected roles, stage directions, costumes, settings, scenes, and final curtains. Cultural scripts reflect what is thought of as the "national character." The same drama may be repeated generation after generation.

Script themes differ from one culture to another. The script can contain themes of suffering, persecution, and hardship (historically, the Jews); it can contain themes of building empires and making conquests (as the Romans once did). Throughout history some nations have acted from a "top-dog" position of the conqueror; some from an "underdog" position of the conquered. In early America, where people came to escape oppression, to exploit the situation, and to explore the unknown, a basic theme was "struggling for survival." In many cases this struggle was acted out by pioneering and settling. Some people managed both.

Early pioneers were always on the move, looking for new "stages," taking risks, and setting the scene for the settlers who followed. Even though some of the scenery, acts, characters, and actions changed, the basic theme often remained the same. Today, a similar pioneering script is being acted out by the astronauts, though with different costumes and settings. Coonskin caps have given way to complicated headgear, horses to space ships, grandma's Sunday pot roasts to food sucked from plastic bags.

The scenery has changed from lands and waters to space and moon dust; the action from self-reliance to technological dependence. Space pioneers, like their earlier counterparts, may be setting a new scene for settlers who will follow. Not all pioneering is geographical, however. The same spirit can be observed on other vast frontiers, those of the scientific and the social worlds.

In contrast to always being on the move, as were the pioneers, the early American settlers' script was to dig in and put down roots. Settlers tilled the soil, built homes and towns, established businesses, worked hard to acquire material goods and to build the population. Their struggle was hard, and their lives short and precarious.

Currently, a large segment of American society—certainly not all of it—is no longer preoccupied with the struggle for individual survival. A modern-day settler has a life expectancy approaching eighty years. Rather than working independently, today's settler is likely to be part of a large corporation or of a government structure. Rather than eking out a bare physical existence, the settler may become caught up in the pleasures and problems of affluence.

As times change, new script themes emerge: getting educated, making money, seeking pleasure, and searching for life's meaning. Today, the American stage is overcrowded with people and goods, and the curtain rises on a new scene. When a large percentage of individuals take on themes that are different from the current premises of their culture, the dramatic style of the entire culture begins to change. Whereas some transitions are relatively painless, others are fraught with anguish and even bloodshed.

Many modern youths, born into a different setting from that of their parents, are rejecting earlier script themes as having no value or relevance to *their* lives. Yet, many are again facing the "struggling for survival" theme as it re-emerges in terms of the survival of the human race and the preservation of the natural environment.

In addition to themes, cultural scripts usually dictate specific roles. Most cultures differentiate—rationally or irrationally—between the roles men are to play and those expected of women [5]. Margaret Mead describes a New Guinea tribe in which men are scripted to be passive and women are scripted to be aggressive. Men are expected to act as nurturing fathers, tending the children and living quarters. Women are expected to be aggressive providers. Yet in the United States a man who chooses to keep the home fires burning while the woman brings home the bacon is likely to be downgraded in some segments of society.

In contrast to the New Guinea tribe, a headhunter tribe near

Burma scripts the boys from birth for battle and brutality. Each boy rehearses his warrior role daily in preparation for his expected violent death scene. Few men live past their prime; women accept their men's being killed off and share those who are left.

A somewhat similar battling pattern exists in the United States; men are expected to fight wars, and women are not. This expectancy is accepted by many, although sharing the men who survive is not so popular. In contrast, both men and women of Israel are expected to learn techniques of fighting, and both sexes are drafted.

Whereas some cultures call for sex roles to be polarized, others call for them to overlap, thus making role interchange easy. No matter what the sex roles, destruction in some form is written into the scripts of most cultures. *Between* cultures it is manifested through economic exploitation and wars. *Within* a culture, suicide, homicide, overpopulation, and upsetting the ecological balance work a different kind of destruction.

Japan has, in the past, encouraged suicide as an honorable final scene and still has one of the world's highest suicide rates. In 1964 West Berlin's suicide rate was extremely high, with men killing themselves at the rate of 56.3 per 100,000 and women at the rate of 30.9. Other countries with high suicide rates are Switzerland, Austria, Sweden, and Denmark.

Although the suicide rate per capita in the United States is half that of Sweden and Denmark, the homicide rate is ten times higher [6]. In the United States violent crime is increasing appreciably. This indicates that a significant number of people are being scripted in one way or another toward violence.

Some cultures, instead of scripting for sudden death, script for a slower form of destruction through the overproduction of "characters." When the cast becomes too large for the capacities of the stage, the inevitable end is death by famine and disease. Overpopulation, such as that of India, is a form of national suicide and is fostered when individuals perpetuate family scripts that call for large families. The population explosion brings a new set of problems. The number of people alive today is half as great as the number of all those who have ever lived [7]!

Cultural scripts have stage directions for the cast of characters. These include such details as acceptable postures, gestures, and actions. Even the show of emotion can be culturally determined. Many Italian men show their feelings easily. Without self-consciousness, they hug each other in warm embrace. In America, where British influence is overriding, such a demonstrative display between men is considered suspect. Most cultures have favorite postures and gestures centered on such things as rituals, sexual behaviors, and manners. The following case illustrates how this aspect of a cultural script is reflected in individual behavior.

Case Illustration

Mai, a beautiful Chinese-American woman, came to a marathon* knowing what she wanted to work on. She stated her contract. "I want to have more freedom in my behavior. We Chinese are always so polite; we never interrupt, we never disagree. Worse than that, we never show our emotions. I do not want to go on in this traditional Chinese way." Mai was asked to use the gestalt technique of thinking and acting in opposites. "What culture has behavior that you think of as quite different from Chinese behavior?" "Oh," she replied instantly, "the Italians'!" It was suggested that she stand in front of the group and address each group member, first with her traditional Chinese behavior, then with her concept of Italian behavior. She did this with increasing enthusiasm, exaggerating her emotions, voice, and expression. Finally she collapsed in a chair, threw up her hands and, with a gale of laughter, said, "Oh, mama mia. Now there are at least two me's—my Chinese me and my Italian me."

Some individuals accept their cultural script, some do not. If individuals' life dramas fit the expectations of their culture, they receive acceptance and approval. For example, if "making money" is the cultural focus, people who do well financially are highly regarded. Their scripts are harmonious with that of their culture.

Other people in the same culture may be considered failures if they choose to pursue their own interests, ideas, or talents and reject the "making money" theme. Because their personal scripts are out of harmony with that of their culture, they are likely to receive disapproval, ridicule, or punishment from others.

In human history many cultural scripts contain themes reflect-

---

* A marathon is intensive group counseling for a concentrated period of time, for a full day or a weekend.

ing supernatural or religious beliefs. These may be anathema to certain individuals within the culture, and consequently the scripts clash. For example, during a time when most decision-making was considered to be a function of the Church, the Italian scientist Galileo (1564–1642) thought for himself, applied his own knowledge, and made his own observations. Against the wishes of the Church, he took a firm stand favoring the theory that the earth revolves around the sun, not the sun around the earth. The Church maintained that human beings had a unique and favored relationship to God; therefore, they and the earth had to be the center of things. Galileo was forced to recant in public, and until his death he was forbidden to take part in further public discussion of religious or political matters.

Similarly, in the 1600s, Anne Hutchinson of Boston challenged the prevailing Puritan theology. Not only was she against the religious dogma, but also against the practice of denying women a voice in the Church. Evidently her personal script, like that of Galileo, gave her permission to think for herself. She openly provoked others, including women, to do the same. For this she suffered a long, miserable trial, was convicted of heresy, excommunicated, and sent into the wilderness for punishment. Eventually she and her family were massacred. The only voice raised in Mrs. Hutchinson's defense was that of a young woman, Mary Dyer. Twenty two years later the same drama seems to have been repeated when she, too, lost her life; she was hanged as a Quaker by the Boston fathers [8].

While it is likely that some individuals will always blame their lack of achievement on the culture, it is also likely that history is filled with men and women who were themselves autonomous, thoughtful people but who existed within a cultural script that could not tolerate their introducing new, dramatic possibilities.

It is also true that history is filled with women and men who were able to remain autonomous and exist and grow even though they were surrounded by a cultural script that was hostile to them. Both Harriet Tubman and George Washington Carver, in the face of racial discrimination, achieved remarkably in their separate areas of endeavor. Bruno Bettelheim and Victor Frankl, although prisoners in Nazi concentration camps, survived, deepened their knowledge, and made significant contributions to the treatment of people with severe emotional disorders.

SUBCULTURAL SCRIPTS

When a culture is large and complex, many subcultures exist within it. Subcultures are often defined by geographical location, ethnic backgrounds, religious beliefs, sex, education, age, or other common bonds. For example, in the past, it was common for youths to imitate the older generations, looking forward to being like them. However, today it is not uncommon for youths to distinguish themselves from their predecessors by dress, hair styles, tastes in music, dance, vocabulary, personal adornment and grooming, and to place a high value on the opinions of their peer group.

Each subculture, whether related to age or some other element, evolves its own dramatic actions. The persons within it may identify themselves by saying "we" and may identify other subcultures by saying "those".

We Texans	Those Hippies
We Easterners	Those squares
We Presbyterians	Those Jews
We Catholics	Those atheists
We Blacks	Those Irish
We Chicanos	Those Germans

Conflict often erupts between subcultural scripts: rich versus poor, liberal versus conservative, Protestant versus Catholic. Conflicts may also occur between scripts of a subculture and scripts of a larger culture: Jews versus Christians, uneducated versus educated, Black versus White. A Mexican-American boy of thirteen demonstrated such conflict when he said, "Wow, if we Chicanos speak Spanish at school, we really get it in the neck from the teachers. At home, if I use English instead of Spanish, my dad blows his stack. Another hang-up I've got is my moustache. My teacher says I have to shave it off, but my mom says it's great—shows I'm getting to be a man. No matter what I do I can't win."

The dramatic differences subcultures can introduce are allowable only in a tolerant larger culture. Yet, even in a tolerant culture there are always individuals who abhor, or are fearful of, differences. Each nation has its own unique script patterns concerning subcultures.

FAMILY SCRIPTS

When cultural and subcultural scripts are perpetuated, it is usually done so through the family. Naturally, all families have dramatic patterns which contain elements of the cultural scripts. Some families, however, develop unique sets of dramas and insist on the children's playing the appropriate traditional roles [9].

A family script contains identifiable traditions and expectations for each family member which are successfully transmitted generation after generation. These scripts are passed from Parent ego states to Parent ego states. Historically, they are observable in royal families or in wealthy families that for generations have produced philanthropists, politicians, professionals, dictators, and so forth. Losers run in families. Winners run in families.

When family scripts are perpetuated, the unity of family members and expectations for certain behavior are indicated by such phrases as:

"We Grahams have always lived off the land and always will."

"We Adamses will always be the life blood of this community."

"We Kellys are known for our good deeds."

"The traditions in our family would not allow us to be cowards."

"In our family, we'd starve rather than ask for help."

"The Edwardses have always been a cut above others."

"Everyone's down on us Joneses."

"The women in our family have always been tough as crabgrass."

"In our family, the home is a man's castle."

Some family scripts include long-held traditions about vocational expectancies:

"There's always been a doctor in our family."

"We Marshalls come from a long line of educators."

"We Smith women have always made good nurses."

"We Goldens have produced three generations of politicians."

"There's always at least one horse thief in our family."

"The sons in our family have a reputation for upholding the traditions of the armed services."

A family member who does not live up to the script expectation is often thought of as the "black sheep." However, a particular family script could call for a black sheep to add intrigue or the possibility of a scapegoat to the family scene.

Many family scripts have an explicit set of directions for each individual in the family, with different expectations for each sex. For example, it is not uncommon for the firstborn son to hold a unique position within the family. One graduate student reporting on her family scripting stated:

Our family script has its roots in Italy. Every son has to be an altar boy. First Communion day is as important as a birthday. The oldest son is always expected to become a priest. At least one daughter is expected to enter the convent. In fact, I remember deciding against being a nun when I was about nine because I couldn't wear high heels at the convent.

Another student reported:

In our family the boys follow in the footsteps of their father. They are expected to be farmers. The girls make their husbands and children their careers, and anything else is attacked for being unfeminine. Mother often said, "The Lord made you female to have children and to take care of a husband. Running the world is for men." It's always been this way in our family. So when I became a teacher, it caused a lot of consternation. Part of me felt proud of myself; another part felt as if I'd done something wrong and disgraced my family. I really felt caught in a bind.

Current research [10] indicates that the kind of scripting for girls which equates intellectual achievement with loss of femininity is a common theme in many American families. When this is the case, the woman who uses her intelligence may tend to belittle her successes and suffer from feelings of guilt over not being "womanly."

As noted in the previous cases, not all families perpetuate family scripts. In fact, many individuals and/or families work at deliberately throwing off the script traditions of the "old country" or those of the older generation. Some traditions simply die because they are difficult to maintain when circumstances are changing rapidly. This can be experienced as "cultural shock." Currently, new scripts are evolving, and the tendency is toward a dwindling sense of community and a weakening family structure. We find:

People turning to government for assistance rather than to their families.

Offspring no longer taking care of aging parents.

Children, parents, and grandparents so separated by distance—either physical, emotional, or intellectual—that they have difficulty even spending holidays together.

More young people becoming involved in social and political commitments.

Family scripts can be changed by an outside influence. Certain families in the United States, poverty stricken for generations, have low expectations for themselves and others. The children are scripted for failure. This is particularly true in reference to education. Thomas Szasz writes:

Since uneducated men cannot compete on equal footing in the game of life with their better educated brothers, they tend to become chronic losers. Players who always lose cannot be expected to harbor affectionate feelings toward either the game or their opponents [11].

If a strong corrective is applied, family scripts of poverty and failure change. Dramatic evidence of this reversal is seen in many American Negro families, who all too often are poor. Under the influence of leaders who claim "Black is beautiful" or "I'm black and I'm proud," failure scripts can be rewritten toward self-respect and achievement. Potential losers can become potential winners.

When old expectations and traditions are thrown off or are no longer possible, new scripts emerge. The experience of change can be painful or pleasurable, disrupting or unifying, for better or for worse, or a mixture of all these things.

Some family scripts promote success, some promote failure. Some families rewrite their scripts by promoting change. However, in the life of any one individual, the most important forces in forming his or her script are the messages received from parents.

PSYCHOLOGICAL SCRIPTS OF AN INDIVIDUAL

The compulsion to live out the preprogrammed, ongoing life drama is a difficult aspect of the personality to understand.* Yet, in daily life most people experience or observe in others a compulsion to perform in a certain way, to live up to a specific identity, and to fulfill a destiny. This is most observable in the individual whose personal drama is destructive, who commits suicide or homicide.

You probably know someone who is moving toward a tragic ending—suicide or one of its equivalents, such as alcoholism, drugs, or obesity.

You probably know someone who is struggling to get to the top, no matter what the cost to self or others.

You probably know someone who enjoys living, exploring, thinking, and changing.

You also may know someone who keeps going around in circles, never getting anywhere and living each day much the same as the day before, or someone who lives like a vegetable, merely existing instead of really living.

According to Eric Berne:

Nearly all human activity is programmed by an ongoing script dating from early childhood, so that the feeling of autonomy is nearly always an illusion—an illusion which is the greatest affliction of the human race because it makes awareness, honesty, creativity, and intimacy possible for only a few fortunate individuals. For the rest of humanity, other people are seen mainly as objects to be manipulated. They must be invited, persuaded, seduced, bribed, or forced into playing the proper roles to reinforce the protagonist's position and fulfill his script, and his preoccupation with these efforts keeps him from torquing in with the real world and his own possibilities in it [12].

A person's script will always be based on three questions that involve personal identity and destiny: Who am I? What am I doing here? and Who are all those others? Experiences may lead a person to conclude:

* At this writing, the theory and nomenclature are still in the process of being developed by theorists. See *Transactional Analysis Bulletin,* Oct., 1969, Vol. 8, p. 112.

I'm a bum. I'll never amount to anything. Other bums put me down.

I've got a good head on my shoulders. I can do whatever I decide to do. Other people will help me.

I'm stupid. I'll never do anything good enough. Other people know what to do.

HOW SCRIPTING OCCURS

Scripting first occurs nonverbally. Infants, almost as if they had radar, begin to pick up messages about themselves and their worth through their first experiences of being touched or being ignored by others. Soon they see facial expressions and respond to them as well as to touch and to sounds. Children who are cuddled affectionately, smiled at, and talked to receive different messages from those who are handled with fright, hostility, or anxiety. Children who receive little touch and who experience parental indifference or hostility are discounted. They learn to feel they are not OK and perhaps may feel like a "nothing."

Children's first feelings about themselves are likely to remain the most powerful force in their life dramas, significantly influencing the psychological positions they take and the roles they play.

Within their first few years, children begin to understand the scripting messages their parents put into words. These messages are instructions that the child later feels compelled to follow:

"You'll be famous some day."

"You'll never amount to anything."

"You're a great kid."

"You're sure nutty."

"Boy, you're something else."

"You're slower than molasses."

"You're a bad seed."

"We'd have been better off without you."

A child is scripted occupationally when parents say:

"George was cut out to be a doctor."

"That kid will never hold a job."

"With your get up and go, you could sell refrigerators to Eskimos."

"What a nurse you'd make!"

"She's too lazy to work."

One man remembers a family friend's looking at him squarely and saying, "You'd make a good lawyer, young man. You've got a gift of gab." This man is now a district attorney.

Each child receives specific script instructions related to his or her sex and marriage. For example, "When you get married . . ." sends a different message from "If you get married . . ." A child's future sexual roles and attitudes are influenced by such judgments as:

"Isn't she the little mother!"

"You're such a scrawny kid, you'll never be a man."

"Why couldn't you have been a boy!"

"Don't be too smart, honey. It might scare the boys away."

"We are Jews and expect you to marry a Jew."

"Play around but don't marry that kind of a girl."

"Marriage is a trap that only fools fall for."

People receive scripting messages about many areas of life. About education a person may hear, "Naturally you'll get to college" or "College is for eggheads." About religion a person may hear, "We expect you to keep the Ten Commandments" or "Church is for the birds." About recreation a person may hear, "Physical exercise is good for you" or "Playing ball is a waste of time." About health a person may hear, "It's all in your mind" or "Be sure your bowels move every day."

Failure or going nowhere scripts may result from unrealistic or inaccurate programming. For example, a person may be encouraged to be a doctor or lawyer but at the same time may not be given any messages about the time, intellectual ability, education, and money it takes to get there.

There is considerable truth in the cliché, "It's not what you say, it's the way that you say it." Sometimes, parents script a child by saying one thing while implying another. This is what Perls emphasizes when he says most talking is a lie. Regardless of what a parent says, a child is most likely to respond to nonverbal messages. A tender, affectionate "Of course I love you" is quite different from an ulterior, incongruent message:

A tense "Of course I love you."

An angry "Of course I love you."

A disinterested "Of course I love you."

SCRIPTS WITH A CURSE

Although parental messages contain varying degrees of constructiveness, destructiveness, or nonproductiveness, some parents, because of their own pathology, send blatantly destructive injunctions to their children. Later in life these destructive orders can be like an electrode in the Child ego state which, when triggered off, compels the person to comply with the command.

Case Illustration

Ronald hanged himself at age twenty-five. He had devoted his life to caring for his ailing twin sister. After her death at age eighteen, he became increasingly depressed and more and more withdrawn. In discussing Ronald's suicide, his parents said:

Mother: I'm not really surprised. It was inevitable. We've had several suicides in our family over the years. In fact, my brother slit his own throat. I warned Ronnie many times he might kill himself. Even his sister wouldn't take her medicine. No wonder she died so young.

Father: All my life I have felt defeated and gloomy. In fact, my father owned a funeral parlor. When Ronnie would ask me for advice, I tried hard not to give it to him and would just quote the parables of Jesus. What else could I have done? For years I've been depressed and have drunk myself off two jobs. Guess I haven't been too good an example. Maybe Ronnie's way wasn't so bad.

Ronald had lived under the expectation that he would kill himself, and his suicide was the result of direct and ulterior messages— a tragic ending to his script. Ulterior messages are like curses that cast a spell on a child [13, 14]. They are destructive injunctions that are given either directly and verbally or indirectly and by implication—like a "witch message." Direct commands a child might hear are:

"You can't do that. Let me do it for you."

"If they gave a prize for being ugly, you'd get it."

"Go play on the freeway."

"Go get lost."

"Kill them if they get in the way."

"You're daddy's little crippled dove."

A child may infer a command based on parental actions:

The boy whose every act of aggression is stopped can infer "Don't be a man."

The child who is criticized for emotions can infer "Don't feel" or "Don't show your feelings."

The child who is punished for disagreeing with his or her elders can infer "Don't think."

The child who is manipulated with guilt often infers "Torture yourself."

These commandments, often given in the form of injunctions or permissions, are felt by the child to be imperatives. They are hard for the person to break because, in a sense, the person is being a "good boy" or a "good girl" by following his or her parents' instructions.

A person who lives under destructive commands—a curse—and

refuses to do his or her own thinking is spellbound. When older, the person may feel helpless in the face of "fate." Spellboundness may be verbalized:

> "I'm trapped."   "I can't help myself."
> "I'm in a rut."   "It's fate."
> "I'm a born loser!"

Every person is born a unique individual who has inherited capacities and potentialities to develop, experience, and express. According to Berne, this means that each child is a potential "prince" or "princess." However, very early in life some children receive messages from significant people that discount them in some way, thus causing them to function below their real potential. They become "frogs" or "beasts" instead of the winners they were born to be.

The "Frog Prince" is one familiar fairy tale which expresses this all too often, real-life experience. It is the story of a handsome prince who, because of a spell cast by a wicked witch, is trapped inside a frog and is destined to live like a frog, waiting for rescue.

People who live their lives under the spell of a curse may refuse to give up blaming their parents. Perls comments:

As you know, parents are never right. They are either too large or too small, too smart or too dumb. If they are stern, they should be soft, and so on. But when do you find parents who are all right? You can always blame the parents if you want to play the blaming game, and make the parents responsible for all your problems. Until you are willing to let go of your parents, you continue to conceive of yourself as a child [15].

COUNTERSCRIPTS

Some people who have scripts with a curse also have what is called a *counterscript*. A counterscript is formed if the messages a child receives in later life go "counter" to the witch messages received as an infant. For example, a small child who receives the message "Get lost," perhaps by nonverbal communication, may later get messages such as "Be careful when you cross the street." In such a case a person has two sets of messages, one appearing more constructive than the other.

Counterscripts are often based on mottos or slogans that are like prescriptions for the child, given from the Parent ego state of a child's father or mother to the Parent ego state of the child. Claude Steiner believes that "The witch or ogre injunction is far more potent and meaningful than the counterscript . . ."[16]. Although the person may vacillate between the destructive script and the more constructive counterscript, the counterscript may fail.

ROLES AND THEMES IN LIFE DRAMAS

As messages are received, the child takes psychological positions and develops the roles necessary to fulfill his or her life dramas. Once the roles are decided upon, a person's Child ego state selects and manipulates others to join his or her cast of characters. For example, intimates tend to base their mate selection on complementary scripts.

An ambitious young man who is scripted to become a top executive needs a marriage partner who is motivated to help him get there. He seeks out a properly educated, hostess-oriented, equally ambitious woman who will not foul up his dramatic plans. In turn, she selects him to fit a required role in her script. Even when planning a party, these two are likely to include others who can play roles that advance their scripts.

The same process of selection happens when a woman, who had taken the position "Men are bums," marries a sequence of "bums." Part of her script is based on "Men are not-OK." She fulfills her own prophecy by nagging, pushing, complaining, and generally making life miserable for her husband (who has his part to play). Eventually, she manipulates him into leaving. Then she can say, "See, I told you. Men are bums who leave you when the going gets rough."

A hypochondriac usually manipulates others from the position of being helpless and weak. His or her partner is likely to react by "coming on" as a rescuer or perhaps persecutor or both and may feel victimized in the process. If the hypochondriac gives up the manipulative position of helplessness, the spouse, who may not be ready to change positions, may aggravate the hypochondriac's illness to reestablish the former role relationship. On the other hand, if the spouse is the first to decide not to play the expected part, the hypochondriac may develop more pronounced symptoms or may seek someone else to play the rescuer/persecutor roles.

Sometimes, a life drama calls for one co-star to exit and a new one to enter the scene. This is frequently observed in marriages of professional men who during long years of training need a leading lady who is a working wife and is careful with money. However, when such a man finally succeeds in his profession and begins to move in a different social circle, his script may require a co-star with different capabilities.

Mates, bosses, friends, and enemies are often selected for their manipulative potential. For this kind of selection to pay off, the co-players must be able to play the "right" games and to fulfill a role requirement that furthers the script. Perls describes two primary manipulative positions as topdog and underdog.

The topdog usually is righteous and authoritarian; he knows best. He is sometimes right, but always righteous. The topdog is a bully, and works with "You should" and "You should not." The topdog manipulates with demands and threats of catastrophe, such as, "If you don't, then—you won't be loved, you won't get to heaven, you will die," and so on.

The underdog manipulates with being defensive, apologetic, wheedling, playing the cry-baby, and such. The underdog has no power. The underdog is the Mickey Mouse. The topdog is the Super Mouse. And the underdog works like this: "Manana." "I try my best." "Look, I try again and again; I can't help it if I fail." "I can't help it if I forgot your birthday." "I have such good intentions." So you see the underdog is cunning, and usually gets the better of the topdog because the underdog is not as primitive as the topdog. So the topdog and underdog strive for control. Like every parent and child, they strive with each other for control [17].

Many roles are played from the topdog and underdog manipulative positions. However, most dramatic roles can be recognized as the persecutor, the rescuer, or the victim.

These roles are *legitimate* if they are not play-acting but are realistically appropriate to the situation. Some legitimate roles are:

A persecutor:	Someone who sets necessary limits on behavior or is charged with enforcing a rule.
A victim:	Someone who qualifies for a job but is denied it because of race, sex, or religion.
A rescuer:	Someone who helps a person who is functioning inadequately to become rehabilitated and self-reliant.

When these roles are like masks, they are *illegitimate* and are for the purpose of manipulation. Subsequently when these three roles are capitalized in this book, they refer to manipulative, illegitimate roles:

A Persecutor: Someone who sets unnecessarily strict limits on behavior or is charged with enforcing the rules but does so with sadistic brutality.

A Victim: Someone who does *not* qualify for a job but falsely claims it is denied because of race, sex, or religion.

A Rescuer: Someone who, in the guise of being helpful, keeps others dependent upon him or her.

Manipulative roles are part of the rackets and games that contribute to a person's script. A person may play a game in imitation of parental behavior. However, games are usually played from the Child ego state. The Child initiates the game, intending to "hook" the Child or Parent in other players. The manipulative roles are used to provoke or to invite others to respond in specific ways, thus reinforcing the Child's early psychological positions.

On life's many stages it is not uncommon for the entire cast of characters to know how to play all the hands in all the games. Each is able to switch and play the three basic roles: Victim, Persecutor, and Rescuer. In transactional analysis this is called the Drama Triangle [18].

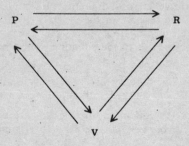

Karpman writes:

Only three roles are necessary in drama analysis to depict the emotional reversals that are drama. These action roles, in contrast with the identity roles referred to above, are the Persecutor, Rescuer, and Victim, or P, R, and V, in the diagram. Drama begins when these roles are established, or are anticipated by the audience. There is no drama unless there is a switch in the roles. . . . Drama compares to transactional games, but drama has a greater number of events, a greater number of switches per event, and one person often plays two or three roles at once. Games are simpler and there is one major switch, i.e., in "I'm Only Trying to Help You" there is one rotation (counter-clockwise) in the drama triangle: the Victim switches to Persecutor and the Rescuer becomes the Victim.

One frequent family drama includes the interplay of three specific games, each initiated from a specific role.

Game	Basic Role
Kick Me	Victim
Now I've Got You, You S.O.B.	Persecutor
I'm Only Trying to Help You	Rescuer

A scene begins when the initiator of *Kick Me* manipulates another person into kicking him or her. As the Victim, the initiator seeks a Persecutor, who obligingly catches the perpetrator in the act and plays the complementary game, *Now I've Got You, You S.O.B.* At this point the stage is set for a Rescuer. A Rescuer who gets into the act with an impotent or unrealistic rescue is rejected and then feels persecuted and kicked. With a line from the Rescuer's favorite game, the third party to the game laments, *I Was Only Trying to Help You.*

The following dialogue may not represent all the transactions in the three games of a family drama; however, it does illustrate the switching of roles.

Son: (as Persecutor, yells angrily at mother)	You know I hate blue. Here you went and bought me another blue shirt!
Mother: (as Victim)	I never do anything right as far as you're concerned.
Father: (rescues mother, persecutes son)	Don't you dare yell at your mother like that, young man. Go to your room and no dinner!

Son: (now as Victim, sulking in his room)	They tell me to be honest, and when I tell them what I don't like, they put me down. How can you satisfy people like that?
Mother: (now Rescuer, sneaks him a tray of food)	Now don't tell your father. We shouldn't get so upset over a shirt.
Mother: (as Persecutor, returning to father)	John, you're so tough with our son. I'll bet he's sitting in his room right now hating you.
Father: (as Victim)	Gee, honey, I was only trying to help you, and you kick me where it hurts the most.
Son: (calling out as Rescuer)	Hey, Mom, lay off, will ya? Dad's just tired.

Every person from time to time plays the parts of Persecutor, Rescuer, or Victim. However, each person tends to confront life and to play games more frequently from a favorite role. The role that is played is not always clear to the player, who may act one way and feel another. For example, it is not uncommon for a person who feels like a Victim to really be persecuting others. Often, the switch in roles creates the drama.

When a husband and wife seek marriage counseling, each may have a self-perception of a Victim suffering under the persecution of the partner. Their expectation may be that the therapist will play into their games as a Rescuer rather than effect a real rescue.

Case Illustration

Ted and Mary came into counseling complaining about the failure of their second honeymoon. Each claimed to have been victimized by the other. He shouted, "You had the gall to take your mother along. She even shared our motel room." She retorted, "And you were very rude to her and embarrassed me." After a number of hostile exchanges, they were asked to tell about their first honeymoon. Ted challenged, "What does that have to do with us now?" Mary retorted, "I'll tell you what. You took *your* parents along on our honeymoon fifteen years ago. You said, 'They never got a chance to go anywhere.' You've been taking advantage of me ever since."

Mary had assumed the role of Victim all these years. She had played the games of *Poor Me* and *See How Hard I Tried* and finally got even by assuming the role of Persecutor herself. Her favorite game became *Now I've Got You, You S.O.B.* For fifteen years the theme of their marriage drama had been Getting Even.

SCRIPT THEMES

Like Mary's theme of Getting Even (which was played out as a Victim switching to Persecutor), all scripts have themes running through them. These themes and roles contribute to the ongoing life drama. Generally, themes can be expressed in short phrases:

Losing My Mind	Driving People Crazy
Being the Best	Committing Suicide
Saving Sinners	Carrying My Cross
Being Helpful	Building Empires
Having a Ball	Being Miserable
Trying Hard	Walking on Eggs
Bossing Others	Missing the Boat
Stumbling but Recovering	Sorry for Being Alive
Succeeding Then Failing	Getting Stepped On
Never Getting Anywhere	Looking for a Pot of Gold
Saving for a Rainy Day	

SCRIPT ROLES AND THEMES IN GREEK MYTHOLOGY

The dramatic roles and themes in human life have been observed and recorded by poets and artists throughout history. In ancient times, one form of dramatic literature that emerged was the myth. A myth is a story which reveals, in symbolic ways, something that is true—not truth that can be proved scientifically—but true in the sense of its basic meaning and universality.

Berne believes that Greek myths contain the script prototypes of contemporary people and can be interpreted psychologically. The mythical figures demonstrate universal types who expressed themselves much as people do today. Two such interesting characters were the brothers Atlas and Prometheus. Each of them went to war against the authority of Zeus, "father of the gods," and was persecuted for it.

For punishment, Zeus doomed Atlas to bear the weight of the heavens on his shoulders. Hercules, the original muscle man, offered to carry this load if Atlas would secure for him the famed golden apples of Hesperides. Atlas complied. But on his return, rather than remaining free of his burden, he was easily "conned" into taking it back on his own shoulders.

The modern-day Atlas has many disguises: the overworked social worker, the business executive who is reluctant to delegate authority and "carries the whole load" for the department, or the exhausted housewife who tries to be everything to everybody. Although Atlases may complain, they tend to perpetuate their own role of Victim and to get a certain pleasure from their miseries.

Dramas that have an Atlas-type character as the central figure have themes such as: Carrying My Cross, Bearing the Weight of the World, Trying Hard, Enjoying My Miseries. Atlas often is masked as a "nice guy" but may actually be playing such games as *Why Does This Always Happen To Me?*, *If It Weren't For Him, Poor Me,* and *Ain't It Awful.* Actually, Atlases would not give up their roles and their misfortunes.

Prometheus and his brother Epimetheus were charged by the gods with creating animals and human beings. Epimetheus was to do the work and Prometheus was to oversee it. Epimetheus gave to the animals such gifts as strength, swiftness, courage, and wings. Little was left to bestow upon humans that would make them superior, so Prometheus effected a rescue. With the aid of Minerva, he lighted his torch from the sun and gave the fire to people. With fire, people could make weapons, tools, and gain dominion over the animals. In addition, Prometheus made human beings upright like the gods and secured for them the best of the sacrificial meat, leaving only fat and bones for the gods.

Zeus was outraged by Prometheus' concern for humanity and sought to punish him. As Persecutor, he chained Prometheus to a rock for perpetual torture. However, after thirteen generations, Hercules rescued him. To this day Prometheus serves as a symbol of "magnanimous endurance of unmerited suffering, and strength of will resisting oppression" [19].

Like the Greek hero, a modern Prometheus is often one who is against authority and the demands of the Establishment. The self-image of a modern Prometheus is that of a savior, of one who identifies with the underdog. But someone who is just playing the role and never really rescuing anyone is acting "as if" he or she were a rescuer rather than being one. A legitimate rescuer sets others on their own feet, often at the risk of becoming the target of a wrathful authority.

Do you have an Atlas or Prometheus in your family? In your neighborhood? At work? Among your friends? Is this position for real, or is it play-acting? Do you know others who are similar to Greek mythological characters? The following may strike a familiar chord.

A Zeus, who sets all the ground rules and controls others by seduction, threat, and brutality, and is a woman chaser.

A Hera, the jealous wife of Zeus, who acts like a detective, always checking up on her playboy husband who, with her, is involved in a "divine" game of *Cops and Robbers*.

An Echo, the little nymph who is doomed to having no thoughts of her own, only repeating what others have already said.

A Pygmalion, a man who really hates women but creates out of stone a perfect one that no real woman could match, then falls in love with this creation, rather than with a woman in the world of reality.

A Narcissus, who is so in love with himself that he is blind to the rest of the world and pines away, spending his life admiring his own reflection.

A Daphne, who flirts with men and when pursued, runs crying to "daddy" for protection.

SCRIPT THEMES IN CHILDREN'S STORIES

Like the ancient myths, a variety of life dramas are popularized in children's stories which are transmitted through books, radio, tele-

PLATE VI

ALL THE WORLD'S A STAGE

Each in his or her time
plays many parts.

vision, or around the fireplace at family gatherings. An individual's script is often reflected in stories that have the basic manipulative roles as well as the plot in which these roles are acted out.

Fairy-tale Persecutors are often wicked stepmothers, witches, ogres, big bad wolves, dragons, or other beasts. The Victims are frogs, waifs, sleeping beauties, poor little match girls, or ugly ducklings and other kinds of "poor things." The Rescuers are good fairies, helpful elves, wise wizards, beautiful princesses, and handsome princes.

To be rescued a Victim must find a Rescuer. A Rescuer in children's stories often has "magic powers." One well-known story showing the complementary functions of Victim and Rescuer is the fairy tale of Beauty and the Beast. Beauty, unlike her selfish sisters, never demands anything for herself. When her father loses his wealth, she sacrificially performs all the menial tasks. For this servile behavior, she receives ridicule from her sisters and praise from her father.

In search of another fortune, Beauty's father falls into the hands of a Beast, who threatens to take his life unless one of the daughters is given to him. Beauty volunteers for the assignment, and her father agrees to be rescued in this way. Although the Beast is very ugly, he is also very kind (a nice guy); and when he becomes ill, Beauty sympathetically marries the pathetic creature. Behold! This magically turns him into a handsome prince.

A young woman who has this type of life pattern assumes from early life experiences with her father that "men are poor things" who need her unselfish devotion.

As casting director for her life drama, a modern Beauty selects a man to marry who is in some way unworthy, or a Beast. He may be downtrodden or miserable looking, a drug addict or an alcoholic, far in debt or in trouble with the law. If Beauty discovers her magic doesn't work, she may, with a sacrificial posture, stay with the Beast. She may get a divorce and seek a new character (also a Beast in some way) to rescue. The Beast, for his part, may continue to wait for a new Rescuer rather than take the initiative for his own life. After all, a wicked witch (likely his mother) cast a terrible spell on him, and a mean ogre (likely his father) showed him how to be a Beast [20].

The same drama can be played out with the sexual roles reversed. In this case, the main characters are Handsome and the Beastly Woman [21].

Another fairy-tale character is Cinderella, a Victim who holds a menial job and is surrounded by cruel, demanding people. Her first Rescuer is a fairy godmother who bestows upon Cinderella a gorgeous gown, glass slippers, and fancy transportation to go to the ball. When she goes, Cinderella attracts another Rescuer—a prince.

Some therapists interpret the prince as acting more like a frog, in that even though he claims to want Cinderella as his bride, he fails to get her name or address. All fairy-tale themes can be followed by either winners or losers. After all, some Cinderellas make it. However, in real life few people "live happily ever after," as magic is in short supply.

A modern Cinderella playing a loser script is one who accepts what she interprets as a menial job, often doing what she claims is other people's "dirty work." She operates under the delusion that if someone magically gave her high-style clothes, a car, and the right situation, she would win her prince and thus be rescued from her mundane existence. Some Cinderellas are shocked to find that after they marry their prince, they have another set of menial tasks to do [22]. Modern-day Cinder-fellows also see themselves as Victims stuck in jobs they don't like, waiting for a magical rescue that in reality may never come.

The Little Lame Prince is another story of a Victim who has been unjustly persecuted and needs rescuing. In the original story a royal family banishes their Little Lame Prince to a tower because of his lameness. A good fairy comes to his rescue by bestowing upon him a magic traveling cloak which enables the Little Lame Prince to "take trips." With his newfound magic, he can fly over No-Man's Land and see and experience trees, flowers, and other beauties of nature for the first time.

W. Ray Poindexter tells of a young man whose life drama follows the story of the Little Lame Prince [23]. The boy's father had decided that his questioning, intellectual son had something "wrong" with him (was lame) because he was not athletic and did not fit the "All American boy" image. Although he had adequate physical care and a good education, the boy had not received acceptance. He felt banished and found refuge in a community of runaways. There, to escape from his "tower," he used drugs as the magic cloak to take "trips."

Storybook characters are common in everyday life dramas. A person can choose isolation like Robinson Crusoe (perhaps with a boy or girl Friday), run away like Huckleberry Finn, fight "windmills" like Don Quixote, fly to the rescue like Superman, refuse to grow up like Peter Pan, deal endlessly with trivia and trauma like the prima donna of melodrama, be a villain, a hero or heroine, a king, a queen, or a fool. A person can be:

miserable like the Little Match Girl,

a miser like Scrooge,

slick with the women and fast with a gun like James Bond,

an unfeeling computer like Star Trek's Mr. Spock,

a knight saving maidens in distress like Sir Lancelot.

People who live their lives in storybook fashion, unwilling to experience their own uniqueness, are often losers.

SUMMARY

Each person has a psychological script and exists in a culture that has scripts. The psychological script contains the ongoing program for the individual's life drama. It is rooted in the messages a child receives from parents, which can be constructive, destructive, or nonproductive, and in the psychological positions the child eventually takes toward self and others. Positions can be related to people in general or directed toward those of a particular sex.

To the extent that the script messages are not in tune with the child's actual potentials and negate his or her will to survive, they create pathology. Pathology has different degrees of seriousness. It can range from being very mild, rarely interfering with the person's ability to function, to being so gross that people become absurd caricatures of their possible selves.

Although all scripts are like spells, some scripts serve the function of giving the person fairly realistic ideas about uses for her or his talents in the society. Others misdirect the person to follow a star that was unrealistically or perhaps resentfully selected. Still other scripts program the Child for destruction, a tragic ending.

Most people at one time or another play roles and mask themselves in some way. If they become aware of themselves when they are putting on a performance, their awareness gives them some freedom to reject phony roles. Playacting can be given up in favor of authenticity.

Aware people can determine the course of their *own* life plans

and rewrite their dramas in accordance with their own uniqueness. Such people can come in touch with their possible selves and
redirect their compulsion to live life within one specific framework. For many, this is not easy. In fact, it is often painful and involves much hard work. Sometimes a real rescuer is needed, as is
depicted in the following paraphrase of James Aggrey's "The Parable of the Eagle" [24].

Once upon a time, while walking through the forest, a certain man found a
young eagle. He took it home and put it in his barnyard where it soon
learned to eat chicken feed and to behave as chickens behave.

One day, a naturalist who was passing by inquired of the owner why it was
that an eagle, the king of all birds, should be confined to live in the barnyard with the chickens.

"Since I have given it chicken feed and trained it to be a chicken, it has
never learned to fly," replied the owner. "It behaves as chickens behave, so
it is no longer an eagle."

"Still," insisted the naturalist, "it has the heart of an eagle and can surely be
taught to fly."

After talking it over, the two men agreed to find out whether this was possible. Gently the naturalist took the eagle in his arms and said, "You belong
to the sky and not to the earth. Stretch forth your wings and fly."

The eagle, however, was confused; he did not know who he was, and,
seeing the chickens eating their food, he jumped down to be with them
again.

Undismayed, the naturalist took the eagle on the following day, up on the
roof of the house, and urged him again, saying, "You are an eagle. Stretch
forth your wings and fly." But the eagle was afraid of his unknown self and
world and jumped down once more for the chicken food.

On the third day the naturalist rose early and took the eagle out of the barnyard to a high mountain. There, he held the king of birds high above him
and encouraged him again, saying, "You are an eagle. You belong to the
sky as well as to the earth. Stretch forth your wings now, and fly."

The eagle looked around, back towards the barnyard and up to the sky.
Still he did not fly. Then the naturalist lifted him straight towards the sun
and it happened that the eagle began to tremble, slowly he stretched his
wings. At last, with a triumphant cry, he soared away into the heavens.

It may be that the eagle still remembers the chickens with nostalgia; it may
even be that he occasionally revisits the barnyard. But as far as anyone
knows, he has never returned to lead the life of a chicken. He was an eagle
though he had been kept and tamed as a chicken.

Just like the eagle, people who have learned to think of themselves as something they aren't, can re-decide in favor of their real potential. They can become winners.

EXPERIMENTS AND EXERCISES

If you wish to begin exploring your script, set aside some time to work through the following experiments and exercises as they interest you.

1. Cultural and Family Scripting

Imagine yourself moving back in time. What were your ancestors like 75 years ago or 150 years ago?

- Does your cultural heritage affect you in any way today (i.e., in your sexual roles, work, educational aspirations)?

- Think of at least one thing you do now that is culturally determined.

- Think of your present life stages. Do some of them involve subcultures?

- Think of the dramatic patterns in the family you grew up in. Are you repeating any of them now? What have you changed?

2. Individual Script

Nonverbal Messages in Your Script (Read the entire experiment before trying it.)

Close your eyes and try to see the earliest facial expressions you can recall. If only parts of faces emerge, such as eyes or mouths, look at these closely. Whose faces do you see?

Now try to recall the nonverbal messages your parents sent through their actions (i.e., pat on the head, clenched fist, angry slap, affectionate kiss).

- What pleasant or unpleasant feelings are aroused in you?

- What messages do the facial expressions and body actions convey?

Verbal Messages in Your Script

Imagine you are the child you used to be. Hear again your family's words. What was said about:

your worth	your abilities	your morals	your sexuality
your looks	your intelligence	your health	your future?

- Say in a sentence what you imagine each of your parent figures thought of you.
- Is your current self-appraisal related in any way to your parents' opinion of you?

Role Identification

Review the last few days and recall how you related to different people. Did you find yourself playing any of the three dramatic roles—Victim, Persecutor, or Rescuer?

- Did your role change when the setting changed?
- Did you play one role more often than the others?
- Are the roles you played similar to those in your favorite myths, fairy tales, or other stories?

As you read through the Parable of the Eagle, did you identify with a specific role? Ask yourself:

- Did anyone keep and tame me? Anyone I've kept and tamed?
- Is there anyone I've really rescued? Anyone who's rescued me?

On stage

Imagine your life drama being performed on a stage.

- Is it a comedy, a farce, a saga, a soap opera, a melodrama, a tragedy, or what?

- Does your play have a script theme? If so, is it success-oriented or failure-oriented—constructive, destructive, or nonproductive?

- Be the audience watching your play. Do you applaud, cry, boo, laugh, go to sleep, want your money back, or what?

Life Stages

Imagine your life as a revolving stage, with each of your settings as a section of it. Diagram your various settings according to the amount of *time* you invest in each. Evaluate a typical month in your life. Eliminate sleeping time unless it is of particular importance to you. Sample diagrams are shown in Fig. 4.2.

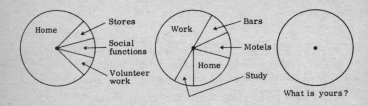

What is yours?

- Is the amount of *energy* you invest in each stage similar to the amount of time?

- Do your real *interests* lie where your time and energies are invested?

- Who seems to be directing your drama on each life stage?

- Are you satisfied with what you invest of yourself in your various settings?

Cast of Characters

Think of the most important people who are currently in your life drama.

- Rank them in terms of the time, energy, and real interest you invest in them.

- Reverse the situation. How much time, energy, and real interest do you believe they invest in you?

- Do you see them as furthering your life plans in any way?

- With whom and on which stages do you play-act "as if"?

- With whom and on which stages are you real—*being* the part, not just *acting* the part?

5

Parenting and the Parent Ego State

It is indeed a desirable thing to be well descended, but the glory belongs to our ancestors.
Plutarch

Some people find it easy to be what they consider "good" parents. Some find it hard. Most have their ups and downs. Some parents enjoy babies. Some resent them. Others are unable to cope with them for a variety of reasons. From time to time some parents experience all three attitudes. "The frightening fact about both heredity and environment is that we parents provide both" [1].

Parents establish an emotional climate which, like atmospheric climate, is warm or cold, mild or harsh, conducive or destructive to growth. Parents give their children firm but tender, loving care through positive strokes, thus encouraging constructive scripts. Or, they discount them, thus encouraging destructive or nonproductive scripts. The best thing parents can do for their children is to evaluate their own script and then decide whether it is worth passing on to another generation.

THE PARENT EGO STATE

For better or for worse, parents serve as models and are imprinted on the brains of their children. The Parent ego state is the incorporation of the attitudes and behavior of all emotionally significant people who serve as parent figures to the child. The Parent ego state does not necessarily function in ways culturally defined as "motherly" or "fatherly." In fact, there is no evidence of maternal or paternal instincts in humans. According to Harlow's studies, this is also true of lower primates [2]. Humans learn how to be parents from their own parents. Monkeys appear to do somewhat the same.

Ego States within the Parent

Each parent has three unique ego states. Consequently, a person's own Parent ego state is likely to incorporate his or her parents' Parent, Adult, and Child, the babysitter's Parent, Adult, and Child, and so forth. At times parents behave toward their children as their parents behaved toward them—moralizing, punishing, nurturing, ignoring. At other times parents reason on the basis of current, objective data—explaining why, demonstrating how, searching for facts, and solving problems. At still other times they use behavior from their own childhood—whining, withdrawing, frolicking, giggling, manipulating, and playing. Therefore, the behavior of a person responding from the Parent ego state may stem from any ego state incorporated from one or more parent figures. The Parent in a person's Parent ego state is most often the grandparents.

Analyzing the ego states within an ego state is called *second-order structural analysis*. Applied to the Parent this means sorting out the Parent, Adult, and Child ego states within the person's Parent ego state. Second-order structural analysis of the Parent can be diagrammed as on page 112.*

This means that at times a person's behavior may resemble grandmother's Adult or babysitter's Parent or father's Child, and so forth. The following story illustrates how certain traditions and beliefs—cultural and family scripts—may go back many generations, although the reasons behind them are long forgotten.

A bride served baked ham, and her husband asked why she cut the ends off. "Well, that's the way mother always did it," she replied.

The next time his mother-in-law stopped by, he asked her why she cut the ends off the ham. "That's the way *my* mother did it," she replied.

* The Parent ego state consists of any and all of the actual parent figures incorporated by a child. The second-order diagram of each person's Parent ego state would reveal a different balance of parental incorporation.

And when grandma visited, she too was asked why she sliced the ends off. She said, "That's the only way I could get it into the pan" [3].

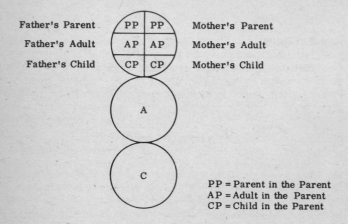

Father's Parent	PP	PP	Mother's Parent
Father's Adult	AP	AP	Mother's Adult
Father's Child	CP	CP	Mother's Child

PP = Parent in the Parent
AP = Adult in the Parent
CP = Child in the Parent

OUTWARD EXPRESSION OF THE PARENT EGO STATE

When a Parent ego state is expressed outwardly, a person transacts with the ego states of others as his or her own parents did (Fig. 5.2).

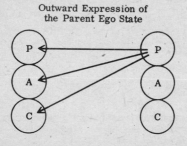

Outward Expression of
the Parent Ego State

Transactions from the Parent are especially evident in child rearing. In many cases people automatically tend to rear their children as they were reared.

Case Illustration

Joe was beaten severely with a strap when his father punished him. He swore to himself that he'd never hit a child as his father had. However, when Joe had his first son, it seemed "natural" to him to strike the child when he misbehaved. It took a determined decision and Adult information for Joe to modify his Parent behavior.

Case Illustration

Mary's mother rarely turned to medical doctors for advice when her children were ill. Mary recalls that whenever she was sick her mother prepared tea and custard pudding. When Mary had a baby and the baby ran its first fever, Mary fed tea to the baby from a bottle.

In addition to copying child-rearing practices, people incorporate postures, stances, gestures, and many forms of body language from parental models. Picture, if you will,

A woman standing with her hands on her hips, scolding someone just as her mother had done.

A man pointing an accusing finger at people in the same way his father had pointed.

A woman lifting her chin, looking down her nose, shrugging her shoulders, and saying, "That's ridiculous," just as her grandmother had done.

A man pounding his desk with his fist to emphasize a point, just as his father had done.

A woman preparing a Thanksgiving feast just as her mother had done.

A man giving a supportive wink and nod of the head as his father had.

People also incorporate the ways their parents put things into words. Later, they use these Parental words with others. Some parents use words like *should, have to,* or *must* to convey the idea

of "oughtness." "Keep everything in its place and you won't have
any problems." "Everyone ought to earn his or her way." Others,
more permissive or indifferent, say things such as "I don't care. It's
up to you," or "Do whatever you want to do, honey."

People also copy their parents' psychological games. A young
wife may play *If It Weren't For You* with her husband in much the
same style as her mother. In this game she blames her prohibiting
husband for her own lack of achievement, when actually she is
afraid to perform.

A teacher may play *Blemish* with his students by looking for and
pointing out unimportant flaws just as his parents had done with
him.

A supervisor may play *Corner* with her workers by being unclear about her standards and then criticizing the workers no matter what they do, just as her parents made her feel that she was
"damned if she did and damned if she didn't."

A young executive may play *Now I've Got You, You S.O.B.* as
he observed his father doing when his father waited for people to
make a mistake and then felt justified in exploding with rage.

INNER INFLUENCE OF THE PARENT EGO STATE

People not only incorporate their parents' behavior, but they also
incorporate a set of parental messages that are later heard in their
heads like tapes. Sometimes two people within the Parent ego
state are talking. Sometimes the Adult hears what the inner Parent
is saying. But most frequently inner dialogue takes place between
the influencing Parent and the Child.

**Inward Influence of
the Parent Ego State**

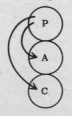

These messages are like replays of old Parental facial expressions, actions, gestures, or statements and instructions. For example, a grown man about to leave food on his plate sees the mental image of father's disapproving frown and cleans up his plate like a good little boy. A teen-age girl wants to steal a scarf, but hears her mother in her head, "Nice girls don't steal." In the same situation another teen-ager hears, "Go ahead, but don't get caught." Still another hears, "I'll beat the hell out of you if you steal." In much the same way, script instructions are heard and followed by the Child.

Some Parental messages are encouraging. Some are not. Some give permission to behave in certain negative or positive ways:

"If at first you don't succeed, try, try again."

"You'll never know until you try."

"You've got a good head, use it."

"You made your bed, so lie in it."

"Get lost."

Since children are not born with an inner censor, their first pangs of conscience result from parent/child transactions. Children learn to value what their parents value. This early sense of conscience can be experienced as inner dialogue between the Parent and Child ego states. This inner dialogue may be permissive, confusing, moral, or rigidly moralistic.

Although the inner conscience is heard, it is not always followed. Even small children can make independent judgments or give in to personal desires. Selma Fraiberg describes such a child:

Thirty-month-old Julia finds herself alone in the kitchen while her mother is on the telephone. A bowl of eggs is on the table. An urge is experienced by Julia to make scrambled eggs. She reaches for the eggs, but now the claims of reality are experienced with equal strength. Her mother would not approve. The resulting conflict within the ego is experienced as "I want" and "No, you mustn't" and the case for both sides is presented and a decision arrived at within the moment. When Julia's mother returns to the kitchen, she finds her daughter cheerfully plopping eggs on the linoleum and scolding herself sharply for each plop, "NoNoNo. Mustn't dood it. NoNoNo. Mustn't dood it!" [4]

All children need some noes to protect them from harm, to enhance their sociability, and to assure them that their parents care about them [5]. However, some people grow up under the burden of inner noes that are prejudicial and unnecessarily prohibitive. Overly restrictive Parental messages inhibit the expression of joy, sensuousness, and creativity.

A child adapted by rigid Parent programming may take the position, "I'm not supposed to think for myself," and succumb to what Karen Horney describes as "the tyranny of the shoulds."

He *should* be the utmost of honesty, generosity, considerateness, justice, dignity, courage, unselfishness. He *should* be the perfect lover, husband, teacher. He *should* be able to endure everything, *should* like everybody, *should* love his parents, his wife, his country; or he *should* not be attached to anything or anybody, nothing *should* matter to him, he *should* never feel hurt, and he *should* always be serene and unruffled. He *should* always enjoy life; or he *should* be above pleasure and enjoyment. He *should* be spontaneous; he *should* always control his feelings. He *should* know, understand, and foresee everything. He *should* be able to solve every problem of his own, or of others, in no time. He *should* be able to overcome every difficulty of his as soon as he sees it. He *should* never be tired or fall ill. He *should* always be able to find a job. He *should* be able to do things in one hour which can only be done in two to three hours [6]. (Italics are ours.)

If influenced in this oppressive way, an individual reading a pleasurable book may suddenly hear an internal parental message, "Work before pleasure." The individual's Child naturally wants to have fun, but in childhood has been programmed to feel guilty about pleasure. Feeling guilty and unable to cope with this uncomfortable feeling, the individual puts down the book and turns to the cleanup project in the garage or kitchen.

Conflicting Inner Dialogue

Many people suffer from a struggle *between* a topdog Parent ego state and an underdog Child ego state. This leads to what Perls calls the "self-torture game":

I'm certain that you are very familiar with this game. One part of you talks to the other part and says, "You should be better, you should not be this way, you should not do that, you shouldn't be what you are, you should be what you are not" [7].

Conflicting dialogue *within* the Parent ego state also creates tension and confusion. Barry Stevens expresses this confusion as she, in her inner world, feels the continuing pressure of outside authorities. She writes:

In the beginning was I, and I was good.

Then came in other I. Outside authority. This was confusing. And then other I became *very* confused because there were so many different outside authorities.

Sit nicely. Leave the room to blow your nose. Don't do that, that's silly. Why, the poor child doesn't even know how to pick a bone! Flush the toilet at night because if you don't it makes it harder to clean. DON'T FLUSH THE TOILET AT NIGHT—you wake people up! Always be nice to people. Even if you don't like them, you mustn't hurt their feelings. Be frank and honest. If you don't tell people what you think of them, that's cowardly. Butter knives. It is important to use butter knives. Butter knives. What foolishness! Speak nicely. Sissy! Kipling is wonderful! Ugh! Kipling (turning away).

The most important thing is to have a career. The most important thing is to get married. The hell with everyone. Be nice to everyone. The most important thing is sex. The most important thing is to have money in the bank. The most important thing is to have everyone like you. The most important thing is to dress well. The most important thing is to be sophisticated and say what you don't mean and don't let anyone know what you feel. The most important thing is to be ahead of everyone else. The most important thing is a black seal coat and china and silver. The most important thing is to be clean. The most important thing is to always pay your debts. The most important thing is not to be taken in by anyone else. The most important thing is to love your parents. The most important thing is to work. The most important thing is to be independent. The most important thing is to speak correct English. The most important thing is to be dutiful to your husband. The most important thing is to see that your children behave well. The most important thing is to go to the right plays and read the right books. The most important thing is to do what others say. And others say all these things [8].

People who have parent figures in their heads who disagree strongly may torture themselves listening to the battle. Such a self-torture game was played by Harvey, who had heard from his mother, "Good boys go to Sunday School." His father had said, "Sunday School is a waste of time and a lot of baloney. Let's go fishing." Harvey found himself fluctuating for periods of time, first doing what his mother said, then doing what his father said.

He complained, "No matter what I do, it doesn't seem right. If I go to church, I feel I should be fishing and enjoying nature. If I go fishing, I feel guilty. What am I supposed to do about my own kids?"

NURTURING PARENT

Most parents are sympathetic, protective, and nurturing on some occasions and critical, prejudicial, moralizing, or punitive on others. Some parents tend to be more nurturing than judgmental and vice versa.

Children who have nurturing parents develop Parent ego states that contain nurturing behavior. Unless deliberately deciding against it, when grown, they may repeat to their own children the same sympathetic, nurturing remarks and gestures they learned from their parents:

"Come on pal, you're tired, I'll carry you awhile."

"Take a nap, honey, then you'll feel rested."

"That's too bad, but don't worry about it."

"Let me rub it where it hurts."

These people also are likely to set the same kind of protective limits on their children that were set on them.

"You can't play on this busy street."

"Don't pet strange dogs."

"Be sure water is clean before you drink it."

A person not only uses nurturing parental behavior toward children, but also "comes on" as a Nurturing Parent toward other adults.

Wife: (to husband)	John, you look discouraged tonight. Is there something special you'd like to do that would make you feel better?
Husband: (to wife)	Now honey, don't cry. Anyone could make that kind of mistake.

Doctor: (to surgery patient)	Trust me and don't worry. I'll take care of everything.
Patient: (to doctor)	Don't feel so bad, Doc, I can take the truth.
Instructor: (to class)	You've been working so hard all semester that today I brought doughnuts for everyone.
Student: (to instructor)	You still look pale from having the flu. Are you sure you feel all right? I could carry those things.
Secretary: (to boss)	I'm so sorry you lost the Anderson account, Mr. Smith. I brought you some homemade cake to cheer you up.
Boss: (to secretary)	You've looked unhappy ever since we put in the new data-processing system. Don't you worry. We still need you.
Worker: (to worker)	You've worked so hard for that promotion. I'm sorry you didn't get it. I'll bet you'll have better luck next time.
Saleslady: (to customer)	Here's a chair. You just sit yourself down and have a nice rest while we wrap the package.

Sometimes the nurturing aspects of the Parent are oversolicitous, and other people resent it. Let's look at a few examples. When some people are ill, they resent having another adult "hover" over them. Some patients would rather have their doctor tell them the truth than "protect" them from it. As one boss complained, "If there's the slightest indication of rain, my secretary insists I carry an umbrella. Sometimes I sneak out before she catches me."

PREJUDICIAL PARENT

The Parent ego state tends to be filled with opinions about religion, politics, traditions, sexual role expectations, life styles, child rearing, proper dress, speech, and all the facets of cultural and family scripts. These opinions, often irrational, may not have been evaluated by the Adult ego state and may be prejudiced.

When operating prejudicially with children, parents attempt to set standards of behavior on the basis of these erroneous opinions rather than on the basis of facts. All parents use prejudicial and critical remarks:

"Boys shouldn't wear long hair."

"Girls should be sweet and quiet."

"Children should be seen and not heard."

"Kids should respect their elders."

People often use their Prejudicial Parent when transacting with other adults:

Wife: (to husband)	Men can't change diapers. That's a woman's job.
Husband: (to wife)	I wish you wouldn't wear pants suits. It isn't feminine.
Nurse: (to patient)	Now if you just "think positive," the medicine will work better. That's what my mother always said.
New patient: (to head nurse)	Who ever heard of a male nurse!
Worker: (to worker)	I don't think he'd be good for the job. Look how wide apart his eyes are set.
Finance department head: (to personnel manager)	Now whatever you do, don't hire a woman. They just can't work with figures.
Instructor: (to instructor)	Kids sure have changed. None of them want to learn anything today.

The Prejudicial Parent is often critical. A person acting from the critical side of the Parent ego state may come on as a bossy, know-it-all whose behavior intimidates the Child in other people. A boss, spouse, teacher, or friend who frequently is a critical Parent may irritate other people and perhaps alienate them.

THE INCOMPLETE PARENT EGO STATE

If a child loses a parent by death or desertion and does not have a substitute parent of the same sex as the one lost, she or he will have an incomplete Parent ego state. It is incomplete because it contains a void. An incomplete Parent ego state may also be caused by a parent's excess absence—either physical or psychological.

When a parent is absent for a long time, a child may turn to fantasy and construct an imaginary, or "ideal," mother or father. Eleanor Roosevelt's father, whom she idolized, was often absent for long periods of time. Nevertheless, for five years she fantasied being mistress of his household. She recalls this period in her life: "Into this world I retired as soon as I went to bed, and as soon as I woke in the morning, and all the time I was walking, and when anybody bored me" [9].

Nietzsche wrote, "When one has not had a good father, one must create one." A child may "make up" a more perfect parent than the lost or absent one. This imaginary parent is likely to have no faults, be capable of filling all needs, ideal in every way. It is easy then to confuse this figment of the imagination with reality. The individual who carries this ideal image of the absent parent may never find anyone who can live up to it.

In a study of American adolescents from middle-class families, Bronfenbrenner found that children whose parents were away from home for long periods of time rated significantly lower than other children on characteristics of responsibility and leadership [10]. After reviewing several related studies of this age group, Bronfenbrenner concluded that children, especially boys, are markedly affected by their father's continuing absence. They are likely to lack ambition, seek immediate gratification, feel not-OK, be followers of their peer group, and revert to juvenile delinquency [11].

The following vignette from *Mrs. Bridge* describes the kind of absentee father experienced by many modern-day children.

Her husband was as astute as he was energetic, and he wanted so much for his family he went to his office quite early in the morning while most men were still asleep, and he often stayed there working until late at night. He worked all day Saturday and part of Sunday, and holidays were nothing but a nuisance. Before very long the word had gone around that Walter Bridge was the man to handle the case.

The family saw very little of him. It was not unusual for an entire week to pass without any of the children seeing him. On Sunday morning they would come downstairs, and he might be at the breakfast table; he greeted them pleasantly and they responded deferentially, and a little wistfully because they missed him. Sensing this, he would redouble his efforts at the office in order to give them everything they wanted [12].

An incomplete Parent ego state often leads to distinctive behavior patterns. For example, some people, from their Child ego state, may continually search for a "lost" parent and may expect "parenting" from other grown-ups, such as a spouse, boss, minister, friend, or even from their own children. Other people, instead of seeking a parent substitute, may reject anyone who acts parental toward them. In either case some people use this kind of handicap to avoid responsibility and to excuse themselves for a bad performance. Later in life they may play the game of *Wooden Leg:* "What can you expect from me? My father died when I was five!"

A person with an incomplete Parent ego state may not appreciate other people who are of the same sex as the lost parent, may downgrade them, mistrust them, or even be hostile toward them.

Case Illustration

When Kate was one year old, her mother and father were killed in an automobile accident, and she was reared by her grandmother. Even though Kate had friends at school and a grandmother who gave her good care, she did not have a substitute father. It was her grandmother who nurtured, trained, judged, and acted both as mother and father to Kate. When Kate became a parent herself, she assumed full responsibility for the children. She disagreed violently with her husband when he tried to guide or direct their children, and exclaimed, "Kids are a woman's job. You tend to your business and let me tend to mine."

A person who "parents" others from an incomplete Parent ego state may do it poorly.

Case Illustration

Carl was the youngest in a large family. His father died when he was four years old. As an adult he was generally competent and self-contained, but suffered from periods of depression.

"I cry every time I talk of my childhood and spend weeks each year in deep depression before the fourth of July. That was the day he died, the day the bottom fell out of my life! I remember being almost squashed between the hearse and another automobile and the thud of the dirt on the casket. Ever since then I've felt an instability in my life.

"Well, after that, I went with my mother to live with my grandmother in a town where I had lots of uncles. I used to hope and hope they would accept me as part of their brood, but they never really noticed me, just patted me on the head and gave me a nickel.

"Now I'm having trouble with my kids. There must be something wrong with me. I can't figure out what. I want to, but somehow I just don't know how to be a good father."

People with an incomplete Parent ego state not only have a difficult time parenting children, they also have difficulty sympathizing appropriately with other adults:

A husband may not know how to comfort his sick wife.

A wife may not know how to sympathize when her husband is laid off work.

A boss may be insensitive to subordinates' human problems.

In these cases the persons need to learn appropriate parenting patterns by programming themselves with information. Not only can they read and attend classes on good parenting, they can also observe and copy others who parent successfully. Furthermore, they can consciously focus their attention on the needs of others and try to meet these needs appropriately. Good parenting does not come automatically—it must be learned.

PLATE VII

THE PARENT EGO STATE IS SOMETIMES NURTURING

People tend to parent children as they were parented.

REPARENTING

Some people have had such woefully inadequate parents that there is little in their Parent ego state that is useful and often much that is defeating. In these cases, counseling directed toward turning off the Parent tapes may be necessary. And in more serious cases, reparenting may be necessary. One way, developed by the Schiffs, is a radical procedure of regressing schizophrenic young people to infancy and then progressing them through their developmental stages, meeting their dependency needs. During this progression, the old Parent is "erased" and the Schiffs are incorporated, thus forming the young people's new Parent ego state [13].

The Parent ego state can also be restructured in a less extreme way by using a method of self-reparenting which is different from that of the Schiffs [14]. In brief, this technique requires people to first recognize the negative characteristics of the parent figures they have incorporated. Negatives are in parents who may have been well meaning but were overcritical, overnurturing, overprotective, inconsistent, conflicting, uninvolved, or emotionally overneedy. The next step in self-reparenting is the observation of parent figures at nursery schools, playgrounds, supermarkets, etc., and reading about parents. This is followed by considerable inner dialogue between a person's Adult and inner Child to determine what particular new parenting needs the Child has. On the basis of all this data, the Adult then acts as a substitute parent. Eventually, this new parenting behavior seems to become part of a restructured Parent ego state. The old parent's negative characteristics have been balanced off by positive ones because a new, more appropriate Parent has been created by the Adult. This new Parent is not necessarily a historical figure, although it may have some characteristics incorporated from favorite teachers, therapists, or friends. Primarily, it is an imaginary Parent, loving and intelligent, created in somewhat the same way that characters in novels are created.

SUMMARY

Those people we are least likely to know in this world are our parents. The dependency position of children makes it almost impossible for them to perceive their parents objectively. Even as adults, people may have delusions of their parents' omnipotence and place them in roles of supernatural beings, not seeing them as mortals who have frailties. People may even feel disloyal if they have negative thoughts about their parents and try to suppress any feelings of anger, hurt, or grief toward them.

Many people see their parents either through "rose-colored glasses" or through a psychological prism that distorts them. They have never seen their parents as they really are, but rather as objects who either met or failed to meet their childhood wants and needs. In any case, when people become aware of who their parents actually are or were, they may become very critical; they may judge or even hate them for awhile. Eventually, they may learn to understand, accept, and forgive them. As Oscar Wilde said, "Children begin by loving their parents; as they grow older they judge them; sometimes they forgive them."

Every person has mental parent figures which form one's Parent ego state. At times the individual acts, speaks, gestures, and thinks as they did. At other times the person is influenced by their inner messages.

Parental transactions are often of a nurturing or prejudicial nature. These patterns are used in transacting with grown-ups as well as with children. For example, the nurturing part of the Parent is appropriately used to respond to a co-worker who is hurt or ill or in some way suffering a temporary dependency need. The Parent ego state is inappropriately used when nurturing, criticism, or discounting are forced upon another person who neither wants it nor needs it.

The Parent ego state is the transmitter of cultural and family scripts. It is valuable for the survival of the human race, since it facilitates the automatic performing of parenting tasks, freeing the Adult ego state to deal with the weightier problems of existence.

When the Parent ego state is incomplete or inadequate in important ways, the Adult can be programmed to do a satisfactory job of parenting. Methods of re-Parenting are also being developed.

You have your own unique Parent ego state which is likely to be a mixture of helpful and hurtful behavior. Awareness of your Parent gives you more choice over your behavior, which in turn can enhance your chances of being a winner and of bringing up your children to be winners.

PLATE VIII

THE PARENT EGO STATE IS SOMETIMES PREJUDICIAL

Some parents send witch
messages that cause a child
to become spellbound.

EXPERIMENTS AND EXERCISES

1. Your Parents as People

To get in touch with your Parent ego state, start by becoming more aware of your actual parents.

- Imagine yourself in a room. In the room is audio-visual equipment you can use to replay your Parent video tapes. Include tapes of mother, father, grandparents, step- or foster parents, older siblings, housekeepers, or any other persons in authority over you during early childhood.

- Imagine the tapes are labeled according to subject matter.

- Read each set of questions, then turn on the video tapes to get the answers. Begin with the one labeled *Money.*

Money

- How did your parents respond to money problems? A threat of losing a job? A sudden, unexpected windfall?

- Did they have to struggle for survival, or did things come easily to them?

- What did they spend their money for? Who controlled the purse strings? How did their expenditures reflect their values?

- How did they talk about money?

Possessions

- Did they have favorite possessions, e.g., house, car, children's pictures? If so, was the care of possessions more important to them than the care of people, or vice versa?

- Were they style conscious? Did they try to keep up with the Joneses?

- Who made the decisions on buying household goods, cars, clothing purchases, and so forth?

Crisis

- What happened in family crises such as death, illness, accident, unwanted pregnancy, divorce, or natural calamities?

- Did your parents respond differently to different types of crises?

- Who could be relied on? Who fell apart?

Fun

- What did they do for fun? Where?

- Did your parents have fun together?

- How did they entertain at home? Whom did they invite to the house? Who did the inviting?

- What did they do for entertainment outside the home?

Sex Roles

- What were your parents' attitudes about maleness and femaleness? Did your father respect your mother, or did he downgrade her? Did your mother respect your father, or did she downgrade him?

- What roles did they play that they assumed were "masculine" or "feminine"? Were household chores assigned on this premise?

- Did they expect you to play these roles?

- Did they have domains in the house and yard designated as "mother's" or "father's"?

- Did you hear common clichés like "Your mother drives just like a crazy woman driver" or "That's just like a man"?

- Were your parents outwardly cool or outwardly affectionate with each other?

- What do you know about their sex life? What do you surmise?

Family Meals

- What kind of atmosphere was created at meal times? Was it "everyone for himself"? Candlelight and wine? What?

- What did your parents talk about at the table? How did they talk about it?

- Did they have any mannerisms that annoyed you?

- Were there family rituals, such as not eating until everyone was seated or until after prayer?

- What opinions did they have about different foods? About how food should be cooked and served?

- What was their expectation about you—what you ate and how you ate it?

- Were meal times a time of pain, pleasure, or a mixture?

Appearance

- What about your parent figures' personal appearance? Was their clothing attractive, clean?

- Were they sloppy at home and dressed up when going out?

- Did they have favorite styles and colors?

- Was either of them extreme—a peacock or a drab?

- Did their dress, size, make-up, shape, physical characteristics, or grooming habits embarrass you? Please you? What?

Education

- What did they say about education? Was education in itself valuable, or was it a means to an end?

- How much education did they have? Were they satisfied with it?

- Did they encourage you to have more? The same? Less?

- Were they interested, indifferent, or hostile toward your education? Schools? Teachers?

Work

- What kinds of jobs did they have? Were they satisfied with them?

- What did they say about the jobs? How do you think they performed them?

- Did they want you to do the same kind of work? Something better?

- Did they have specific attitudes about what was a woman's

work and what was man's work in the business and professional world?

Values [15]

• What were the moral and ethical values your parents taught you?

• Were these values related to a religious background or not?

• Were your parents atheists? Agnostics? Were they affiliated with a particular religious group? If the latter, were you included and how?

• Did they have definite attitudes toward people of different religious beliefs? How did they express their attitudes? Did they use "religion" to control your behavior? Did they use it to give you a sense of appreciation for the wonder of life? To give you comfort and security? To explain natural phenomena? What did they say about religious beliefs? Did they agree?

• How did they practice their beliefs? Were what they said and what they did consistent?

• Did your parents act friendly, hostile, cool, or fearful toward people of different color? Different ethnic backgrounds? What did they say? What did they do?

Speech Patterns

• How did they speak to each other?

• How did they speak to other people such as *their* parents? Friends? Servants? You? Can you recall their words and tone of voice?

• Did they use one kind of language with some people and another kind with others?

Listening Patterns

• Did they listen to other people? To you?

• Did they listen with a closed mind? Indulgently? With understanding? Absentmindedly? Responsively?

• What was said about listening?

Script Themes and Roles

- What seemed to make them happy? Sad? Angry? Frustrated? Helpless?

- Did they have a life theme, such as "Drinking themselves to death," "Committing suicide," "Making it," "Succeeding in business," "Never quite making it," "Building a family," "Enjoying life"?

- Did your parents have different life themes? Were the themes in conflict, or were they complementary?

- Think of your parent figures in their various roles. How did they play the parts of Victims, Persecutors, or Rescuers? What roles did you play in relation to them?

Parenting Practices

- How did they act as parents? Were they affectionate, cruel, loud, silent?

- What were their facial expressions? Body postures?

- How did they scold, punish, or praise you?

- If you had brothers and/or sisters, did your parents show favoritism?

- Did they express anger, hate, or love toward you? How?

- How did they manipulate you? With guilt? Fear? Criticism? Sweetness? False compliments? How?

- What mottoes and sayings were you reared on? Were they helpful? Hurtful? Irrelevant?

- Were your parents generally trustworthy or unpredictable?

- Were they in competition with each other or with you?

- Did you feel they were on your side?

- What did you like and dislike about them? Why?

- Do you think they felt like winners or losers? Do you think they encouraged you to be a winner or loser?

2. Your Parents' Attitudes

How would your parents react to

• A sick child crying out in the night.

• A child's birthday approaching.

• A child breaking a family treasure or doing something forbidden.

• A child's having been sexually molested.

• A child's wanting a pet.

• A teen-ager running away or getting pregnant.

• A teen-ager enlisting in military service.

• The marriage of the last child in the family.

• A new neighbor of a different religion or race.

• A presidential campaign in full force.

• A relative's wanting to come to live at your home.

• A panhandler in soiled, ragged clothes asking for a handout.

• A relative who needs custodial care.

• Having a car accident.

• The coming weekend, Monday morning, or holidays.

3. How Are You Like Your Parents?

After discovering more of what your parents were really like, become aware of how you're like them.

• Review the questions and responses in Experiments 1 and 2, asking yourself the question, "How do I copy them?"

• What is your Nurturing Parent like and how do you use it? With family? Friends? Co-workers?

• What is your Prejudicial Parent like and how do you use it? With family? Friends? Co-workers?

- What mannerisms, gestures, tones of voice do you now use that are like those of your parents?

If you work with children, how much of your behavior comes from your Parent ego state?

- Imagine yourself talking to children in different moods. How would you respond to: a whiny child, a hurt child, a naughty child, a boastful child, an inquisitive child, a giggling child?

   Which parent figures in you would talk in that way? Is it appropriate? How do you use these same modes of expression toward grownups?

Now take a pencil and paper and write out your idea of a perfect child.

- Do you think this is what your parent figures would write?

- Did you live up to or fall short of this image?

- Do you now expect children or other adults to live up to this image?

4. Try these exercises to become aware of your inner dialogue. It may help to diagram them.

- Imagine yourself at a PTA meeting. About twenty-five people are gathered informally. The speaker calls the group to attention and then says, "I need five of you to volunteer so that I can demonstrate some of the principles of our new approach to mathematics."

   Close your eyes; what would be going on in your head when you were confronted with this request? Who is talking (in your head)? Who wins?

- Imagine yourself about to take a final examination in an important course. Listen to your inner dialogue.

   What are your parent figures saying? How is your inner Child responding? What are your body feelings? Associate them. Do any previous teachers come into your head?

- Imagine you receive notification from the Internal Revenue Department that they wish you to come in to document your income tax return.

What is the inner dialogue?

• Imagine you are at a banquet and your name is called unexpectedly. You are asked to stand up and come to the front table. Imagine, as you stand there, that the speaker suddenly launches into a paean of praise for your "good works."

What do the parent figures in your head say to you? How does your Child respond?

• Imagine several emotional or traumatic situations. Listen to your internal dialogue. What is actually said?

5. Your Parent Ego States

Write in the important messages your two most significant parent figures sent to you from each of their ego states.

(P) _____

(A) _____

(C) _____

(P) _____

(A) _____

(C) _____

Which of these messages have you incorporated in your own ego states? Include feelings, thoughts, and behavior.

(P) _____

(A) _____

(C) _____

6. Naikan Therapy (Japanese Self-observation Method)

If you are familiar with Zen or other forms of ascetic medita-
tion, you may want to try this Japanese self-observation method called *Naikan therapy.* "It is a process in which the disciplinant examines and reflects on his past experiences, and through
the reflection completes the self-reformation" [16].

In Japan, Naikan takes one week, with the person sitting on his
or her legs in a small room, meditating from 5 a.m. to 9 p.m. A
teacher (Sensei) comes into the room from time to time and
asks the person to meditate only on the people who have mold-
ed the individual's personality, beginning with the person's
mother. The disciplinant is asked to focus on what *he* or *she* did
or said to the person's mother at the time being remembered,
not just what she did or said. The emphasis is on self-observation rather than on other-observation.

A modification of Naikan could be:

• Go someplace where you will have absolutely no sensory distractions for an extended period.

• Imagine you are looking at a black TV screen in your mind.

• Then bring your mother to the screen. When pictures of incidents with your mother emerge, ask yourself, "What did *I* do
  or say at the time?" Keep your focus on what *you* did, or
  failed to do, or had no intention of doing.

• Repeat this with other parent figures.

• What do you learn about *yourself?*

6

Childhood and the Child Ego State

But what am I?
An infant crying in the night?
An infant crying for the light:
And with no language but a cry!
  Alfred Tennyson

Every child is born with inherited characteristics, born into a specific social, economic, and emotional environment, and trained in certain ways by authority figures. Every child experiences significant events such as a death in the family, illness, pain, accidents, geographical dislocation, and economic crises. These influences contribute to the uniqueness of childhood for each person. No two children, even in the same family, have the same childhood.

THE CHILD EGO STATE

Each of us carries within our brain and nervous system permanent recordings of the way we experienced our own impulses as a child, the way we experienced the world, the way we felt about the world we experienced, and the way we adapted to it. The Parent ego state incorporates the personalities of emotionally significant authorities; the Child ego state is the inner world of feelings and experiences and adaptations.

A person who responds as a child does—inquisitive, affectionate, selfish, mean, playful, whining, manipulative—is responding from the Child ego state. The Child ego state develops into three discernible parts: the Natural Child, the Little Professor, and the Adapted Child.

The Natural Child is that part of the Child ego state that is the very young, impulsive, untrained, expressive infant still inside

139

each person. It is often like a self-centered, pleasure-loving baby whose response is cozy affection when needs are met or angry rebellion when they are not met.

The Little Professor is the unschooled wisdom of a child. It is that part of the Child ego state that is intuitive, responding to non-verbal messages and playing hunches. With it, a child figures things out, things such as when to cry, when to be quiet, and how to manipulate mama into smiling. The Little Professor is also highly creative.

The Adapted Child is that part of the Child ego state that exhibits a modification of the Natural Child's inclinations. These adaptations of natural impulses occur in response to traumas, experiences, training, and, most importantly, to demands from significant authority figures. For example, a child is naturally programed to eat when hungry. Shortly after birth, however, this natural urge may be adapted, so that the child's eating schedule is determined by the child's parents. A child would also do and take what's wanted naturally, on impulse, but may be adapted to share and to be courteous toward others in ways also determined by parents. On the next page is a second-order diagram of the Child ego state.

THE NATURAL CHILD

The Natural Child within each person's Child ego state is what a baby would be "naturally," if there were no other influence. The Natural Child is

> affectionate,
>> impulsive,
>>> sensuous,
>>>> uncensored,
>>>>> curious.

By nature, an infant responds to the skin-to-skin touch with mother and good feelings of a full belly. If the mother is pleased with her baby, smiles of satisfaction pass between them. They are close and like it.

Infants respond impulsively to their bodily feelings, crying when hungry or wet and cooing when full or comfortable. Infants react spontaneously to changes in their situation. By nature seeking pleasure over pain, infants are unashamedly sensuous. They enjoy pleasurable feelings such as rolling on a rug, splashing the water, warming in the sun, sucking on a thumb, chewing on a blanket, slurping lustily on a bottle. They explore their bodies and are often delighted in what they find. Infants are without an inner censor that might say "No."

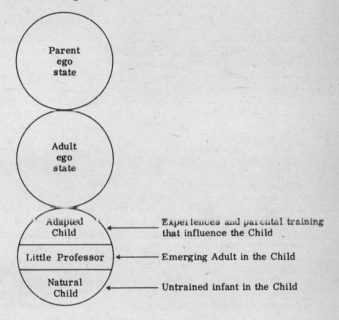

An infant is curious about the surrounding world—looking at it, feeling it, and often trying to taste it. The fuzz of a teddy bear tickles the infant; the movement of a mobile above the infant's crib captures attention. These and other things the infant sees, hears, smells, and touches are shaped into primitive mental images from which the infant builds an uncensored fantasy life. Later in life these preverbal fantasies may take the form of recurring dreams, often of a symbolic nature.

When children begin to use language, their fantasies become more sophisticated. They are frequently of unrestricted pleasure

PLATE IX

THE NATURAL CHILD

- is aggressive
- impulsive
- sensuous
- rebellious
- affectionate
- curious
- self-centered

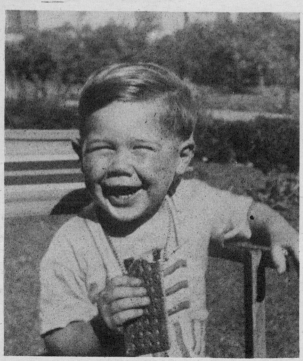

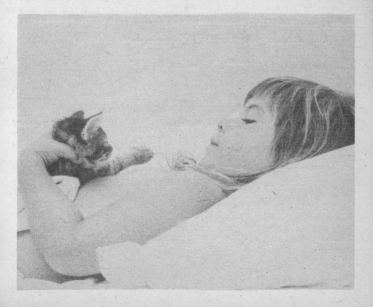

PLATE IX (continued)

or aggression. In a grown man these fantasies may take the form of imagining he is surrounded by beautiful women who bring him comfort and delight, asking nothing in return. Or, they may take the form of aggressively telling off a boss or beating someone up. Fantasying is one way a grown-up experiences the internal Natural Child.

Have you ever noticed an elderly man licking an ice cream cone with obvious delight on a park bench, or a middle-aged woman skipping along an ocean beach, or a couple dancing together in joyful abandonment? If so, you saw the Natural Child still being expressed. Regardless of how old a person is, the Natural Child has value. It adds charm and warmth to the person's personality, just as a real child can add charm and warmth to a family. A person who maintains the child's capabilities for affection, spontaneity, sensuousness, curiosity, and imagination is likely to enjoy life and is fun to be around.

However, the Natural Child is not just charming, but also

fearful,

self-indulgent,

self-centered,

rebellious,

aggressive.

By nature, children are fearful. They have primal fears of being dropped or abandoned. What would happen if no one came to protect or care for them? Being naturally self-indulgent, children want everything their own way—sometimes at a specific moment, which is usually right now. Children appear to experience themselves as the center of the universe.

The self-centered child is insensitive to other people's feelings. This child is selfish and doesn't like to share or to take turns. He or she can gleefully pull the legs off a spider and aggressively hit a friend on the head with a toy. The self-centered child is willful and sometimes asserts this will with force.

When frustrated, the Natural Child responds rebelliously. Children may assert this will by throwing a bottle, refusing to eat, screaming with anger. A rebellious child says "No" in many ways. Some children express rebelliousness by having temper tantrums. When used in adult life, such behavior is self-defeating.

PLATE X

THE NATURAL CHILD HAS
VALUE TO ADULTS

It adds charm and warmth to a person's personality.

Case Illustration

When Mary was a little girl, if she couldn't have what she wanted, she would fall to the floor, kick her feet wildly, and scream. Her mother inevitably gave in to her demands.

As a grown woman, Mary was a competent secretary and in line to become personnel manager. However, when her request for certain vacation dates was denied, Mary responded by yelling, "I want those dates, and if I can't have *that* much, you can all go to blazes around here!" She then stamped her foot, marched out of her supervisor's office, and slammed the door as she went. As a result, the supervisor submitted such a negative report that Mary not only failed to get her preferred vacation time, she also failed to be advanced to personnel manager.

Unless they make self-centered demands, some children would perish. Yet, if aggressiveness and rebelliousness go completely unchecked, people, when grown, may blindly demand self-gratification without regard either for personal health or safety or for that of others. Such persons may drive like fools, drink too much, and eat like gluttons. Their unadapted Natural Child may emerge in many roles:

bosses who want things their way, on their time schedule, without regard for others.

relatives who selfishly take more than their share.

parents who use their aggression to batter their children.

Conversely, if feelings of aggressiveness and rebelliousness are completely squelched in childhood, people become unable to assert themselves, even when necessary. They lose their sense of personal rights and often allow others to take advantage of them.

A healthy, happy person allows the *appropriate* expression of the Natural Child every day.

THE LITTLE PROFESSOR

The Little Professor is that part of the Child ego state that is innately

intuitive,

creative,

manipulative.

With no knowledge of psychology, a child intuits much of what is going on. Debby looks at her mother's face and figures out she'd better stop what she's doing. She catches her mother's nonverbal message sent through a disapproving look and responds to it. She then attempts to solve her problem with the use of her Little Professor, who "psychs out" the best move in a given situation.

Winnie-the-Pooh [1], a walking, talking teddy bear, is a literary prototype of the intuitive Little Professor. Pooh wants honey from the top of a tree, but fails in his first attempt to get it. He then begins to create his plan and calls for his six-year-old friend, Christopher Robin, to give him a balloon. Thus he can float to the top of the tree.

"It's like this," he said. "When you go after honey with a balloon, the great thing is not to let the bees know you're coming. Now, if you have a green balloon, they might think you were only part of the tree, and not notice you, and if you have a blue balloon, they might think you were only part of the sky, and not notice you, and the question is: Which is most likely?"

To further his plan, Pooh rolls himself in the mud. He inflates a blue balloon and, hanging onto it, rises above the treetops to become "a little black cloud in the sky." But the bees see through his disguise, so his plan fails. Although Pooh had given much thought to solving his problem, he lacked information about the intelligence and visual acuity of the bees.

Like Pooh, the Little Professor in the Child ego state is not always well informed. The child has neither lived enough years nor had enough experience to be so. The child often makes wrong decisions and draws wrong conclusions. For example, six-year-old Raymond, who had been watching television westerns, said to his grandmother, "Look out for robbers when you open the door."

PLATE XI

EVERYONE HAS A LITTLE PROFESSOR

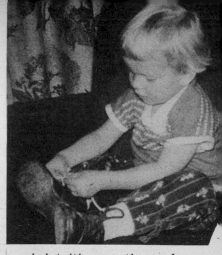

. . . is intuitive, creative, and manipulative.

The Little Professor figures
things out and often believes in magic.

She responded, "How will I know a robber if I see one?" With scorn the boy said, "Oh, Grandma, you can always tell the bad guys; they wear black hats!"

The intuitive Little Professor is still active after a person has grown up. For example, a person can intuit the meaning of the boss's tense jaw or the twinkle in a friend's eye. However, the Little Professor is sometimes wrong. The boss may have a toothache, and the friend may be enjoying a fantasy.

The Little Professor, who can create something original without guilt or fear, is not inclined to "stay within the lines" in the coloring book, but can originate new boundaries and make a different picture. The Little Professor can make a castle out of sand and water, a building out of blocks, pies out of mud, and a drama with high heels and long skirts, cowboy hats, and holsters.

People who express their creativity purposefully use their Little Professor in conjunction with their Adult ego state. When a person experiences a moment of genius, the Little Professor is probably in on it. The Adult and the Little Professor make a good team. Together they can:

design a new building,   write a book,

compose a musical score,   improve human relationships,

make a home attractive,   create a relevant curriculum,

develop a mathematical formula, and so forth.

Having fantasies is necessary for creativity. The Little Professor creatively designs fantasies which may be realistic. When a man visualizes the excitement his wife will feel on receiving his flowers, he may be correct. When a woman, tired after working hard, pictures herself lolling on the beach, she may be visualizing a possibility that can become reality.

However, the creative Little Professor's fantasies may be quite unrealistic. One young man felt sure he could have had a good relationship with his uncaring and unresponsive father if they could have "just gone to a ball game together." One woman who dabbled in painting fantasied an unveiling ceremony and the breathless anticipation of a large audience, although she had no evidence whatever to substantiate the idea that she was talented.

Every child, even without acting lessons, discovers at an early age how to manipulate people and things. Almost every infant has to figure out how to bring someone close by. Often by trial and error, the infant finds that a feigned fear or illness will make mother come quickly. If these early manipulations are effective, the child is likely to attribute these successes to magic. "Like all magicians he believes that his wishes, his thoughts, his words are the instruments of his magic powers"[2]. After all, a child can make the world disappear by closing his or her eyes.

Young children also attribute magic powers to parent figures and may fear that they have the power to turn them into snakes, toads, or ugly ducklings, or make them disappear altogether. Actually, parents do hold the power of life and death over their children. It is no wonder that children learn to think of parents as powerful giants or witches to be outwitted, and of themselves as powerless. (Powerless Me, I'm not OK, Powerful You, You're OK.) Some authorities take advantage of a child's belief in magic when they imply they have eyes in the back of their heads or teach that someone is always watching. As one boy wrote:

Mothers are people with X-ray eyes. They always know where you are, what you are doing, how you're doing it, who you're doing it with, and where you're doing it. They are the first ones to find out what you don't want anyone to know.

Jack [3]

Children frequently believe in the magic of objects and events. They become superstitious about a lucky penny, a rabbit's foot, a four-leaf clover, a black cat, a tooth under a pillow, a shadow crossing the moon, breaking a mirror, stepping on a crack, wishing on a star, and walking under a ladder. Some people, when grown, are unable to distinguish the magical thinking of the Little Professor from the factual information that can be data processed by their Adult. Such people easily confuse fact and fantasy. Consequently, they may act either omnipotent or helpless, or just wait and do nothing.

Omnipotent-acting people manipulate from the top-dog position. They try to rule the lives of others, under the delusion that they hold a special power and are always right.

Helpless-acting people manipulate from the under-dog position. They refuse to assume responsibility for their helplessness and/or find it difficult to make direct decisions.

Many people retain a childhood belief that wishing will make it so. They wish and wait for the magical event to improve their

PLATE XII
THE CREATIVE LITTLE PROFESSOR

. . . often remains active in adult life.

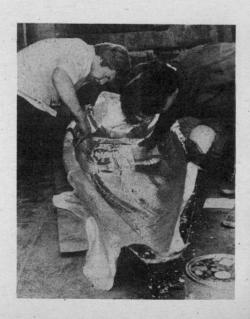

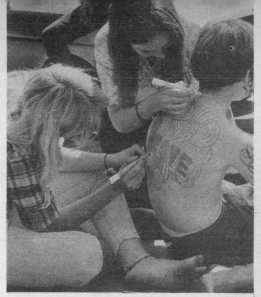

People who express their
creativity purposefully use
their Little Professor in
conjunction with their Adult
ego state.

lives. Meanwhile, time runs out, and they manipulate themselves into going nowhere. Berne refers to this as *waiting for Santa Claus*. He writes:

For most, Santa Claus never comes: if there is a knock on the door, at best it is only the milkman. For the others, when he does come he leaves not the magic orb which the original childhood tales of Santa Claus led them to expect, but only a tinsel ornament, a piece of paper, or a big little red wagon which can be duplicated in any auto showroom. Healthy people learn to resign this quest in favor of what the real world has to offer but, to some extent, feel the despair that comes from such resignations [4].

This belief in magic continues into adult life. According to Selma Fraiberg, "Long after reason has deprived the magician of his magic, and for all the days of his life, the belief that wishes can bring about real events will persist in a secret part of the self" [5]. One fisherman, climbing down a bank, was overheard saying to another, "If you just don't pay attention to the poison oak, you won't get it."

The manipulative skills of a child seem to have magical powers over others. With an active Little Professor, a person can manipulate a spouse, parent, teacher, boss, or friend.

Within a family, a husband may try to manipulate his wife with a bouquet of flowers and sweet talk if he comes home late. She may seize the opportunity to have him take her out to dinner or give her money for a new dress. Their son may manipulate to get the family car by having to "go to the library to study." Each is likely to be pulling the same old tricks that worked in early childhood. Manipulative skills may sometimes be necessary for survival, but dependence upon them leads to a game-playing, cliché level of living.

Have you ever seen: A woman secretary get what she wants from her male boss by using a quivering chin and teary eyes as she tells him how hard she tries to keep up with the work? The boss get what he wants from her by sighing, "My wife just doesn't understand me"? A salesperson clinch a deal by saying, "That car looks as if it was made for you"? If so, you have watched the manipulative Little Professor at work.

THE ADAPTED CHILD

A child's first adaptations to the world begin in the mother's womb as her emotions, chemical make-up, nutrition, and health leave their effects on her unborn child. Following these experiences is the trauma of birth—an infant's first thrust into separateness and first contact with the outer emotional and physical environment. This new environment may range from dire impoverishment to gross overstimulation or overprotection, contributing to the OK or not-OK feelings the infant will gradually develop.

Immediately after birth, an infant begins to adapt to the demands of outside authority, doing this out of a will to survive and a need for approval and/or the anxiety of fear. Born without a sense of what is right or wrong, a child's first sense of conscience develops very slowly from interaction with the environment, particularly with parent figures.

Smiling and flattering responses from parent figures convey to the child the idea of approval for doing what is right. Cold or angry parental responses convey a sense of punishment and pain for wrong-doing. Young children usually learn what they ought to do by being praised or punished. They figure out, with the aid of their Little Professor, how to avoid pain and how to get approval. They adapt, in some way, to the "oughts."

A child's adaptations result in what Berne calls the Adapted Child. The Adapted Child is the part of the Child ego state that is influenced primarily by parents.

Whereas some adaptation of natural impulses is essential, many children experience training that is unnecessarily repressive. For example, children who hear:

"I'll give you something to really cry about!"

"I expect you to do what I say and like it!"

"I can't stand it! Don't ask me another dumb question!"

"I'll beat you within an inch of your life if you say that again."

may adapt by losing their ability to feel for themselves, to be curious about the world, to give and receive affection. Their natural expressiveness becomes overly inhibited.

When children are adapted rationally, they learn to be aware of other people—to share, to take turns, to be courteous, to be sociable. They learn social skills that help them relate to others and enable them to fulfill their own needs sociably.

Whereas the Natural Child does what he or she wants to do and feels OK about it, the Adapted Child is likely to do what parents insist on, rational or irrational, and may learn to feel not-OK. Common patterns of adaptation are:

complying,

withdrawing,

procrastinating.

Some children choose to comply in order to get along. They find that complying without question is easier, more practical, and less anxiety-provoking than battling for their own position or ideas.

They may comply by copying a parent figure or by obeying one. Some children get the message "Do as I do," and comply by copying their parents. For example, "I made captain of the team, son; no reason why you can't do the same," encourages a boy to copy his father. Other children get the message "Don't do what I do, do what I say." They comply by obeying in spite of an obvious double standard. For example, "We expect good manners around here, young man!" shouted by a father with a mouth full of food encourages the son toward a standard his father doesn't apply to himself.

Although many children comply with parental demands, they often do not do so graciously. Frequently, children choose to sulk. Something happens in early life which makes them mad at authority figures. Instead of rebelling, they hang on to their resentments, grudgingly doing what is asked, continuing to sulk, and then blaming others when things go wrong [6].

Sometimes, sulking and blaming behavior may result from a traumatic experience that causes deep psychological injury to a child.

Case Illustration

Betty was known in the counseling group as "The Sulk." She appeared to be pouting much of the time and spoke infrequently. Although she persistently denied saving up resentments, at one session she went into a rage because someone moved to another group. This outburst led her to get in touch with old feelings of anger she had felt when her mother was institutionalized and her father had allowed it to happen.

When she was only three, Betty had nearly been killed. Her mentally ill mother attempted to jump with her from a window ledge of a hotel. Her father, aware of the possible suicide, entered the room unexpectedly and pulled them from the ledge. After this, Betty's mother was permanently institutionalized.

Betty was sent to live with an aunt whom she obeyed, but always grudgingly. Her father rarely visited her, and she spent long periods in her room sulking. When things went wrong at school, she always blamed "that stupid old teacher."

When Betty started dating, one of her steadies was a young man who rarely kept his promises and often kept her waiting for hours. After each disappointing experience, Betty complained, "Why does this always happen to me?"

Betty was eventually able to admit that she had held a grudge all her life against her mother and father for abandoning her. In counseling, comparable behavior is often observed in clients who lose a parent in early childhood.

Other children in a similar situation might respond differently. Instead of sulking like Betty, they might act openly hostile or they might withdraw in fear. Children who adapt by withdrawing pull into themselves. They feel unable to cope with their external world in a direct way. They often isolate themselves from others by frequent illnesses or with activities, such as hobbies, which they can pursue alone. They may hide out in fields, alleys, treehouses, bedrooms, or in their inner world of fantasy.

A dramatic withdrawal can be illustrated by the case of a man who disappeared for two days after a family argument. His frantic wife discovered him huddled in a corner of the cellar. Later, talking about his childhood, he revealed that when his mother and father engaged in loud conflict, he hid for hours under a bed with a blanket over his ears. His family was so large that he was seldom missed. As a grown man, when he withdrew from conflict with his

PLATE XIII

THE ADAPTED CHILD IS SOCIALIZED

Children may be adapted to be courteous and to conform to rituals and to standards of dress.

wife, he was reliving the same pattern of adaptation. This was a re-play of a common childhood scene.

Children who adapt by withdrawing may do so emotionally rather than physically. In a sense, such children "tune out" and often act as if they don't hear. Thus they avoid external demands. When "tuned out," they often create their own world of fantasy which protects them from conflict and the possible hurt and in-volvement that go with it.

Fantasies of the Adapted Child frequently reflect early training or experience. A young boy caught stealing a cookie by his mother may imagine being sent away to jail because he's such a "bad" boy. A young girl scared by her brother's unexpectedly jumping out of a closet with a loud yell may fantasy that there could be a man in every closet. A common fantasy of people trained as chil-dren to be "seen but not heard" is of being in a situation where they need to speak or yell but can't make a sound.

The mass media, as well as parental expectations, may influ-ence a child to distort reality. This distortion may take the form of copying or fantasies in which the child is

The swaggering cowboy who causes others to cower when he enters the room.

The superperson whose X-ray vision foils the robbery of the city treasury.

The helpless woman who is rescued from her dingy laundry by a handsome man with the right product.

The teenager who gains friends by dazzling white teeth and a bikini-clad figure.

Procrastination is another common pattern of the Adapted Child. Because the Natural Child wants to rebel and say, "I won't," and the Adapted Child doesn't dare, the Little Professor decides to stall. By stalling, a child partly placates the authorities and at the same time satisfies an inner wish to rebel. Eventually, procrastination becomes an adaptive pattern.

A boy hearing his mother call, "Freddy, it's time to come in for dinner," may respond nicely, "Just a minute, mother." By this technique he neither openly defies her nor jumps to her com-mand. A girl reminded to set the table may counter with, "Just as soon as the program is over, Mom." Often, the procrastination continues with "just one more program" or "I'll do it at the next commercial." Children learn to procrastinate for many reasons:

They hear too many parental commands.

If they finish their chores too soon, they'll get more to do.

Superior performance might make their friends and siblings jealous.

No matter what they do and how they do it, it won't be good enough.

If they stall long enough, someone else will do it.

Procrastination can become an integral part of the psychological script—a way of acting out the life drama. This acting is seen in a person who is constantly late: to class, to dinner, to a job, to meetings. Even the ring of the morning alarm clock can trigger the response, "Just ten more minutes and I'll get up." Many procrastinators balk at deadlines and often ask for a little more time.

The pattern of procrastination is sometimes revealed in a counseling technique in which the person is asked to imagine her or his epitaph. Frequently, the epitaph is a capsuled summary of the essence of the person's life drama. Epitaphs from clients that indicate procrastination are

She always meant to, but something always interfered.

She tried and she tried, but she finally died.

He ran out of time.

He never got started.

One man's epitaph took a poetic form:

Here lies a person named Paul,
Who, in truth, was not very tall.
He tried and he tried, till the day that he died,
But Paul never made it at all.

The famed Winchester House in San Jose, California, which has corridors going on and on and doors opening onto nothing or onto blank walls, might have been built by a woman who believed that as long as she procrastinated on finishing the house, she would not die.

The inner Adapted Child is very often the troubled part of the personality. This is particularly true when a child, born to win, develops the self-image of a loser, as not-OK, and begins to act not-OK. When a grown man hides in his den rather than face family conflict, when a woman says "Yes, dear," to all requests even though she resents them, or when a person feels confused and can't think independently, it is likely that the Adapted Child is in control of the person's personality at that moment. When this is the case, a person may act (from the Adapted Child) like a

clinging vine,   know-it-all,   vicious bully,
seductive siren, witch, pure saint, ornery ogre, or down-in-the-mouth Victim.

The possibilities are myriad. The overly adapted person often needs professional counseling in order to recover the Natural Child and recapture the ability to laugh, love, and play with zest.

SHIFTS BETWEEN THE NATURAL AND ADAPTED CHILD

Within the Child ego states of some people, there is a perpetual battle between their Natural Child and their Adapted Child. In those cases, their feelings and behavior fluctuate relentlessly between compliance to parental interference and rebellion against it. The conflict is often seen in a person whose parents permitted the child happiness and pleasure only if she or he met certain rigid conditions. As a grown person, the confused inner Child may pursue an insatiable quest for approval and, according to Berne, ". . . apologetic clumsiness replaces authenticity in his social behavior" [7].

Case Illustration

Although forty, Harold continually worried about his relationship with his mother. Between visits to her home he would rehearse in his head how to tell her that he and his wife had agreed that their children no longer had to attend Sunday School. However, when Harold actually faced his mother, he could not tell her of this decision. Instead, he fabricated

PLATE XIV

THE ADAPTED CHILD MAY COMPLY

• with parents' expectations,

• or withdraw, feeling not OK.

stories about the children that pleased her. As for the children, they were in great conflict about what they were supposed to say and do in front of grandmother.

Harold's mother was the most important person in his drama and continued to direct it. Although he felt miserable—vacillating between wanting to comply with her wishes and wanting to rebel against them—her approval was always sought after in the end.

A letter received by columnist Ann Landers illustrates the same personality problem:

Dear Ann Landers:

This problem has bothered me for years and I have been tempted to write you many times. Now I feel I must. It is about my mother.

Although I am a grown woman and have children of my own, my mother is still the most important person in my life. I have always felt that she never loved me, and no matter how hard I try to please her I *somehow* fall short of the mark.

My sisters and brother practically ignore Mother, yet she treats them much better than she treats me. She is always telephoning them and going to their homes (inviting herself, actually). I find myself begging her to come to our home.

This problem is ruining my married life and casting a dark cloud over everything. Please tell me what is wrong with me and what I can do about it. My husband says "forget it."

Unloved Daughter [8]

The search for parental approval that is never forthcoming can so preoccupy people that they cannot function in the "here and now," in their current relationships. Instead of dealing with the present scene, they are still playing the past scene of inner conflict.

ACTIVATING THE CHILD EGO STATE

Camus, in *The Fall*, claims, "At the end of all freedom is a court sentence; that's why freedom is too heavy to bear, especially when you're down with a fever, or are distressed, or love nobody." It is at times like these—when people are injured, ill, tired, worried, or otherwise under stress—that their Child ego state is likely to surface. Feeling partially or fully incapacitated, they respond with their unique childhood patterns:

Withdrawing from other people

 Trying harder and harder

  Whining about aches and pains

   Making demands for service

    Covering stress by acting cheerful

Sick people commonly desire the same foods—tea, milk-toast, custard, or chicken soup—that they adapted to when they were sick as children. Their Little Professor may think of these foods as magic potions, and they may eat them, even though their Natural Child may want only ice cream and jello [9].

When people are tired, their Natural Child may want to sleep or do nothing. Their Adapted Child may not dare give in to these feelings, especially if goodness is equated with keeping busy. To settle the inner conflict the Little Professor may figure out how to get by with a cat nap.

When people are worried, their Natural Child often wants something to suck on: a cigarette, a piece of gum or candy, a drink. Their Adapted Child may procrastinate and not face the problem or may expect others to solve it. If their Little Professor gets into the act, the individuals may come up with a creative solution or may call on some form of magic to make the problem go away.

When people are badly hurt, their Natural Child wants to scream, cry, and demand care. Their Adapted Child may withdraw in silent agony, especially if they learned in childhood that crying brought spanking. Their Little Professor may figure out that looking pathetic results in needs being met or that hiding the injury avoids the trip to the doctor. Every person has his or her own individual responses. Many situations, such as a party, a test, a day off, a vacation, a sudden windfall, a promotion, or being fired, activate the Child ego state.

For example, at a party a person's Adapted Child may feel shy or unliked, and may wish he or she hadn't come. Then the Little Professor discovers that alcohol knocks out the inhibiting Parent, and the person becomes less shy. Continued drinking also knocks out the Adult, leaving the person at the mercy of the unguarded Child. Having lost inner control, the person may express unpredictable behavior from any part of the Child ego state and may fight, swear, sing, dance, insult the hostess, or become amorous.

Eventually, the Child may succumb to the alcohol, and the person "passes out."

Another person may arrive at the party with his or her Natural Child ready to laugh, play, and have fun. A person whose Parent is less inhibiting than in the case above may not feel the same need for alcohol and may be a delight to be with; or, if untempered by reason, the person may selfishly hog the stage for the evening. If the latter is true, she or he is likely to provoke someone else's critical Parent or resentful Child who also wants a place in the spotlight.

In addition to stress and specific situations, certain transactions also tend to activate the Child. When one person "comes on" with the Parent ego state, the other is likely to experience his or her Child. Parental comments like the following usually "hook" the Child.

Husband to wife: (critically)	This place is a mess. What have you been doing all day!
Secretary to boss: (protectively)	Now don't forget to take your umbrella when you go to lunch. You don't want to catch a cold, do you!
Eight-year-old to eight-year-old: (scornfully)	You can't do anything right. You can't even catch a ball.

Child ego state comments like the following might also "hook" the Child ego state in another.

Boy to girl: (admiringly)	Gee you're pretty.
Girl to boy: (admiringly)	You're so big and strong.
Salesperson to salesperson: (eyes gleaming)	How about a drink after work?
Employee to employee: (angrily)	I'm so mad at you for embarrassing me in front of the boss, I could just spit in your face.

Although certain situations and transactions tend to activate the Child, the Child doesn't have to be expressed. Many people function well from their Adult ego state in spite of the internal replay of their Child memory tapes.

SUMMARY

Everyone has an internal little boy or little girl. When you now act and feel as you did in childhood, you are in your Child ego state.

The Natural Child feels free and does what he or she wants to do. When you are being expressive, affectionate, playful, selfish, or are standing up for your own rights, you are very likely expressing your Natural Child.

The Little Professor is the smart little kid in each person. When you are feeling intuitive, experiencing a moment of genius, creating for the fun of it, or manipulating someone else to get what you want, your Little Professor is involved.

The Adapted Child is the trained child who develops social awareness but sometimes feels very not-OK. When you are being courteous, compliant, avoiding confrontation, procrastinating, or feeling not-OK, you are likely to be expressing your Adapted Child.

The Child ego state becomes active if someone else comes on like a parent. It may also be activated during times of dependency, such as when one is sick, or where there is fun to be had, such as at a party.

The Child is the foundation of a person's self-image. Your feelings of being a winner or a loser are likely to stem from your Child ego state.

EXPERIMENTS AND EXERCISES

People have different levels of recall about their childhood. Some recall a great deal, a few find it difficult to remember anything. If you desire to stimulate recall, to re-experience childhood feelings, and to gather data about your Child ego state, set aside time for the following experiments and exercises. Some will give you emotional, as well as intellectual, insight.

Emotional insight comes with an expansion of awareness. It is that moment of self-discovery when the person says "ahah." Perls describes the ahah experience as "Whenever something clicks, falls into place; each time a gestalt closes, there is this 'Ahah!'"

click, the shock of recognition"[10]. Intelligent insight comes with the gathering of data. It is a thinking process, often analytical, in which the person often concludes, "So *that's* the way it is!"

1. Your Childhood Home

Close your eyes. Imagine yourself back in the first home you can remember. Let the pictures emerge. Don't include what you think *ought* to be there. Just what you *see* is there.

• What do you actually see? People? Furniture? Other objects?

• Look around the room for details—colors, shapes, decorations, doors, windows, etc.

Next, try to re-experience your other senses in relation to this home.

• What do you hear? Smell? Taste? Touch?

• Notice your emotions as you re-experience the past.

Now become aware of the people who are there in your childhood home.

• Look at their faces, gestures, postures, clothes.

• How are they interacting? How do they interact with you?

• What kind of drama is going on? A Comedy? Farce? Tragedy? Saga? What?

• What roles are being played? Who are the Victims, Rescuers, Persecutors? What are your roles in the drama?

It may take you more than one visit to recover the memories of your childhood home. You may also have more than one home to visit.

2. Getting in Touch With Your Childhood

Get out your family album or any picture of you as a child. Study the pictures slowly. Let your memories emerge:

• Were these happy times? Sad times? Serious times?

- What was going on in your life then?

- Compare yourself as an infant, a toddler, a school child.

- What do you see in these pictures that you see in yourself now?

- Do you see anything in the pictures that you would like to see in yourself now?

After you have a picture of yourself as a child, take this child on an imaginary walk to a quiet place, perhaps a favorite childhood haunt. Get acquainted.

- Listen to the hurts, happinesses, and longings of your inner Child.

- What does this child believe about itself?

- Stick with this until you learn something brand new about yourself as a child.

3. The Child in You Now

Try to discover what currently activates your Child ego state. Begin by becoming aware of how you act

- When under stress, sick, tired, disappointed, etc.

- When someone "comes on Parent" to you.

- When the Child in another person provokes or invites the Child in you.

- When you go to a party.

- When you want something from someone else.

Next, try to discover if you have a pattern of "coming on" Child inappropriately.

- Do you do or say things that elicit frowns or ridicule from others?

- Do you do or say things that turn people off or embarrass them?

- Are there certain people that you habitually respond to from your Child ego state? If so, why? When you transact with them, how do you feel and how do you act? What responsibility do you take for the nature of the transaction?

If you discover inappropriate Child behavior patterns, explore alternative ways you could act.

4. Fantasy Awareness

Next time you "tune out" from what's going on around you, become aware of what's going on inside you.

- Are you taking a fantasy trip to a special place?

- Talking to a special person? Debating? Seducing? Pleading? Fighting?

- Rehearsing for a future event?

- Playing a superman or superwoman role or otherwise engaging in wishful thinking?

- Can you identify which part of your Child ego state is fantasying?

- What happens to your ability to hear others when you are fantasying?

5. Your Childhood Adaptations

Think back to the methods—verbal and nonverbal—that were used to train you. Try to compare what you *wanted* to do (i.e., climb on Daddy's lap, stay up late, play outside with the kids) with what you *had* to do (i.e., act stoic, go to bed early, do your chores before playing).

- What words, looks, etc., were used to keep you in line?

- What words, looks, etc., were used to encourage you?

- What limitations were set on your activities?

- Were these rational and necessary, or were they unnecessarily inhibiting?

Now select a specific incident and in your imagination re-experience it.

- See again who was there.

- Hear what was said.

- Feel again what you felt then.

Now ask yourself:

- When do you feel this way now?

- Do you act toward someone else *now* as your parents acted toward you then?

What were your patterns of adaptation to parental demands?

- Did you comply? When?

- Did you withdraw? When?

- Did you procrastinate? When and how?

- Was one of these behavior patterns more predominant than the others?

- How do you see these patterns operating in your life drama now?

How appropriate are your childhood adaptations to your life now? Which adaptations did you learn that remain:

- Helpful to you?

- Confusing to you?

- Inhibiting of your potential?

- Destructive of you or of others?

If you have discovered adaptive patterns that now hinder you, think of *opposite* behavior.

- If you usually comply with people's demands, what would it be like if you refused?

- If you frequently withdraw from others, what would it be like if you got involved with them?

- If procrastination is your style, what would it be like if you stopped stalling and made some rapid decisions?

When you thought about opposite behavior, was an old Parent memory tape activated inside your head?

- If so, play the words back again. Then say the words out loud.

- What memory tapes in your Child do the words activate?

- Sit in a chair. Imagine your Parent sitting opposite you. Use the words you heard to start your dialogue.

- Next, tell your Parent you're going to experiment with different behavior, but that you are not going to do anything destructive, either to yourself or to anyone else.

Your Adapted Child frequently takes an under-dog position. Your Parent ego state frequently takes the top-dog position. These may represent poles in your personality. An overdemanding Parent may be one pole; the balky, compliant, or withdrawn Child the other.

- Can you admit to any top-dog and/or under-dog positions within yourself?

- Can you relate these to your Parent and Child ego states?

After you have clarified polarities within yourself, let your two fists represent these polarities. Decide which fist will represent your top-dog position, which will represent your under-dog. Let your two fists talk to each other.

- Does one win over the other? Is this the best way for it to end? If not, attempt a compromise or reconciliation or take a firm stand against the opposition.

6. Loss of a Parent

This experiment is for a person who has lost a parent by some means other than death—i.e., divorce, desertion, hospitalization, going away to war, taking extended business trips.

If this happened to you, ask yourself:

- How was the parent's absence explained? Were you allowed to talk about it?

- What were your questions? How were they dealt with?

- Did you blame someone for the absence of the parent?

- If the parent came back from time to time, were you happy? Confused? Resentful? What?

- Did things change when the parent returned?

Now use the chair technique. Tell the parent how you felt about being left. Allow the parent to talk back to you. Express your feelings. When it feels right, try forgiving your parent.

This experiment is for a person who as a child lost a parent by death. Do it when you feel strong, not "down." Let yourself re-experience as much as you can tolerate. You may want to do this at intervals and in small doses.

In your imagination go back to the day your parent died.

- Who told you? What did you do?

- How did you feel? Sad? Mad? Deserted?

- What did other people do and say?

Now imagine this parent in the chair opposite you. Tell him or her what happened to you at that time and how you felt about it. Express your feelings.

- After you feel you've expressed everything you need to (which may take several sessions), say "Goodbye."

7. Your Little Professor

How accurate is your intuition—your ability to tune in to non-verbal messages or play your hunches?

- Select several people in different situations who would be willing to give you honest feedback on their thoughts and feelings. They may be at your dinner table, in your car pool, on your office staff, etc. Include people who are different—different in sex, age, race, etc.

- Ask yourself, "What is that person feeling about me or the situation? Thinking about me (the situation)?"

- Immediately check with the other person to see if what you intuit is correct.

- How accurate is your intuition? Are you correct most of the time? Some of the time? Seldom?

- Do you "read" some kinds of people easier than others?

Review your creativeness.

- In the past week have you tried something in a new way? Dreamed up a fresh idea? Given new shapes to old materials, ideas, relationships?

- Can you trace your creativeness or lack of creativeness to any childhood event or circumstance?

- Do you have memory tapes that give you discouraging or encouraging messages in reference to your creativity?

- If you find you lack creative expressiveness, try doing something a new way this week.

Recall your manipulative skills.

- What did you do to get what you wanted? Act sick? Obey? Turn on the charm? Sulk? Throw a tantrum? What?

- Whom did you manipulate easily?

- Was there anyone you felt unable to sway?

- Now think of the people you are currently involved with. How do you think you manipulate them? If possible, ask them what you do.

Do you remember what seemed magical to you as a child?

- Seeing something appear or disappear?

- Feeling like a giant or like a dwarf surrounded by giants?

- Believing someone or something would rescue you?

- Wearing or carrying a lucky charm?

How does this carry over into your adult life?

- Are you still wanting to be rescued?

- Do you still sometimes feel like a dwarf or a nothing?

- Do you count on the "magic" of your smile? Your touch? The way you speak? Your gestures?

Do some people around you now seem to have a magical quality?

- Is there anyone in your life who seems like a witch? An ogre? A fairy godmother? A wizard?

- Do they have any similarities to people in your past?

- Are they characters in your script?

8. You as a Natural Child

You may be one of those many people who have lost some of their childlike ability to sense the world in their own unique way. This experiment will enable you to get in touch with your senses more fully.

- Go to a place where you feel comfortable, preferably outside. Focus your eyes on an object as if you've never seen it before. Become aware of its size, shape, color, texture, etc. Now let it fade away and allow the background to come into focus. Repeat this with other objects.

- Next, focus your attention on listening to something outside of you. What sounds are constant? What are intermittent? Be aware of the intensity and pitch.

- Next, focus on any odors. When you distend your nostrils and inhale, what smells are you aware of?

- Next, focus on the taste in your mouth. What is it like? Run your tongue over your teeth. What do you feel?

- Next, focus on the surface of your skin. Do you feel warm, cold, pain? Shift your focus to different parts of your body, moving from the top of your head to your toes.

- Repeat the experiment above every day for a few minutes. Let sensory awareness become a habit.

What did you really enjoy doing in your early childhood? Choose something that's all right to do but that you haven't done for a long time. Try it again.

- If you liked to lie on your back and make pictures out of the clouds, take some time to find a spot where you can lie on your back again and watch the clouds.

- If you liked to take off your shoes and walk in the mud or run through the wet sand or kick your way through the autumn leaves, why not do it again at the first opportunity?

- Let the sun shine on your skin and concentrate on the feelings it gives your body.

- Find a tree you can climb and sit there a while.

- Fly a kite. Take a hike. Suck a popsicle.

- Like a child, have fun. Enjoy yourself. Winners do.

7

Personal and Sexual Identity

We shall not cease from exploration
And the end of all our exploring
Will be to arrive where we started
And know the place for the first time.
   T. S. Eliot

Everyone experiences natural impulses, "psychs out" how to manage the world, and adapts in unique ways. Everyone, no matter how old, how sophisticated, or how well educated, acts at times from the Child ego state. The Child ego state contains a person's first sense of identity, life script, games played, life positions, and winning and losing streaks—all of which are likely to be reinforced by the Parent ego state. If the Parent is saying internally, "Why did you have to be born?" the Child ego state is likely to hold the position "I'm no good" or "I don't deserve to live."

NAMES AND IDENTITY

Paramount to a person's identity is his or her name. Even though this name should not change one's character, it often contributes to the person's script, either negatively or positively, because of the message it sends to the child.

On a birth certificate, a boy's name could read James William Stone. However, he might be called:

Jim (by a friend)

   James (by his father)

      Jimmy (by his mother when pleased)

         James William Stone (by his mother when displeased)

179

Each of these variations on the boy's name reflects an emotional feeling of the person using them. Each gives the boy a different message to live up to. Each activates a different response in him.

Egbert, now a banker, relates that at age seven he decided to change his name to Butch. This exercise of his Little Professor successfully stopped the other children from picking on him and calling him sissy. Another man reported that he had to defend himself continually because of his family name of Francis. Bertha, an attractive housewife, changed her name to Maria because of the images of an elephant that always came to mind when she heard the name Bertha. Some people indicate their dislike for the identity their first name holds for them by choosing to use their middle name or their initials.

Many children labeled Junior or the "III" assume that they should follow in their father's footsteps. The same can occur with designations such as "Big" Bill and "Little" Bill for a father and son. In either case there is a risk the son will feel he can never measure up to dad. Consequently, he ends up feeling guilty or inadequate or in some way not-OK. In addition, he may feel like a carbon copy rather than an original, confusing his own identity with his father's.

Many children are given symbolic names from literature, family genealogy, or history and are expected to live up to them. For example, children with biblical names such as David or Solomon, Martha or Mary, may learn to identify with, or choose to fight against, the implied expectations. A Solomon may assume he is wiser than he really is. A Martha may resent the implication that her interests lie in the kitchen rather than "in things of the spirit."

Case Illustration

When the twelfth child was born to Philip and Sarah, Philip, a minister, opened his Bible at random for a scripture verse to help him select a proper name for his new son. His eyes fell on the passage "You shall call his name Jesus." Both parents were inspired by this, and Sarah commented that the child had been born without pain. In fear that their neighbors would think them unduly proud, the parents adapted the name Jesus to Joseph. He was the family favorite and treated as a special child that would do great things.

Joe was thirty-three when he and his wife entered therapy. She was threatening to leave him and complained, "He either demands to be treated like a king or goes around the house acting like a martyr." One of Joe's favorite comments about his job as a probation officer was that he felt "nailed to the cross."

Foreign-sounding names, as well as symbolic names, are often burdensome. In both World Wars many families with German names were persecuted or rejected. Throughout history many Jewish families have suffered the same fate. It is common for families with difficult foreign names to shorten or anglicize them as a way of fitting into a new cultural script. However, in disowning their identity based on traditions they often end up with a sense of rootlessness and with a generation split between those of the "old" country and those born on new soil.

Surnames usually reflect the family heritage and give some clues—pleasant or unpleasant—to the cultural scripting of a person. Some people are so closely identified with their family name that they use it almost exclusively.

The importance of a family name differs in various cultures. In Japan, for example:

The primacy of the family name and its survival is such that if a couple with adequate means have only a daughter, they will often adopt the man she wishes to marry. He will then take her family's name, thus insuring its survival. This practice, called *mukotori*, is accepted as a commonplace in Japan. In the event that a prosperous family has an only daughter who marries a man not free for his own family reasons to change his name, it will sometimes adopt officially an adult couple who will then assume its name. This practice is often used to preserve and continue a family trade or business. In both these practices, we can see the intenseness of the Japanese concern for the family name! [1]

Traditionally, it has been a common American practice for a woman, when marrying, to drop the use of her surname and take on that of her husband. "Spanish cultures, in contrast, add the mother's maiden name to surnames, recognizing both lines of descent instead of the father's alone" [2].

Although a practice similar to that used by the Spanish was common in early America, today it is infrequent. Consequently, many married women—often without their awareness—lose the sense of the early identity associated with their maiden name. As one woman recounted, "One day when home alone and bored, I took out my college photo albums and turned the pages. I was amazed at the dynamic young woman pictured there—receiving scholarships, being politically active, debating on the team. This was *me!* What happened along the way? Did becoming Mrs. Roberts make me a different person?"

A "psychic symbiotic union" is a phrase of Eric Fromm's which describes two grownups living off each other much like an unborn child lives off its pregnant mother [3]. Symbiotic attachment, sometimes symbolized by use of a surname, can lead to the neurotic pattern of incorporation/identification. This attachment can occur in marriage, work relationships, even friendships. As Anthony Storr puts it:

To incorporate another person is to swallow him up, to overwhelm him, and to destroy him; and thus to treat him ultimately as less than a whole person. To identify with another person is to lose oneself, to submerge one's own identity in that of the other, to be overwhelmed, and hence to treat oneself ultimately as less than a whole person [4].

Although both given names and surnames affect the sense of identity and destiny, nicknames, pet names, and being called names have even more influence on some people. These names are descriptive and may be affectionate or demeaning, and their effect either positive or negative. If nicknames script children unrealistically or unfairly, the effect is always negative, discounting the person.

Some nicknames conjure up physical images. Fatso, Stringbean, Freckles, Venus, Blondie, Piano-legs, Shortie, Fish-face, and Dimples, all focus on appearance.

Some nicknames imply behavioral characteristics. Stupid, Sweetie-pie, Monster, Knuckle-head, The Clod, Angel, Red-the-Hothead, all give a child "permission" to act in specific ways.

Case Illustration

"Kicker" was the nickname of a four-year-old boy. It was given to him by his father, who had had a strong frog kick as a swimmer on a college team and was proud of the strength in his infant son's legs. He continually commented, "He's a real kicker." In nursery school, the boy frequently kicked other children to get what he wanted and even attacked the teacher. When she tried to correct him he bragged, "But I'm a real kicker, just ask my daddy."

In a sense Kicker was acting out his nickname, but in an aggressive way, not related to the original, constructive, "good" meaning. He was making life miserable for his family, friends, and schoolmates. In counseling, his parents became aware of the script implications of his nickname. They had unintentionally given him "permission" to act aggressively toward others. He had adapted his script theme to become "kicking up a fuss." They dropped the use of this nickname and used only his given name, Alan, and they asked others to do the same. The child's behavior soon began to improve, and he eventually gave up being The Kicker.

Some children are summoned or chastised with derogatory epithets. This namecalling is a vicious form of discounting. Some children are almost totally ignored or are called "Hey you" or "Kid." Some children enter kindergarten without even knowing their name. Lacking a sense of identity, such children feel unreal or like a nothing.

When a name gives a child unnecessary pain, perhaps the old jingle "Sticks and stones can break my bones, but names can never hurt me" is *less* true than the Anatolian proverb that says, "The hurt of a stick dies away, but words hurt forever."

IDENTITY THROUGH PLAY

A name is only one of the many ways by which a child develops a sense of self-identity. Play is another. It is one of the most natural. Play involves physical or mental activity for the sake of diversion, amusement, and growth. Play is a child's way of "trying out" life and of discovering her or his world.

Often, a child's ability to laugh and to play go hand in hand. A personal sense of identity may include such feelings as reserve, soberness, playfulness, or wit. For better or for worse, a grownup expresses some Child aspects.

A child can play actively, testing strength and skills, acting out emotions, fantasies, and future expectations. Or, a child can be passive, an observer, rather than an active participant in life. Most active play requires the child's direct bodily participation, a test-

PLATE XV

REHEARSING FOR
FUTURE ROLES

Parents often define roles
as masculine or feminine.

ing of muscle strength and a sharpening of wits. This may be un-structured play—an infant rolling on the grass, a toddler chasing a moth, a child dancing freely to music—or it may be highly struct-ured, with predetermined rules that require specialized skills and some Adult programming.

If the Natural Child engages in active play, there are likely to be giggles, laughter, and shouts of joy. If the Adapted Child is playing, beating an opponent may be more important than having fun.

Some active play is a rehearsal for future roles. Playing house, "You be the mommy, I'll be the daddy, and she'll be the baby," is play-acting future sexual roles. Playing war games with good guys and bad guys may be acting out roles seen on television or in movies and practicing, perhaps, in line with future expectations. Playing doctor, explorer, teacher, chemist, carpenter, etc., is often the Little Professor in action, figuring out future vocational possi-bilities. Or, it may be the Adapted Child copying parents or re-hearsing for roles assigned by parent expectations. In one family a boy who was always very active in competitive sports is now a coach. His brother, whose favorite game was "cops and robbers," is now a sheriff. Their sister, who was always ready to go to their rescue with Band-Aids, is now a nurse.

The passive child lives vicariously through other people's expe-riences, often fantasying what it would be like to be a character on the screen or a part of the team. All children enjoy being specta-tors. However, when most of their free time involves watching others, they do not develop their own body skills, cooperativeness, competitiveness, or creativity. Their natural expressiveness is stunted, and they adapt to observing life rather than living it.

As an adult, this person is likely to sit around the fringes of so-cial gatherings, watching others swim, dance, laugh, and have fun, perhaps resenting those who are the attention-getters, or simply feeling helpless and inadequate.

A passive observer may select to take on a job as an objective observer. For example, such a person may write about problems of society but be totally uninvolved, may write about social events but never give a party, may write about romance but never get close to anyone.

Where a person played during childhood often has as much sig-nificance in adult life as how she or he played. One man we knew hated camping, wouldn't travel, and even disliked going out for an evening. He said, "I'm just like I used to be as a kid. I've never been able to get out of my own back yard to play." In contrast, many people find it impossible to play, to laugh, and to have fun in their own homes. Usually, this is because of old Parent tapes that discouraged such activity in their childhood and that continue to be heard by the Child ego state.

"Go outside, the house is not to play in."

"Be quiet, mother has a headache."

"Be quiet, you'll upset your father."

"I don't want any messes in this house."

"No dancing in this house. If you're going to stay inside, go watch TV."

Married couples, reared under the injunction "Don't play in the house," may discover the only time they can really have fun is when they go "out."

Conflict often erupts in marriage when one person enjoys more active kinds of recreation than the other. One couple got into violent fights because of the husband's enjoyment of hiking. His wife interpreted, "He doesn't love me or he'd spend the time home with me. Why does he always have to do such strenuous things!"

Another couple always fought over how to spend their vacation. In childhood the husband had gone hunting with his father. He enjoyed the rugged outdoors and every year looked forward to getting to the mountains during hunting season to do a "little shooting." His wife, however, had spent her childhood vacations at the beach, playing in the sand and surf. Now when it came time to "play," she wanted to go to the beach, and he wanted to go to the mountains. Each accused the other, "You don't even care whether I have a good time or not."

No matter what they finally did, one partner withdrew resentfully, and vacations were far from fun. After studying Transactional Analysis they were able to understand that their Child ego states were simply programmed differently. Their Adult ego states were then able to work out satisfactory compromises so that they each got a "turn" without the other's resenting it. They also experimented by going to new places and trying new activities that neither had known as a child. Vacations became fun.

It is not uncommon in marriage for one person, from the Child ego state, to be continually on stage as the main performer and for the spouse to feel compelled to be a passive observer. The center-stage role may be, for example, that of a clown, a wit, or a tragic queen. The audience is expected to applaud or weep. Conflict often emerges in a marriage if the passive partner wants a share of the spotlight.

Some grown-ups have lost the capacity to play. The child of a person who cannot play is likely to feel guilty under the influence of an internal Parent dialogue such as "Playing is a waste of time," "You can't play till all the work is done," "You don't deserve to have fun," or "Idle hands are the devil's workshop." This kind of person may pick a job that is all work and no play. If other workers are cutting up, this person's Child may feel uncomfortable while the Parent disapproves.

Other adults find it easy to play and laugh. Their Natural Child laughs out of a sense of pleasure, often a "belly laugh" or a de-lighted giggle. Their Little Professor laughs at the humor or absur-dity of a situation. Their Adapted Child laughs out of nervousness and politeness and at what they've been taught to laugh at. Such people may have learned to play the role of a clown to get atten-tion and to make others laugh. Or, they may have learned to play the clown to cover up a tragic feeling in their Adapted Child. One man expressed this when he said, "At a party I always play the role of a Jewish comedian. I'm good at making people laugh. But sometimes when they laugh at me, I really hate their guts." This man used his talent to collect hurt and angry feelings.

The person who cannot laugh or bring laughter to others, whether at age seven or seventy, is probably adapted to fear the potential intimacy that shared laughter is likely to bring. Shared laughter is also a way of being transparent, and some people al-ways have their guard up.

CHILDHOOD PSYCHOLOGICAL GAMES AND ROLE IDENTITY

Not all play is innocent. Ulterior motives are involved when a child rehearses psychological games to be played later in life. A future Rescuer may bandage his unwilling and complaining three-year-old patient. When the young patient finally bursts into tears, the would-be Rescuer throws up his hands in despair with, "I'm just trying to make your hurts better, you crybaby." *(I'm Only Trying to Help You)* Another future Rescuer is the young girl who while baby-sitting her little brother lets him wander away. When he screams in terror after climbing up a fence and falling off, she picks him up, brushes him off with, "You always hurt yourself if I'm not there to take care of you." *(What Would You Do Without Me?)*

A future Persecutor may "accidentally" leave a bicycle on the school grounds, later catch a friend stealing it red-handed, and at this point threaten, "I saw you. You're gonna get in trouble!" *(Now I've Got You, You S.O.B.)* Another type of future Persecutor is the little girl who baits the neighbor boy by calling sweetly to him, "Why don't you come over and play with me?" When he arrives, she looks down her nose at him and sneers, "Oh, you're too dirty, my mama wouldn't want me to play with you." *(Rapo)*

When little Johnny, also practicing a Persecutor role, taunts Jane with, "My daddy is bigger than your daddy," he's delivering the first line of a fight. If Jane responds with, "Oh no he isn't. My daddy is bigger," the game is on. Their attack/defense continues until Johnny outbullies her and she runs away crying. *(Uproar)*

A future Victim, invited to a party that he's afraid to attend, may turn down an invitation with, "I could go if it weren't for mom. She never lets me have any fun." *(If It Weren't for Her)* Another future-rehearsing Victim whines to his would-be competitors, "I can't run in the race. If I run too fast, I might get a stomachache like my little brother." With this move he successfully uses an imaginary illness to avoid performing. *(Wooden Leg* After all, what can you expect of a person with a wooden leg!) And still another young Victim, seeing that the cookies are nearly gone, passes them all to his friends and then moans, "There are never any good things left for me." *(Poor Me)*

Later in life, games are likely to be played harder, with the Adult ego state used to cover up the ulterior motives of the Child.

SEXUAL IDENTITY

In addition to developing an identity as a person, everyone also develops a sexual identity. Even as most children have a basic feeling about themselves as being OK or not-OK as a person, they also feel OK or not-OK as a person of a particular sex [5]. Some children develop a sexual identity that is healthy and realistic; others do not.

Although maleness and femaleness are biological facts, the acceptance or rejection of oneself as either masculine or feminine is psychologically determined by feelings learned in childhood. From the moment of birth, a child whose parents wanted a baby of the opposite sex may start out on the wrong foot (not-OK male/female). Although most parents learn to love what they get, some never get over their disappointment, and the children get the message—a supreme discount of what they were born to be. As Merle Miller recalls:

Almost the first words I remember hearing, maybe the first words I choose to remember hearing, were my mother's, saying, "We ordered a little girl, and when you came along, we were somewhat disappointed." She always claimed that I came from Montgomery Ward, and when I would point out that there was no baby department in the Monkey Ward catalogue, she would say, "This was special."

I never knew what that meant, but I never asked. I knew enough. I knew that I was a disappointment. "But we love you just the same," my mother would say, "and we'll have to make do." . . . My baby blankets were all pink, purchased before the disaster, my birth. The lace on my baby dress was pink; my bonnet was fringed with pink, and little old ladies were forever peering into the baby buggy and crib, saying, "What an adorable little girl" [6].

Children whose sex is rejected by their parents are likely to reject their own sex. They may try to live up to their parents' expectations, often at the expense of their own realistic sexual identification. A little girl who tries to be "daddy's little boy" may alienate her natural feminine qualities. A little boy who tries to be "mommie's little girl" may alienate his natural masculine qualities. Although these influences seldom lead to homosexuality or lesbianism, they can, in some cases, contribute to deviation.

One young homosexual reported that his mother reminded him several times every day that he should have been a girl. A vivid memory from his childhood is of being walked past store windows and told that if he were "just a girl, we could buy those pretty, little dresses." Another homosexual said that the first time he felt like a man was when he tore up the many pictures his mother had saved of him dressed as a girl and with curls.

Homosexual behavior can occur in people for a variety of reasons including psychological, sociological, biological, and situational circumstances. The bent toward homosexual behavior is probably related to the primal feelings in the Natural Child and to the lack of adequate heterosexual adaptation. At birth, infants are not programmed to know toward whom their sexual feelings should be directed. They want only to satisfy their own urges and experience their own pleasure. The Natural Child seems to be sexually nondiscriminatory. The later development of heterosexual *preference* is highly influenced by childhood experiences in the earliest years.

Current research [7] indicates some important aspects contributing to this heterosexual adjustment are:

lack of fear of members of the opposite sex,

opportunities for contact with members of the opposite sex,

a personal sexual identity that is a realistic acceptance of one's own sex.

Sexual identity is strongly influenced by the parent of the opposite sex—father to daughter, mother to son. If a father holds that women are not-OK, a daughter is likely to adapt by negating her own femininity. She may also see other women as not-OK because she looks at them through her father's eyes. The mother-son relation is comparable.

A man who trusts women and believes that they are OK will tend to marry a woman who will serve as a good model for their daughters. In a like manner, a woman who trusts and appreciates men will tend to pick a good model for the father of her future son. On the other hand, men and women who do not like the opposite sex tend to select partners who will be poor models for their children. This is often part of their script.

The parent of the same sex is important as a model. Boys tend to identify with their male parent figures. From them they conclude what men *should be*, copying their behavior and incorporating their negative or positive attitudes toward the sexes. Similarly, girls copy their female models, incorporating their behavior and attitudes. A girl whose father appropriately endorses her femininity and whose mother feels OK-feminine is likely to feel like a winner as a woman.

Children who do not have an adequate model of the same sex often resent or distrust people like themselves. Men express this adaptation when they isolate themselves from other men at work and in recreation. Women do the same when they refuse to work for a woman supervisor or prefer men's company exclusively.

The extended family of the past offered many substitute parent models of both sexes. The current nuclear family, however, frequently limits a child's adult contacts. Children with limited adult associations often turn to their peers for sex standards or to the mass media, where their models are likely to be phony images of masculinity and femininity projected for the purpose of selling. The feelings of being OK or not-OK, masculine or feminine, are most powerfully influenced by parents' expectations and their definitions of "masculine" and "feminine" behavior.

If a little girl swinging from a tree is admonished, "That's not feminine," or "We Smiths never do such unladylike things," she may question the fact that she is really a girl. If her boisterous activity does not seem "proper" to her parents and she then adapts by being overcautious or quiet, one side of her personality will be fragmented or underdeveloped.

Many women strive to appear shy, emotional, fragile, sentimental, helpless, and intellectually incompetent in order to live up to their adapted image of a "real" woman or to appear "feminine" to others [8].

Although American cultural scripting often calls for discounting the intellect and aggression of girls, it encourages these aspects in boys. Boys are more likely to have their feelings and tender actions discounted. A little boy, playing cowboys and Indians, may cut his leg and run to mother crying. If he is met with a stern, "Boys don't cry!" he receives a message about masculinity which translated is "To be a real man is to hide feelings." A sensitive, quiet boy, who prefers reading and noncompetitive activities to more aggressive activities, may also receive a negative message about masculinity which translated can be, "You're not living up to our expectancies of a real man." This may contribute to a script similar to The Little Lame Prince.

Studies by Jourard point to the danger of parental messages which deny children their honest reactions to pain or fear. This denial, most often given to boys, may later contribute to the poor health and premature death of men who feel they are not men unless they appear "tough, objective, striving, achieving, unsentimental and emotionally unexpressive" [9].

Many boys hear, "Dolls are for girls," an injunction which often frustrates the natural desire to re-enact their emotional life drama using dolls as substitute people. Many girls hear, "Trucks are for boys," which often frustrates the natural desire to shape and manipulate objects. This kind of scripting perpetuates traditional sexual roles in the American culture, where taking care of people is largely assigned to women and taking care of machinery is largely assigned to men. When society draws a rigid line between masculine and feminine play, crossing over the line is often expressed in disguised forms. As one aware man said, "Camping is the male way of playing house," which prompted a woman to say, "Driving a school bus is my way of feeling powerful."

Often, the burly, brusque man is one who has disowned his softer qualities; the frail, fluffy woman is one who has disowned her aggressive tendencies. Each suffers a deprivation. According to the noted psychoanalyst Carl Jung, every person has both masculine and feminine components, and all aspects of a personality need to be recognized and developed for the personality to be whole. This does not deny or discount the genuine differences between the sexes that nature provides [10, 11].

SEXUAL EXPRESSION

In addition to feeling OK or not-OK as a masculine or feminine person, each individual also has archaic feelings in the Child ego state about whether the body's sexual aspects are OK or not-OK.

Children are sexual people. They actively seek to discover their sensuousness through exploring all parts of themselves. In fact, they may find their sexual organs a source of good feelings and pleasure. For example, it is common for children to explore their genitals while playing in the bath water or when napping and to be curious about the genitals of others. This kind of exploration is natural, but needs adaptation for the child to be socially accepted. However, if children are slapped, scolded, threatened, and told that part of their body is "nasty," an attitude of "nastiness" can persist. Frequently, people who suffer from sexual inadequacies have been made to feel ashamed of their bodies or to feel afraid of the consequences of their sexual exploration. Clients, who as children were caught touching themselves or others, have reported Parent tapes which threatened them with

"You'll go crazy."

"You'll be paralyzed."

"You won't be able to have babies."

"It will drop right off."

"God will punish you."

People who feel that their sexual organs are dirty or bad or that sexual pleasure is sinful, have usually been "caught" and ridiculed at an early age for their sexual inquisitiveness. Ridicule fosters a sense of shame.

According to Erikson, "Shame supposes that one is completely exposed and conscious of being looked at . . . 'with one's pants down.' Shame is early expressed in an impulse to bury one's face, or to sink, right then and there, into the ground" [12]. One man, severely punished as a child for peeking through a keyhole at his mother dressing, was for many years unable to look any woman straight in the face. If by chance a woman caught his eye, he blushed uncontrollably.

Children also pick up attitudes about their genitals while being toilet trained. One woman reported that as a child she was resistant to her mother's demands for immediate performance on the toilet. For punishment a potty was tied to her buttocks and she was displayed to visitors. As a wife this woman undressed in the closet and experienced an overwhelming sense of shame not only if she needed to use the bathroom but also if anyone saw her nude—including her husband.

Some parents believe that anything to do with sex is bad and try to convince their children of the same. Some parents brutalize and use their children for their own sexual gratification. Some parents are so excessively permissive that their children lack judgment about appropriate sexual behavior, while others vicariously live their own unfulfilled sex lives through their children. Yet most parents struggle with the dilemma of how to create healthy attitudes about sexuality while placing on a child the restrictions that seem personally and socially necessary.

Parents who are fearful or ignorant of their children's need for sexual self-understanding, fail to give them accurate words with which to think and talk. Although parents may glow with pride when their son points to his eye and says "eye" and points to his nose and says "nose," they may carefully avoid any reference to sexual organs or close off transactions with, "we don't talk about that."

When parents do use sexual words, the words they choose are frequently euphemisms, such as "privates" or "your thing," instead of straight scientific words, such as: anus, penis, testicles, vulva, clitoris, vagina [13]. Occasionally, a knowledgeable child is discounted by someone who "should know better." This was the case when a doctor sat three-year-old Mark on the table and commented, "I'm going to examine your water works, young man" and Mark, with a puzzled look, asked his mother, "Does he mean my penis?"

In order to refer to sexual organs, children frequently design their own substitute words: weiner, peter, ding-dong, carrot, pussy, slit, bun, and boobs. Many children also develop a sexual vocabulary of "four-letter words" frequently considered obscene. Because of their negative connotations, such words can easily block talking about sexual problems with grown-ups. Sometimes, four-letter words take on a hostile or violent meaning used to put others down. They become a sign of rebellion against authority. They are used to shock people, to start fights, and to initiate psychological games. In some instances, the use of obscenities is an indication of pathology [14].

Many young people (and some not so young) need to strengthen their Adult ego states by collecting accurate biological, psychological, and sociological information about sex. However, data-collecting is often discouraged by parents, school authorities, or librarians who operate from their own prejudicial Parent, saying:

"Don't have such a dirty mind."

"You'll find out soon enough."

"You'll understand after you're married."

"You don't need to know about things like that."

"What you don't know won't hurt you."

In matters of sex, the internal Little Professor often outwits or outguesses parents, "psyching out" parental messages and trying to figure out what parents consider right or wrong in sexual behavior. The child gathers information from keyholes and alleys, from movies and magazines, and tries to make sense of the bombardment of sexual innuendos. The child also tries to figure out how to manipulate others into sexual play and, when possible, do what he or she wants to do—which is often when no one is looking.

As children mature, they frequently disguise their natural interest in sex by playing such games as "doctor" or "nurse" or a "peeking" game in which there is some kind of exposure.

When a person grows up, the Little Professor remains active concerning sex, continuing to "psych out" partners for sexual games, how to appear desirable or seductive, when and where to make an overture, how to set the scene to "turn someone on," how to put someone off, and how to "fake" a sexual response.

As grown-ups, some people seek a profession in which their interest in sex is acted out in culturally acceptable ways. Some, however, continue to play a childhood peeking game, hiding pornography under the bed or, more seriously, peeking into someone's window. Voyeurism is common in American culture where sexual scripting has been traditionally puritanical.

All cultures have scripts which dictate expected sexual expression. Most sexual taboos and permissions grow out of the need for a social order that contributes to group survival. Cultural mores, family sexual values, and traumatic sexual experiences all influence the Adapted Child.

Many movies, television shows, records, and current dress styles with "the nude look" indicate an increasing preoccupation with and permissiveness toward sex. For better or for worse, the Natural Child is being allowed freer reign. In many persons, the Adapted Child is taking on standards different from those of their counterparts in previous generations. American cultural scripting concerning sexual behavior is changing rapidly.

The Adapted Child contains the person's feelings about personal sexual identity. It also contains the individual's feelings, based on childhood experiences, about persons of the opposite sex. In some people the Adapted Child is trained to be aware of others—not to hurt, not to embarrass, not to insist. When this is the case, the adaptations are appropriate, and the person, when grown, will be able to

appreciate people of the same sex,

relate affectionately to members of the opposite sex,

take responsibility for personal sexual activity,

function adequately in a sexual role,

enjoy the exciting feelings of sexual intercourse,

delay immediate gratification if appropriate.

If adaptations are inappropriate, the person will suffer from sexual problems, some mild, some of a serious nature. Sexual pathology can lie in the Adapted Child like a curse from a witch or ogre. If the curse is activated, the person can feel compelled to try to be the opposite sex,

indulge in sadistic or masochistic sexual behavior with other adults,

engage in child molestation,

be impotent or frigid.

When sexual problems are severe, professional counseling is strongly indicated. Professional counseling is often useful in less serious cases.

Case Illustration

Ted and Alma, a married couple in a Transactional Analysis group, reported that they genuinely liked each other, were committed to their marriage, but were confused as to why their sex life was so unsatisfying. Alma said she rarely felt sexually aroused and was embarrassed by "too much touching." Ted claimed he "wanted to make their sex life better but didn't know what to do."

Both had been given Parent tapes on sex which included the injunctions: "Keep your hands to yourself," "Shame on you for touching yourself there," and "You'll really get it if I catch you again."

Ted and Alma soon became aware that their Parent tapes were very prohibitive and activated uncomfortable feelings in the Adapted Child. Each felt guilty about touch. Each was fearful of sensuousness. Each lacked creativity and sensitivity in sexual expression. Consequently, their natural sexual impulses were almost totally suppressed. These problems were compounded because their Adult ego states were both uninformed and misinformed.

In treatment, Ted and Alma were instructed in techniques for increasing bodily awareness. They were given a reading list of books that would strengthen their Adult ego states with accurate information and vocabulary. They were also encouraged to express more sensuousness from their Natural Child. Eventually, they learned not to base their sexual activities on old, negative memory tapes.

The inclination of the Natural Child's urges for sexual self-satisfaction can be used either in constructive or in destructive ways. Destructively, the unadapted Natural Child in a person may act out selfish and/or sadistic feelings, using another person as a sexual object rather than as one who also has desires and needs that should be respected. Overadaptation of the Natural Child also has a destructive effect. The ability to be aware of one's own needs can be completely squelched or the desire to fulfill them can be totally subordinated to the needs of another. When this happens a person often feels victimized—may act the sulk, feel resentful, engage in self-pity, and manipulate others from the underdog position.

Natural sexual capacities can usually be recovered in spite of their having been unduly repressed. However, the task of recovering the joyful aspects of the Natural Child is a delicate one. As the sensuous Natural Child emerges, some rational restraints, decided upon by the Adult ego state, are always necessary. The possibility of venereal disease or of pregnancy and of damage to the person's sense of human worth are ever present for Adult consideration.

When the Natural Child with Adult cooperation is used constructively, a person is able to "let go" and can then, with pleasure, express the warm, affectionate, curious, and spontaneous capacities with which she or he was born. This ability to experience bodily pleasure and give pleasure to others may add years to life and add zest to the life that is lived [15].

SUMMARY

A person's sense of identity develops in response to many early influences. Even the name put on a birth certificate often reflects the parents' background and expectations for their child. When a child's name, nickname, or change of name carries meaning— either negative or positive—to the parents, this meaning may influence a child's sense of identity.

When playing, a child is also involved in the process of finding self-identity and rehearsing future roles. Some play is active, and the child uses his or her body to develop skills and act out emotions. Other play is more passive, and the child experiences emotions and the body as a spectator of life rather than as a full participant. This child is like a person in the bleachers rather than like one on the playing field. The active and passive styles of childhood play—the how, where, when, and with whom of childhood play—sometimes are reflected later in the person's choice of vocation and use of leisure time.

Children play psychological games to reinforce their early sense of identity. The games are rehearsals for future scenes in which the roles of Victim, Persecutor, and Rescuer will be played.

The development of sexual identity is also related to early life transactions. A person whose sex is accepted and appreciated by parents is likely to feel basically OK about being male or female. If experiences with the opposite sex are healthy, this person is likely to take a positive position about the sexual identity of others.

You have an identity both as a person and as a sexual person. The messages you received about your name, what and where you played, the way you felt about being a boy or a girl, and how you learned to feel about the opposite sex have all affected your identity. If these are healthy, you have the basic I'm OK, You're OK winner position. If they are not, old attitudes can be discarded.

EXPERIMENTS AND EXERCISES

1. Identity and Your Name

Consider your name in relation to your script. What identity did it give you?

- Who named you? Why?

- Were you named after someone? If so, did the name hold special expectations?

- Were you proud of your name or did you dislike it?

- Were you called a name that didn't seem appropriate to your sex, or one that invited ridicule?

- Was your name so popular that you felt part of a mob, or so uncommon that you felt odd?

- Did you have a nickname? A pet name? How did you get it?

- How did your names, or other terms you were called, influence your self-image?

- What are you called now? By whom?

- If you are married, do you call your spouse mommie or daddy? Why?

- Are you called one name at home and another name at work? If so, what are the implications?

- What do you prefer to be called? Why?

- Would you rather have a different name? Why? Is there any Adult reason for changing your name? For keeping the one you have?

For married women only

- If you dropped your maiden name when married, how has it affected your identity?

- When someone says, "Who are you?" do you answer, "Mrs. John Doe," or do you say "Mary Doe"? Why?

- If you are divorced or widowed, what name do you use and why?

- If you use a professional name different from that of your husband's, how do people respond?

2. Your Childhood Play

Do this experiment slowly. Close your eyes. Try to see yourself as a young child at play. You will probably catch glimpses of yourself at different ages and stages. Hold on to some of the imagery and experience it more fully.

Now go into the imaginary room in your head where you store video tapes. Take out a tape labeled Parents and Play. Put it on your imaginary tape recorder. Turn on the switch. Listen.

- What do your parents say about play?

- What nonverbal messages do they give?

- Were you given time to play, or was your time overstructured?

- Were restrictions placed on your play because of your sex?

Now use the following questions to gather data:

- What were your active forms of play?

- Where did you play? Back yard? Street? Barn? Alley? Park? Which was your favorite place? Why?

- Did you play alone? Did you have playmates? If so, were they relatives? Neighbors? Schoolmates? Did you have an imaginary playmate?

- Were your playmates similar to one another? If not, what were the differences?

- Did your size, sex, appearance, skills, etc., keep you on the sidelines, get you on the team, or let you be the star performer?

- Were you primarily a leader, a follower, or a referee? Which role did you prefer? Was it a topdog or an underdog role?

- What was the most fun thing you ever did?

- What were your passive forms of play? Did they include a lot of reading, radio, or TV?

- What were your favorite programs? Comedy acts that made you laugh? Soap operas that made you cry? Adventure stories that took you out of this world?

- Did they motivate you to action? Lull you into further passivity?

- With which characters did you identify? Why?

- In what way was your play a rehearsal for your present roles? Domestic, occupational, etc.?

Now imagine another video tape, labeled "Childhood Laughter." Turn it on. Hear the sound of your laughter.

- What made you laugh?

- Does the sound seem to come from a particular part of your Child ego state? Free-flowing Natural Child? Manipulative, intuitive Little Professor? Polite Adapted Child?

- Is anyone telling you not to laugh, that "It's not funny"?

- Do you see or hear anyone laughing at you? If so, does it make you feel good or bad?

3. Your Current Play

To some people, play is the major focus in their lives; others seek a balance of work and play. Still others seldom play. Their lives, especially when off the job, tend to be dull and joyless. How about you?

- Do you have enough recreation or play in your life? Too much? What are your favorite forms of play?

- Is recreation an important part of your life? Or do you see it as a waste of time?

- Where do you like to play? Is it similar to where you played in childhood? With whom do you like to play? Is your recreation active or passive?

For married couples

- Do you find your recreation in pursuits shared by your spouse? Do you allow your spouse to pursue recreation and fun without you?

- Who makes the vacation plans in your family? How are these plans related to your childhood vacations?

- Is your favorite source of recreation in conflict with that of your spouse? In what ways?

- If you have a conflict, sit down together and, without accusation, tell each other what you really would like to do for fun and relaxation and why.

- Give feedback to each other to indicate you really understand the other person. Your task, at this point, is to *hear* the other person and make sure you understand what *he* or *she* likes. Avoid being judgmental, indifferent, or defensive.

- Next, discuss possible alternatives. What would each of you be willing to try? What would be intolerable to either? What might be exciting?

- Attempt to make plans for having more fun and pleasure together. Consider taking turns planning the weekend activity. Do your best and try to enjoy the other person's plans.

- Try this for two months. Then discuss your experiences. Level with each other as to what was enjoyable, what was tolerable, what was impossible. Could anything have been done to increase the fun? Are there agreements that need to be reached to make it better in the future?

- Now, with the purpose of bringing as much pleasure as possible to the other person, take turns planning a creative fun activity that you think would most delight your spouse.

- Finally, explore some fun activities which neither of you have tried but would like to. Which of these would be practical to experiment with? Make your plans. Give them a try. Assess your results.

This fantasy experiment is for those who have forgotten, are afraid, or feel unable to play. Do the experiments gradually. Stop if you become too anxious. Wait a while and start again. Don't rush yourself.

- Imagine yourself getting ready to go play a game of volleyball.

- Select what to wear. Visualize yourself dressed and ready to play.

- Imagine that the other players will also be beginners, more interested in fun than in competition.

- Imagine yourself on the way to the game.

- See yourself and others arriving at the court.

- Visualize yourself on the court hitting some good shots and missing others.

- Let your excitement flow freely. See yourself smiling, laughing, yelling, running, leaping, scooping up the ball, and having fun.

Now think of a playful activity you've had a sneaking "yen" to try. Seek out play situations where you would feel safe, say the "Y," a recreation center, or an adult program. Select people to play with who are nonthreatening.

- Repeat the same process as above. Do this for several days.

Become aware of your increasing confidence. When it feels right, turn your fantasy into reality.

• Remember to play for fun, not for "keeps."

4. Your Psychological Games

Limiting this experiment to the games discussed in this chapter, first write in the basic manipulative role—Victim, Persecutor, Rescuer—from which each game is played.

Now consider which psychological games you, your playmates, or siblings played in childhood.

Name of the Game	Manipulative Role	Your Game Involvement
I'm Only Trying to Help You	_____	_____
What Would You Do Without Me?	_____	_____
Now I've Got You, You S.O.B.	_____	_____
Rapo	_____	_____
Uproar	_____	_____
If It Weren't For Her/Him	_____	_____
Wooden Leg	_____	_____
Poor Me	_____	_____

If you played any of these games in childhood, do you play them now?

• How do you act out roles of Rescuer, Persecutor, or Victim?

• In what situations and with whom?

• At what level of intensity do you play your games?

5. Your Sexual Identity and Expression

Re-experiencing your childhood feelings about your sexual identity and your sexual experiences may give you important clues to your present attitudes and behavior regarding your sexuality.

Think back to what was said about your birth.

- Was anything, either positive or negative, said about the pain you caused your mother?
- Do you know what your parents felt about your sex when you were born? Were you what they wanted?
- If so, how did you come to know this?
- If not, how did you get the message and how did you feel about it?

Who were your male and female models? Were they adequate?

- Did you have sufficient opportunities to be with persons of the opposite sex? The same sex?
- Were you generally afraid, or did you enjoy persons of the opposite sex in your childhood? Persons of your own sex?
- What images of masculinity or femininity have you incorporated? Rejected? Are still confused about?
- Did your father believe women were OK and treat them as such?
- Did your mother believe men were OK and treat them as such?
- What were the attitudes and behavior of your other parent figures in relation to persons of the opposite sex?
- Which of these attitudes have you incorporated?

Now activate your Parent video tapes labeled SEX.

- What do you hear about your sexual curiosity? Are the remarks rational? Prejudicial? Threatening? Destructive? Indulgent?
- Are they ignoring the subject or saying nothing? Are you ridiculed or shamed?
- What words or phrases are used to keep you in line?
- What are your sexual organs called? How did they teach you "the facts of life"?

- Did they teach you to protect yourself sexually? Did they abuse you sexually? Fail to protect you sexually? Flirt with you? Tease you? Tell you dirty stories to arouse you?

- Do either of your parents get vicarious satisfaction from your sexual experiences? Did they seem unduly interested?

Now activate your Child feelings about sex.

- What is your primary feeling about your body, especially your sex organs? Guilt? Joy? Shame? What?

- Recall the sexual experiences you had as a child. What feelings in your Child ego state accompany this recall?

Let your Adult try to separate your Natural Child feelings from those of your Adapted Child. Were your adaptations appropriate? Overprohibitive? Insufficient? What?

- Did you need to hide your sexual curiosity? If so, how did your Little Professor manage it?

6. Your Sexual Feelings and Behavior Now

Consider the following questions in relation to your present feelings and behavior.

- What are your feelings about your body now, particularly your sexual organs?

- What are your feelings about persons of the opposite sex?

- At your age and stage of life, what do you consider appropriate sexual behavior? Do you have Adult data and logical reasons to support your conclusions?

- Which ego state rules in terms of your feelings? Your behavior?

- Are you acting in accordance with, or in rebellion against, your Parent ego state? Does your Adult, on the basis of real data, agree with your Parent?

- If you are at an appropriate age for an intimate partner, evaluate your sexual transactions. Are they adequate? Joyful? Frustrating? Exploitative? Mutually satisfying? What?

This experiment is only for those who have a sexual problem. [16]

• Do your Parent tapes contribute to your problem now? If they do, figure out a way to turn them off.

One way is to interrupt the internal dialogue by focusing on your sensuousness. Become aware of your body feelings and what feels good. If your parents resume negative talking in your head, say to them, "That's past history." Verbalizing your body feelings will help turn off the tape. Focus your attention again on how you feel, *now*.

• Do your Child tapes contribute to the problem? What are the desires of your Natural Child? Which of these are you able to express? Do you need more control? Less control?

• How does your Little Professor affect the problem? Is its intuition and creativity turned off? Does it manipulate reasonably or attempt to exploit others?

Because so many sexual problems developed in the Adapted Child, examine your adaptations carefully.

• What feelings did you learn to have about sex? Guilt? Fear? Contempt? What? Are these feelings related to traumatic incidents in your childhood or to long-term negative conditioning?

• Is your Adapted Child choosing to maintain the sexual problem in order to prove its early psychological positions?

• How does the problem contribute to your script?

Now, using your fists or the chair, develop a dialogue on sex between your Parent and Child. Do the same with your Adapted Child and Natural Child. Say whatever you want to say.

• After you have exhausted the conversation (which may take several tries), let your Adult tell your Parent that you are now and hereafter responsible for your own sexual behavior.

Now examine your Adult ego state.

• Do you have adequate information about your sexuality and that of the opposite sex? If not, gather more data by reading, attending classes, or talking to professionals.

- Is the clear thinking of your Adult contaminated by Parent prejudices and/or Child experiences and distortions?

- What sexual behavior is appropriate to your life now? What does your behavior mean to others now? What could it mean? Could you make someone happier?

- Is there something you could do about your problem but haven't? Do you need to see a counselor? Have a physical examination? Take a vacation from work? Rearrange some of your environment? What?

- What new decisions do you need to make? What new guidelines could your Adult decide upon?

8

Stamp Collecting and Game Playing

*Life is like an onion; you peel off one
layer at a time, and sometimes you weep.*
  Carl Sandburg

Opinions and traditions, for most people, tend to be centered in
the Parent ego state; factual data and computation centered in the
Adult; and natural and adapted feelings centered in the Child.

Children are born capable of all feelings, ranging from affection to rage. In the beginning they respond genuinely with how
they feel—screaming, cooing, cuddling. In due time, however,
children adapt their feelings according to their experiences. For
example, children are naturally cuddly, yet can learn to become
rigid and to withdraw in fear when someone approaches the crib.
Children naturally seek pleasure over pain, yet can adapt to seek
pain, even death. Children are naturally self-centered, yet can
learn to feel guilty about wanting anything for themselves.

Children are not born with their feelings already programmed
toward objects and people. Each child learns toward whom and
what to show affection. Each learns toward whom and about what
to feel guilty. Each learns whom and what to fear. Each learns
whom and what to hate.

Although each child experiences all feelings, each eventually
adapts with a "favorite" feeling. This is what was commonly felt
when things "got tough" around the house.

A child who continually hears	Adapts to feel
"I'm ashamed of you!" or "You should be ashamed of yourself!"	guilty.

"Just wait until your father gets
home; he'll beat you good."   afraid.

"Don't speak to those
Jews/Catholics/Protestants,
they can't be trusted."   hate or suspicion.

Although these feelings may have been an understandable response to the original childhood situations, later in life people
tend to seek out situations in which they re-experience the old
feelings. In fact, these feelings are often collected.

PSYCHOLOGICAL TRADING STAMPS

In TA the particular feelings the Child ego state collects are called
"trading stamps." The term "stamps" is borrowed from the practice in some parts of the country of collecting trading stamps when
making purchases and later redeeming them for merchandise [1].
A similar phenomenon is observable in human behavior. People
make collections of archaic feelings and then later cash them in
for a psychological prize.

   When people collect their stamps, they manipulate others to
hurt them, to belittle them, to anger them, to frighten them, to
arouse their guilt, etc. They accomplish this by provoking or inviting others to play certain roles or by imagining that another person has done something to them.

   When people manipulate others to re-experience and collect
these old feelings, they are indulging themselves (often with the
permission and encouragement of the Parent ego state). This form
of self-indulgence is a *racket*. Berne defines rackets as "Self-indulgence in feelings of guilt, inadequacy, hurt, fear, and resentment.
. . ." [2]

   Not all feelings are rackets. Some are genuine. For example, if a
person feels guilty about having misbehaved, learns from past
mistakes, and changes behavior patterns, he or she is acting realistically and doing so from the Adult. This person is becoming a
winner.

   In contrast, a loser may feel guilty about some actions, but do
nothing to alter that behavior. In fact, a loser is self-indulgent,
deliberately seeking situations that provoke those guilt feelings. A
loser is like a child making promises with "fingers crossed." A

loser who succeeds in re-experiencing "that old feeling," perhaps by playing games, manages to maintain the status quo.

The following case illustrates how two people handle their guilt feelings differently.

Case Illustration

Several men had requested a transfer out of Division B of an electronics laboratory. This caused the supervisor to call a meeting at which the men were encouraged to ventilate their resentments. The issue became clear when one man exploded with, "I'm sick and tired of Sam and Ed's always taking a two-hour lunch period and leaving the extra work for the rest of us." Both Sam and Ed confessed to being guilty, apologized, and promised to do better.

Sam lived up to his promise. Ed, however, didn't. He continued his long lunch hours, offering excuses of "Gee, fellows, I'm sure sorry. It seems like something always happens, even when I have good intentions. I feel terrible about it, and I know I've just got to try harder." The reprimands from the supervisor became more frequent. Ed was finally laid off.

The ego state transactions between the supervisor and Ed were very different from those between the supervisor and Sam. (See Fig. 8.1) Sam recognized the fact that his long lunch hours put an unfair burden on others and shaped up. Ed collected guilt stamps by playing a hard game of *Kick Me* and got his payoff by being fired. *Kick Me* is a common game of job losers.

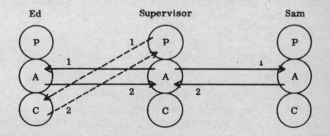

A child whose "favorite" feeling response was inadequacy, later in life tends to collect feelings of inadequacy (sometimes referred to as *brown stamps* or *gray stamps*). This person usually has an I'm not-OK position and manipulates from the Victim role.

One game played to collect feelings of inadequacy is *Stupid*. The following conversation, reported by Ginott [3], illustrates a son's strong determination to collect an inadequacy stamp from his father and his father's willingness to give it.

Son: I am stupid.

Father: You are not stupid.

Son: Yes, I am.

Father: You are not. Remember how smart you were at camp? The counselor thought you were one of the brightest.

Son: How do you know what he thought?

Father: He told me so.

Son: Yah, how come he called me Stupe all the time?

Father: He was just kidding.

Son: I am stupid, and I know it. Look at my grades in school.

Father: You just have to work harder.

Son: I already work harder and it doesn't help. I have no brains.

Father: You are smart, I know.

Son: I am stupid. *I* know.

Father: You are not stupid!
            (loudly)

Son: Yes I am!

Father: You are not stupid, Stupid!

If people who feel stupid can't find someone to call them "Stupid," they may *imagine* that someone is sneering at them. Thus, they collect a *counterfeit* stupid stamp.

People who respond to discounting in childhood by feeling hurt and depressed* later tend to indulge themselves by collecting feelings of depression (sometimes referred to as blue stamps). One woman, accustomed to collecting feelings of depression, discovered that when her day was too bright, she could always collect a few depression stamps by calling her mother-in-law. One man collected his depression stamps by consistently showing up late to department meetings, thus provoking a "kick" from the chairman. Later, he always complained, "Those meetings really depress me. They ruin my day."

A person who collects depression stamps usually operates from a psychological position of I'm not-OK and manipulates others by playing a Victim role. This type of person is easily hurt by casual comments and actually tries to get hurt in order to feel depressed.

Playing *Harried* offers an opportunity to collect depression stamps. A Harried player eventually justifies a serious depression and complete collapse. Berne describes the typical housewife who plays this game:

She agrees with her husband's criticisms and accepts all her children's demands. If she has to entertain at dinner, she not only feels she must function impeccably as a conversationalist, chatelaine over the household and servants, interior decorator, caterer, glamour girl, virgin queen, and diplomat; she will also volunteer that morning to bake a cake and take the children to the dentist. If she already feels harassed, she makes the day even more harried. Then in the middle of the afternoon she justifiably collapses, and nothing gets done. She lets down her husband, the children and their guests, and her self-reproaches add to her misery. After this happens two or three times, her marriage is in jeopardy, the children are confused, she loses weight, her hair is untidy, her face is drawn, and her shoes are scuffed [5].

Executives who play Harried say "Yes" to everything, volunteer to come early and work late, take on weekend assignments, and carry work home in a briefcase—perhaps even studying it on the commuter bus. For a while they are able to act like superman or superwoman, but eventually their appearance begins to reflect their harried state. They come to work a bit disheveled, perhaps unshaven or with bloodshot eyes. They are unable to finish their work. Their physical and mental health deteriorate. They collect

* Depression is not the same as despair. Despair is an authentic reaction in which a person faces unpleasant facts of life. Depression, on the other hand, is based on a replay of old memory tapes where the child felt powerless in relation to his or her parents. [4].

and save so many feelings of depression that they finally collapse, so depressed they are unable to function.

Many people collect angry and hostile feelings (sometimes referred to as red stamps). This kind of stamp collector usually operates from the position of I'm OK, You're not-OK. Such a person may be accidentally tripped in the hallway and become furious when the other person tries to apologize. One salesman frequently misplaced his contracts, then felt mad at his secretary for not keeping his desk in order.

A game which is sometimes played to collect anger stamps is *See What You Made Me Do*. [6] This game is played in the office if a typist makes a mistake while the supervisor is watching. Rather than taking personal responsibility for the error, the typist turns to the supervisor and angrily says, *See What You Made Me Do!* The typist collects an anger stamp by the act of blaming someone else for a mistake. If this happens often enough, the supervisor may collect enough fear or guilt stamps and leave the typist alone; thus the purpose of the game is fulfilled—isolation. Another *See What You Made Me Do* player may collect feelings of purity, "After all, it's not *my* fault. It's *your* fault I made my mistake."

Some people can collect feelings of purity, blamelessness, and self-righteousness (sometimes referred to as white stamps). A mother, out to give herself a self-righteous stamp, may complain, "It's not my fault no one will come to dinner. Even with a headache I do everything I can to make it nice." A child, out to get a purity stamp from a teacher, may tattle excessively and receives the desired white stamp when the teacher replies, "I'm certainly glad you told me who's passing those nasty notes around." A supervisor, collecting white stamps, may fail to distribute the work load and then stay "faithfully" overtime to complete the job.

Lunch Bag is a favorite game of executives who collect purity and self-righteous stamps. An executive who plays this game uses self-righteousness to manipulate and control others. The game has a payoff, both at home and at the office.

The husband, who can well afford to have lunch at a good restaurant, nevertheless makes himself a few sandwiches every morning, which he takes to the office in a paper bag. In this way he uses up crusts of bread, leftovers from dinner and paper bags which his wife saves for him. This gives him complete control over the family finances, for what wife would dare buy herself a mink stole in the face of such self-sacrifice? The husband reaps numerous other advantages, such as the privilege of eating lunch by himself and of catching up on his work during lunch hour [7].

In such a case the executive saves up enough purity stamps to ward off the "frivolous" demands of others. The ulterior message is, "If a person like me can be this frugal, so can you." By collecting so much self-righteousness and humility, the executive makes others feel too guilty or too fearful and in this way wards off their demands.

The color that we assign to psychological trading stamps is, of course, unimportant. The important point is the fact that psychological trading stamps represent an indulgence in archaic feelings which are saved up and eventually "redeemed."

One way people can get in touch with the old feelings that they keep reinforcing is to become aware of feelings that seem inappropriate in the situation. When people know that their feeling response is not rational, they may be able to trace it back to its origin, as Diana did in the following case.

Case Illustration

Diana described herself as depressed and anxious when her husband watched television in the evening. She said her feelings were unreasonable, because in reality he worked hard, was responsible at home, and was devoted to their two sons.

One evening, overcome by depression, Diana went to her bedroom to try to trace her feelings to their origin. Using a technique she had learned in counseling, she began by clarifying to herself how she really felt. She then asked herself, "What does this remind me of?" "When did I feel this way before?"

After a few minutes, childhood memories of her father came to mind. When things were difficult for him, he withdrew into mental illness. This was manifested by his sitting for long periods of time in a chair, staring blankly at nothing. When Diana's father behaved in this way, she felt depression first, then panic. Yet when she struggled to talk about it, her mother protested, "It's better not to talk about things like that. It just upsets everybody."

Diana reported that experiencing these old memories was painful and precipitated a torrent of tears. However, she discovered that subsequently she could see her husband watching television from his chair without experiencing the old feelings from her past.

The person who is in the process of becoming a winner will often decide to give up collecting negative stamps and consciously collect *gold stamps*—feelings of self-appreciation. Rather than rejecting positive strokes and saving old loser feelings, the person learns new responses:

To the Stimulus:	That was a lovely dinner, Sally.
Old Response:	Oh, it wasn't anything.
New Response:	Thank you. Shish kebab is my specialty.
To the Stimulus:	That estimate you made for the job was good. In fact, it was so close you must have ESP.
Old Response:	Yeh, well, but I'm sorry it wasn't finished sooner.
New Response:	Thanks, I'm pleased it worked out so well. It might help us get more contracts.
To the Stimulus:	Your solo was great at the concert.
Old Response:	I didn't think I was so hot.
New Response:	Gee, thanks. Glad you liked it.

Giving oneself gold stamps makes the Child feel good. However, they can be phony. A person whose generosity with money is really a bribe to "buy" friendship is really collecting a counterfeit gold stamp which gives a temporary or false sense of OKness.

A person who has gained enough inner support no longer feels a compulsive need to collect psychological trading stamps of any kind—even gold stamps. It's a rare person who can achieve this degree of independence. Most of us find it comforting to have a few gold stamps for a "rainy day"—even winners.

THE TIME OF REDEMPTION

Psychological trading stamps are eventually cashed in for a prize. By this "time of redemption," so many resentments in conjunction with this special stamp collection have been saved up that the person feels justified in acting them out. The process is

collecting $\rightarrow$ growing $\rightarrow$ justification
stamps resentment for behavior.

A person redeems these trading stamps through self-injury, flunking a test, striking out at someone, sitting and brooding, and so forth. A person who has been collecting gold stamps may seek for ways to improve his or her job, take a pleasurable vacation, make new friends, patch up differences with old friends, give up a destructive relationship, and so forth.

People acquire collections of different sizes and have different compulsions as to when, where, and how to redeem their collections. Some people wait years to cash in a single negative stamp. This was true in Ken's case. He recounted how his brother cashed in an anger stamp that he'd saved against him for many years. One day at play, his older brother had demanded that he remove a piece of bread from their toy railroad track. Although Ken was only five, he had stubbornly refused. His brother threatened, "I'll never forget that. Some day I'll really get even with you." Their relationship was good until some twenty years later, when Ken called his brother for help when his car broke down out in the country. Although his brother had helped him often before, this time he "got even" and cashed in his stamp with "Not this time, Buster. Just remember the bread on the track!"

Some people collect the equivalent of a page of stamps and turn them in for relatively small prizes—weeping in the bedroom, having a headache, throwing a dish, dropping a pie, dressing-down an employee, spilling a file drawer, or mailing a letter in the wrong envelope. For some people, the prize is somewhat bigger.

Case Illustration

All day long Jane allowed her small son to enter the house with muddy feet. She acted patient, cleaned up the mud, and sent him outside again. Later, he colored her new chair with a crayon. Still without showing disapproval, she moved him to another room and cleaned up the chair. The boy continued his transgressions and she continued to accept them. Finally, at the end of the day, Jane had "had enough" (her page was full and it was time to redeem her collection). When her son came in for dinner, again with mud on his feet, she angrily slapped him, scolded him, and sent him off to his room.

Some people save several "books" of stamps and then feel justified when they do such things as wreck the car, run away from home, injure themselves, loot a store, fire a valued employee, quit a job when most needed, have an affair, and so forth.

Some people make even larger collections, cashing them in for larger prizes—a mental breakdown, imprisonment, dropping out of society, or divorce. A married couple sometimes express the many resentments they have collected for years during their first visit to a counselor.

A wife may say,

> "Why, the day after we were married he. . . ."
> "And on June 8, 1959, he. . . ."
> "And on my 35th birthday, he. . . ."

And a husband may say,

> "At our wedding she even. . . ."
> "When we bought our first house, she. . . ."
> "And then when I brought my boss home for dinner, she. . . ."

The ultimate prizes when cashing in a lifelong collection of negative stamps are suicide and/or homicide. Redemption time is often announced when a person says:

"I've taken this long enough!"

"That's the last straw."

"I'm at the end of my rope."

"That does it!"

"I've had it!"

Translated, such exclamations mean, "That's the last stamp I need. It's time to cash in for a prize worthy of my collection." It usually happens that this last stamp represents a small thing compared to what follows.

Redeeming gold stamps may be announced with expressions such as

"I'm ready for a new challenge."

"I feel good about doing this."

"I'm going to ask for a raise and I bet I get it."

THE SWEATSHIRT MESSAGE

The inner Child—often with the aid of the Little Professor—sends a pertinent message to others in order to engage them in rackets, games, and stamp collecting. Sending such a message is much like wearing a sign on one's chest and is colloquially referred to as the *sweatshirt*. This term was taken from a youth fad of wearing sweatshirts imprinted with messages.

People whose shoulders droop, who whine and look anxious, may wear a sweatshirt message that says, "Please Don't Kick Me. I'm a Victim." Their invisible messages give their associates a come-on, either to put them down or to try to help them.

People who look wide-eyed and confused may also be playing Victim, wearing sweatshirts saying, "Gee Whiz, what can you expect from a fool like me?" They "act" dumb and then can't understand why others are exasperated.

A man wearing a tweed jacket with leather elbow patches, leaning back in his chair and looking sympathetically at his visitor while casually lighting his pipe may project a Rescuer sweatshirt, "You can tell me all your troubles."

A man who scowls with his chin jutting out, walks with a heavy step, and directs an accusing finger toward others wears a Persecutor sweatshirt, "You Better Do What I Say, or Else."

A woman who wears a revealing costume, flutters her eyelashes, and wiggles her hips has on an "I'm available" sweatshirt. She may want men to think she can Rescue them. Actually, she is a Persecutor with her favorite game of *Rapo*. She complains like a Victim, "The women at the office are a bunch of crabs, and the men are always making passes at me."

Other popular sweatshirt messages readily observable are

I'm Going to Get You If You Don't Watch Out

Lean on Me, I'm the Rock of Gibraltar

Don't Worry, I'll Take Care of You

You've Just Got to Love Me

I'm Better Than You

Catch Me If You Can

Keep Your Distance

I'm So Fragile

One woman reported having several sweatshirt messages, some more obvious than others. She analyzed the front of her sweatshirt as "I'm so Good and Pure." On the back, however, she carried the message, "Do Not Disturb. I May Not Be So Pure." On her blouse, beneath her sweatshirt, was a third message, which she described as "Screw You! (I love humanity but can't stand my neighbors)." The multiple messages helped her with two stamp collections, white for purity and red for anger.

These messages were part of her script pattern, which was seducing people into false intimacy by righteously helping them and then holding them at a distance. When they got too close, she would switch and give them the brush-off through the use of sarcasm or by undermining their reputations with gossip. This was her version of the *Bear-trapper* game. Perls describes a person who plays this game as follows.

The bear-trappers suck you in and give you the come-on, and when you're sucked in, down comes the hatchet and you stand there with a bloody nose, head, or whatever. And if you are fool enough to ram your head against the wall until you begin to bleed and be exasperated, then the bear-trapper enjoys himself and enjoys the control he has over you, to render you inadequate, impotent, and he enjoys his victorious self which does a lot for his feeble self-esteem. [8]

When hiring workers Bear-trappers tend to send the message, "Just trust me." They look like nice people, appear to listen, are polite, and make promises (the bait):

"You'll only be on this job for a year."

"Of course, you'll be free to do pure research."

"You've got a great future here."

Later, the trap falls when the employee finds out that the job is not going to change, "pure" research means company-oriented, or there is no future with this organization [9].

GAMES PLAYED FROM THE CHILD EGO STATE

When games are played from the Child ego state, the person plays them to reinforce life positions and to advance his or her script. Games are usually played from the Persecutor or Rescuer roles to reinforce a negative position about others, You are not-OK (you need to be punished or rescued). Games are played from the Victim role to reinforce a negative position about oneself, I'm not-OK (I need you to punish me or rescue me). Let's examine these games.

Theme	Name of the Game	Purpose: to prove
Blaming others	*If It Weren't for You* *See What You Made Me Do*	You're not-OK
Saving others	*I'm Only Trying to Help You* *What Would You Do Without Me*	You're not-OK
Finding fault	*Blemish* *Corner*	You're not-OK
Getting even	*Rapo* *Now I've Got You, You S.O.B.*	You're not-OK
Provoking put downs	*Kick Me* *Stupid*	I'm not-OK

Enjoying misery	*Poor Me*	I'm not-OK
	Wooden Leg	
Copping out	*Harried*	I'm not-OK
	Frigid Woman	
	(Man)	

The dramatic action of a game starts with an invitation to one or more potential players. The invitation is often aided by the sweatshirt message or some other "hook" such as

a car left unlocked, with valuables visible through the window or with keys in the ignition,

money or matches left on a low table where there are young children,

inadequate instructions given to co-workers or subordinates,

staying up too late to get to work on time,

having four martinis at lunch,

forgetting to turn in a vital report.

If the other player shows interest in the game, he or she is hooked and the drama begins. Subsequent moves are complementary and have an ulterior motive leading to the final payoff. The payoff includes a stamp, perhaps the last stamp of the collection.

One radio entertainer reports a woman's unbelievable compulsion to play a dangerous game. While driving down a darkened street in the wee hours of the morning, he saw a man holding a woman to the sidewalk and beating her about the face and shoulders. The entertainer jumped from his car, kicked the man away from the woman, and shouted "Police!" The bloodied woman sat up and retorted indignantly, "This is none of your business."

Each game has its roles, its point of discount, its number of players, its level of intensity, its length, and its ulterior messages. Each game has its own dramatic style and can be played in different settings. Further illustrations of games follow.

THE "YES, BUT" GAME

The game is likely to be *Yes, But* if the chairperson in a business meeting presents a problem and then shoots down all suggestions, if a principal does the same with teachers at a faculty meeting, if a woman rejects all the helpful suggestions given by her friends. People who play *Yes, But* maintain the position "Nobody's going to tell me what to do." In childhood they had parents who tried to give them all the answers or who didn't give them any answers, so they took a stand against their parents (You are not-OK).

To initiate this game, one player presents a problem in the guise of soliciting advice from one or more other players. If hooked, the other player advises, "Why don't you. . . ." The initiator discounts all suggestions with, "Yes, but. . ." followed by "reasons" why the advice won't work. Eventually, the *Why Don't You* advice-givers give up and fall silent. This is the payoff of the game to prove the position "Parents Can't Tell Me Anything."

In this game the Child ego state "hooks" the Nurturing Parent in the other players. Although the transactions may appear to be Adult to Adult on the surface ("I've got a problem. Tell me the answer."), the ulterior transaction is Child to Parent ("I've got a problem. Just try to tell me the answer. I won't let you.").

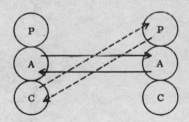

THE "LET'S YOU AND HIM FIGHT" GAME

A game that is usually played three-handed is *Let's You and Him Fight*. In this game one person stirs up a fight between others to gratify his or her psychological position, "People are fools."

One wife, adept at this game, would dutifully listen to her hus-

PLATE XVI

LET'S YOU AND
HER FIGHT

"Are you going to let her get away with that?"

"I heard her say
something pretty
bad about you the
other day. . . ."

"Wow, look at those two fools fight!"

band recounting an unpleasant encounter with his boss. She would then try to prod him into a fight with, "You're not going to take *that* from him are you? You ought to give him a piece of your mind." She gets her payoff the next evening, when he tells of the foolish fight he had with his boss.

A man might start this game with an associate at work by saying, "Gee, Bill, I think you ought to know what Mr. Anderson said about you. It was terrible." He gets his payoff when Bill and Mr. Anderson have "words" with each other.

This game can be played with a sexual dimension. For example, a woman can get two men fighting over her and then run off with the third, laughing to herself and thinking, "Men are really fools."

THE "SEE WHAT YOU MADE ME DO" GAME

A common game played to reinforce the position "You're not-OK" is *See What You Made Me Do*. It is for the purpose of isolating oneself by angrily blaming others rather than accepting responsibility for one's own mistakes. If a mother cuts her finger while peeling potatoes and shouts angrily to her intruding children, "See what you made me do," she may be playing the game to keep them from bothering her further. (After all, if their very presence causes mother to injure herself, it's best to stay away.) A similar blaming game is played if a foreman stops to look over the work of a mechanic who then drops a small part and accuses the foreman with, "See what you made me do." A harder degree of *See What You Made Me Do* is played if a manager solicits and accepts suggestions from junior partners, but then blames these subordinates if the outcome is less than satisfactory.

THE "UPROAR" GAME

In the game of *Uproar* both players are fighters, but one is the accuser and one is the defendant. It often starts with a critical remark implying an ulterior You're not-OK. The payoff is to avoid closeness.

If a father plays *Uproar* with his teenage daughter, he may start with, "Where in the hell have you been? Can't you even tell what time it is?" The daughter then defends herself. A shouting argument follows, which is climaxed when she begins to cry, runs off to her room, and slams the door. A mother might start a game with her son by saying, "You look like a girl in that outfit. No wonder the teachers don't like you."

Although Berne describes *Uproar* as a game played by two people to avoid sexual intimacy, variations of *Uproar* are played in offices and classrooms. The initial attack, which always contains a discount, might be:

Boss: Haven't you learned how to write a report yet!
(to subordinate)

Secretary: You'd misfile your head if it wasn't fastened
(to file clerk)   on.

Salesperson: What's the matter with you? Are you too stupid
(to salesperson)   to read the fine print in the contract?

If some form of defensive statement is made in response to the attack, the fight is on. The payoff comes when the defendant gives up in angry frustration and the two stamp away from each other.

THE "COURTROOM" GAME

Uproar sometimes leads to *Courtroom*. In the case above of father and his teenage daughter, both might seek out mother to be the judge in their arguments. *Courtroom* is played with three or more players. The persons who play *Courtroom* frequently are those who in childhood learned how to manipulate authority figures to side with them and to be against their opponents. Their position is I'm OK, You're not-OK. The basic roles are plaintiff, defendant, and judge. Sometimes, there is a jury—the children, office staff, personnel review board, or whatever.

Married couples often take their "case" to a counselor to judge; office workers may take their grievances to the boss or to those at the coffee break; an instructor and student can take their grievances to the principal, dean, or Board of Regents. Each presents the case to the counselor, hoping that the other will be judged guilty.

To Counselor
    Wife as plaintiff: I've always been careful about
                                 money. Then he overdraws the check
                                 book so now we can't pay our bills.

PLATE XVII

STUPID

"Now look! You've made
that same mistake
again."

"You mean that little mistake?"

"It may be little to you, but it's important to me.
I've told you the same thing a dozen times."

"How stupid of me,
I forgot."

Husband as defendant:	She gives me such a small allowance I can't even afford to buy my friends a drink.

To Supervisor

Office worker # 1:	I've got more seniority with the company than he has. Yet he gets July for vacation time and I get stuck with September.
Office worker # 2:	I can't help it if July is the only time my wife can get off. I can't be expected to take my vacation alone, can I?

To Dean

Instructor as plaintiff:	He deserved that low grade. He was always late with his assignments. Even when I gave him extra time, he still didn't turn in some of them.
Student as defendant:	She gives more assignments than anyone else in this whole college. When I came to her for help after class, I thought this was making up some of my work.

Courtroom can be played out as a criminal game in which two people present their cases before an actual judge and one is found guilty and the other acquitted. This game is required by many state divorce laws.

THE "COPS AND ROBBERS" GAME

Some criminals are motivated by profit; others engage in crime to play the game of *Cops and Robbers*. The game is much like a children's game of hide-and-seek in which the "robber" hides but gets the real payoff by acting chagrined when caught. In fact, a "robber" who has hidden too well may cough or drop something as a clue to the "cop."

A *Cops and Robbers* player who is a burglar or a bank robber manages to leave a clue behind or to commit unnecessary violence or vandalism. The "robber" is indulging Child feelings and compulsion to lose by venting anger and provoking the cops in order to get caught. In contrast, the professional criminal meticulously leaves no clues behind, avoids unnecessary violence, and does not intend to get caught.

The dynamics of *Cops and Robbers* are similar to two games that complement each other, *Now I've Got You, You S.O.B.* and *Kick Me.*

GIVING UP GAMES

Games reinforce old decisions. Old decisions are not permanent and can be changed. People who decide to give up these games devote their time to becoming aware of the games, particularly the games they initiate. They figure out how to recognize them, how to identify their roles in them, how to interrupt them, how to avoid them, how to give and get *positive* strokes, and how to structure their time more appropriately in the here and now. They get in touch with their potentials and become more of what they were born to be [10, 11].

The game may be foiled by a refusal to play or a refusal to give a payoff. For example, refusing to give advice or suggestions to a *Yes, But* player usually stops the game. This is stopping a game by using a crossed transaction [12]. Giving permission instead of authoritarian restriction to an *If It Weren't For You* player also foils a game. Refusing to be defensive in the face of a critical remark or refraining from being overly critical stops the game of *Uproar*.

One young woman who played *Uproar* with her father for years learned to break up this game by not being defensive when he criticized her. Instead, she reflected on how she thought he felt, using the feedback transaction. When he stormed into the kitchen yelling about the fact that she hadn't made his lunch, rather than defending herself, she said, "You seem very upset because I haven't made your lunch." With a startled look, he blurted out, "That's not what you're supposed to say!" The feedback transaction often thwarts a game.

Leveling with the body, a method developed by Franklin Ernst [13], can also be used by a person who does not want to initiate or participate in a game. To level physically, the person sits or stands, feet flat on the floor, arms uncrossed parallel to the body, back straight, head untipped, and chin parallel to the floor. It is harder to play a crooked game if the body is coming on straight.

Giving up discounting is another way to stop a game. The person doing this must first find the game's point of discount. For example, in *Uproar* a discount is usually part of the first transaction. In *Rapo* or *Bear-trapper* it is usually the last transaction, when someone is cut down. It is not necessary to know the name of the game to stop playing it. Persons who give up discounting themselves or others also give up their games.

Giving up a game can result in a sense of despair and a feeling of "Now what?" Some people settle for playing a less hurtful and milder form of a game. However, when a game is stopped altogether, something is usually needed to take its place. To fill the gap people need to get their strokes more legitimately and to structure their time more constructively. They may follow their interests into further activities and may allow themselves the freedom of more intimacy. Both are signs of a winner.

SUMMARY

People collect stamps to reinforce old childhood feelings. One way to collect stamps is to play games. Game players, as well as getting stamps, get stroking (though it may be negative), structure their time (though it may be a waste), reinforce their psychological positions (though they may be irrational), further their script (though it may be destructive), feel justified in cashing in old resentments (though they overindulge themselves), and avoid authentic encounter (though they may be *acting* as if that's what they want). Serious game players reject opportunities for being winners.

Winners refrain from collecting negative stamps and playing the same old games, thus diminishing their negative "cashing in" episodes. By learning to deal more realistically with the here and now, handling their resentments as quickly and as openly as is practical, they cut down their losing streak and become more like the persons they were born to be.

EXPERIMENTS AND EXERCISES

Whenever you make a move toward autonomy, old feelings may remind you of how you "used to be." Being aware of how you feel, even if it doesn't seem rational, gives you a chance to change.

1. Your Stamp Collection

Some feelings are genuine and relevant. However, if you exploit your feelings, if they are inappropriate to the current situations, you are saving stamps. To discover your collection, consider the following questions.

- In childhood when things were tough, emotions high, or trouble was brewing, how did you usually feel?

- What did you see, hear, or intuit that caused you to feel that way?

- What feelings (stamps) do you experience most commonly as a grown-up when things go wrong? Fear? Inadequacy? Anger? Guilt? Helplessness? Anxiety? What?

- In what kind of situation does this old feeling emerge? Is it similar to a childhood situation?

- Do you cash in your stamps frequently by indulging in a long sulk? Blowing off steam? Having a crying jag? Going on a binge? Overdrawing your account? Exploding at someone?

- Do you save your stamps for a big collection?

- If you are now collecting, how do you intend to cash them in? Do you have a prize in mind?

- Where do you redeem your stamps?

- Do you collect them in one setting and redeem them in another, for example, collect at work and cash in at home?

2. Integrating Old Feelings

The following exercises will help you integrate specific feelings that were conditioned in the past and are bothersome in the present. Try them when an archaic memory tape which is irrelevant to the present situation is activated.

Use the experiments most relevant to the feelings you're most likely to collect in the form of stamps. If you find them too disturbing, stop. A good mirror—preferably full-length—is a handy prop.

Inadequacy

If you have feelings of inadequacy, try exaggerating your feelings and actions.

- Talk to yourself about how inadequate and stupid you are. Look stupid. Exaggerate your facial expression.

- Acting stupid and inept, move about the room.

Now reverse your feelings.

- Look yourself squarely in the face in the mirror and say, "I'm OK!"

- Say this aloud every day for at least a week and silently to yourself whenever you catch your reflection in a glass or mirror. Continue this until the "I'm OK" feels good.

- Ask yourself, "How was I ever convinced that I was not OK?"

Turn on your private tape recorder and listen to the Parent tapes about your inadequacy.

- For the next two days be aware of all the ways you put yourself down.

- Then for the following two days interrupt yourself every time you put yourself down; refuse to take put-downs from others.

- Next, make a list of all the things you do competently. Don't overlook any detail of living you perform adequately.

- Start a gold stamp collection and give yourself a gold stamp every time you perform confidently. Say to yourself, "I did that well."

Helplessness

Start your exercise by focusing your awareness on the reality of your physical age.

- Look at yourself in a full-length mirror. Examine how you appear front, rear, sideways.

- Start a close examination from the top of your head to the base of your neck. See your skin, features, and hair as they really are.

- Now continue on down to your toes.

- Does the image you carry in your mind fit with the reality you see? Notice anything you hadn't noticed before? Does it make you frown or smile?

- Do you feel one way—like a child—or do you know who you are, a grown man (woman)?

Next, in what areas do you act inappropriately dependent or helpless?

- With money? Making decisions? Driving? Selecting clothes? What?

- With whom do you act helpless? With whom do you act competent? Why the difference?

- What advantages do you have by acting helpless? Does it give you control over someone? Does it "save" you from some thing?

If you are overly dependent upon others for support, imagine the opposite. Visualize yourself in a situation with others who are able to depend on you. Do this for short periods over a week's time.

- When you feel ready, do in a small way what you have imagined yourself doing.

- Then try your competencies on a larger scale. Try out a new skill, volunteer to help in community problems, plan a weekend excursion, make a decision that has been hanging over your head, do something for yourself that you've always let others do for you.

Perfection

If you fuss unduly over details at work, your car, clothes, files, desk, the yard, the house, etc., make up an exercise that *exaggerates* your compulsive perfectionism.

- For example, if you try to have everything perfect, exaggerate your movements, i.e., fuss with the dust, straighten and re-straighten the papers on your desk.

- Verbalize as well as act out your symptoms. "See how perfect I am. I admire me because I'm so perfect. I can control people because I'm so perfect. No one can put me down, I'm so perfect."

- When you begin to feel driven by your perfectionism, repeat this exercise exaggerating your behavior.

Consider these questions:

- What old memory tape am I playing that says I have to be perfect?

- What feelings do I avoid by trying to act perfect?

- How does perfectionism affect my use of time?

- What is important enough to be done perfectly? What isn't?

Depression

When the blues start, take a good look at yourself in the mirror.

- Study your face carefully. What do you look like when you're depressed?

- Now look at your entire body. How are you holding your shoulders, your hands, your abdomen, etc.?

- Do you resemble a parent figure?

Now exaggerate your symptoms of depression.

- First, exaggerate your facial and body expressions.

- If you tend to withdraw and sulk, curl up in a ball, cover up your head, stick out your lower lip, and sulk in a big way.

- If you cry, get a few imaginary buckets and fill them with imaginary tears.

- Exaggerate any symptom you're aware of.

Now become aware of how your body *feels* when depressed.

- If you feel up tight around your shoulders and neck, try to discover whether the tenseness is related to a particular person.

- If it is, say softly, "Get off my back." If this phrase "fits," say it louder and louder, increasing your power until you are shouting.

Now ask yourself:

- What else could I do with this time if I weren't sitting here feeling miserable?

Next, *reverse* your depression symptoms.

- If your eyes look sad, your mouth droops down or something similar, reverse your expression.
- If your head is hanging low and your shoulders are drooped, raise your head high and pull your shoulders back. Thrust your chest forward and say, "I am not responsible for everything and everybody!" or "I'm OK."

Fear

Sit down and think of all the things or people you're afraid of. Write a list of them.

- Take your list and imagine being confronted with each item on your list, one at a time.
- Exaggerate the experience (after all, it's only fantasy).
- What's the worst thing that could happen?
- How would you cope with the worst?

Now try the opposite feeling of fear—fierceness.

- Look fierce enough to make someone afraid of you.
- Move about the room being fierce toward objects in the room. Feel your power when being fierce.

Now switch back and forth, first exaggerate your fearfulness (be afraid of all the objects in the room), and then exaggerate your fierceness. Did you get any messages? If your fear is of a person you know, pretend the person is behind you.

- How do you feel?
- Turn this person into a huge bear or some other frightening animal. Now how do you feel?

• In your fantasy world, look around for something that would please this animal. Turn calmly and do something good for this fierce creature. What happens?

If you are bothered with recurrent frightening dreams that someone or something is chasing you, tell yourself that the next time you have such a dream, you will turn and face your adversary. Remain confident and calm. You will be in control of the situation.

• Now in fantasy imagine yourself chasing whomever or whatever frightened you in the dream. Visualize yourself as being big and strong.

Guilt

If you frequently feel guilty, it is likely that you are punishing yourself. Imagine yourself in a courtroom. You are on trial. Look the scene over carefully.

• Who is at the trial?

• Who is the judge?

• If there is a jury, who is on it?

• Is there someone there to defend you? To prosecute (persecute) you?

• Are there observers? If so, what do they want the verdict to be?

• Is the verdict guilty or not guilty? If guilty, what is the punishment?

• Now defend yourself. Speak up on your own behalf.

If in your inner dialogue you play a self-torture game between your Parent as judge and your Child as defendant, be these two polarities, using the two chairs.

• Put the judge (top-dog) on one and the judged (under-dog) on the other. Start your dialogue with an accusation. Then, switching to the other chair, present your defense.

• If you feel guilty during your everyday activities, stop a moment and verbalize your top-dog and under-dog inner dialogue.

Now consider the questions:

- Do you frequently apologize and/or look guilty to avoid responsibility for your actions?

- Have you been trained to collect guilt stamps, or are you really guilty in some significant way?

If your guilt comes from a "crime" you have actually committed against another or from an important thing you failed to do, ask yourself:

- What is this burden doing to my life in the present?

- What am I doing to others because of it? Is there now something I can do to rectify the situation?

- If not, can I learn to accept this as past history, which cannot be changed?

- Have I ever seriously considered forgiving myself? What could forgiveness mean in my life?

Sometimes, talking about it helps. Seek out someone who is a good listener, who will not betray your confidence, who will neither condemn nor condone your behavior. Talk to that person about it.

Forgiveness may be easier if you "make it up" in some way toward someone who needs a second chance or a helping hand. Involving yourself in correcting some of society's injustices may help you as well as society. Don't play the role of Rescuer, be one!

Anxiety

If you frequently experience anxiety, ask yourself:

- Am I destroying the moment by concentrating on the future?

- Am I anxious because of exaggerating a problem or procrastinating?

- Is there anything I can do *now* to allay the anxiety—finish a report, make a list, return the book, call that person, study for the exam, make that appointment, design an outline, finish that cleaning job?

Next, try a "now" experience. It's difficult to be anxious if you're fully in the here and now. Focus your complete attention on the *external* world. (See Exercise 8, pp. 177-178.)

• Tune in your senses. Become aware of the sights, sounds, odors around you.

• Verbalize in a literal way what you experience. Start your statement with "Here and now I am aware. . . ."

Next, focus your complete attention on your *internal* world.

• Tune in to the world of your body—your skin, muscles, breathing, heartbeat, etc.

• Again verbalize statements with "Here and now I am aware. . . ."

After doing this for a few minutes, ask yourself:

• Did I use some of my senses and not others?

• When I focused on my body, did I ignore certain parts of it? (In this experiment many people ignore the fact that they have genitals and excretory organs.)

• If you find that you have not used all your senses or have been unaware of parts of your body, repeat the exercise, paying special attention to the ignored areas.

• Each time you feel yourself becoming anxious, have a *now* experience.

Anxiety and breathing difficulty go together. When you become anxious, pay attention to your breathing. Perls suggests the following exercise:

Exhale thoroughly, four or five times. Then breathe softly, making sure of the exhalation, but without forcing. Can you feel the stream of air in your throat, in your mouth, in your head? Allow the air to blow from your mouth and feel the stream of it with your hand. Do you keep your chest expanded even when no air is coming in? Do you hold in your stomach during inhalation? Can you feel the inhalation softly down to the pit of the stomach and the pelvis? Can you feel your ribs expand on your sides and back? Notice the tautness of your throat; of your jaws; the closure of the nose. Pay attention especially to the tightness of the midriff (diaphragm). Concentrate on these tensions and allow developments [14].

The next time you feel excitement over a person, situation, etc., become aware of your breathing [15].

• Do you hold your breath?

• If so, what are you holding back?

• Try breathing more deeply.

Anger

The desire to hurt and destroy others often accompanies feelings of anger.

If in childhood you frequently felt angry toward a parent figure and currently collect feelings of anger against your boss, spouse, fellow employees, teachers, students, etc., try role-playing. Use the chair technique.

• Imagine the person who bothers you sitting opposite you. Say aloud how angry you are and why.

• Become aware of your body's response to your anger. Do you restrict or hold back with some part of your body? Clench your teeth? Fist? Colon? Exaggerate your restriction. What do you discover?

• When you feel ready, reverse your roles and *be* that person. Respond as if the other person were actually there.

• Continue the dialogue, switching back and forth.

• If you strike a phrase that fits or feels good, such as "Stop trying to run my life," "Stop hurting me," "Stop embarrassing me," "Why didn't you protect me?" repeat the phrase several times, each time louder and louder until you are really shouting.

Next, stand on a sturdy stool. Imagine the person toward whom you feel anger is cowering beneath you.

• Look down at this person and state what you are angry about and why. Say all the things you've always wanted to say and never dared.

• If you feel like changing positions, do it.

Some people need safe methods for dispelling their anger physically. This requires a "letting go" [16]. The following exercise is only for those in good physical condition.

- Stand by a bed or a sofa, raise your arms above your head, clench your fists, arch your back. Bring down your fists and pound. Increase your force. Make noise—grunt, groan, weep, scream. As words emerge, say them out loud. Yell. Exhaust yourself.

- When you come to this point of exhaustion or relief, lie down and tune in to your body and to your feelings. Take at least five minutes. What do you discover?

- As a variation try beating on a punching bag or shadowboxing with strong movements. Make sounds with your movements.

Resentment

Any negative stamp collection is usually accompanied by feelings of resentment. Resentment is often a "demand that *the other person feel guilty*" [17].

When you become aware that your resentment is growing, handle each situation as it occurs and with whom it occurs rather than collecting and holding your feelings and perhaps cashing them in for a big prize or on an "innocent" person.

- Try to talk the problem over with whoever is bugging you.

- When you attempt this, avoid accusing the other.

- Tell the other person how the situation is affecting you. Use the pronoun "I" instead of an accusative "you." (For example, "I don't like smoke; it bothers me," instead of "You're really thoughtless the way you blow your smoke around.")

If you are in a family group, try to establish resentment and appreciation sessions. To be effective the procedure has definite rules to follow:

- Each person in turn verbally states the *resentments* she or he holds against the others. (It is important that the others listen but *do not defend themselves*. The statements of resentment are to be let out but not reacted to.)

- After resentments have been stated, each person tells the others what is appreciated about them.

- When first learning how to conduct this kind of session, do it daily. Later, after it can be done with ease, do it on a weekly basis.

In some working situations resentment and appreciation sessions could be useful, particularly where people work together closely and personal irritations occur easily.

- If it is tried, *all* members should agree to a trial period—say two months.

- At the end of this period the usefulness of the procedure could be re-evaluated. If the participants decided to continue, they could decide on adaptations and establish regular session times—meeting once every two or three weeks or whatever seemed practical.

Other Feelings

If you have a bothersome feeling that has not been dealt with in the previous exercises,

- Exaggerate your symptom—move around, make sounds, look at yourself.

- Keep in touch with your body and exaggerate your body reaction.

- Reverse your feelings and experience the opposite.

- Develop a top-dog/under-dog dialogue.

- Assume some responsibility for your own feelings. For example, instead of saying that "it/she/he depresses me," say, "I am allowing myself to be depressed."

3. Tracing Old Feelings

The next time you are aware that you have overreacted or reacted inappropriately in a situation, try tracing your feelings back to the original scene* [18].

- As soon as the situation occurs, ask yourself, "What am I feeling right now?"

* Diana (p. 215) used this technique. You may wish to review this case.

- Is there another feeling under the surface feeling? Anger under the guilt? Fear under the hate? Helplessness under the anger?

- What does it remind you of? When did you feel this before?

- Go back to the original scene.

  - Where was it?

  - Who was the director?

  - Who were the characters?

  - What roles were played?

  - How did you feel?

Role-play the scene if you have other people to work with. If you don't, try to act out the various parts yourself.

4. Your Sweatshirt Messages

Do you send people messages that cause them to say that you are

as wise as an owl,   a snake in the grass,   a wolf,
proud as a peacock,   a skunk,   hen-pecked,
stubborn as a mule,   stupid/strong as an ox,
little more than a stud,   a poor fish,   an old crab,
crazy as a loon,   sly as a fox,   happy as a lark,
sneaky as a weasel,   gentle as a lamb, or
clumsy as a bull in a china shop?

- If so, how do you give them this impression? What posture, facial expression, gesture, tone of voice, etc., do you use?

Now ask at least five other people [19] how they would visualize you as

a color,   a country,   a kind of food,   music,
a famous person,   a kind of weather,   kind of dog,
part of the body,   article of clothing,   a type of literature,
a piece of furniture.

After gathering the above feedback, study it. Then consider these questions:

- What messages do you send others to cause them to see you this way?

- Which of these messages are come-ons? Put-offs? Put-downs?

- Do you have a collection of sweatshirts that you wear different places with different people?

- Are these the messages you want to send? If not, what could you do differently?

5. Script Check List

Read the following quickly. Write in the first thing that comes to mind. Then go back and fill in the blanks after further thought. Work on completing the check list [20] as you finish this book.

Rate how you feel about yourself and others most of the time.

I am OK _____ I am not-OK

Others
are OK _____ Others
are not-OK

Things I feel OK about _____

Things I feel not-OK about _____

Now rate yourself in reference to sexual identity.

I am OK . . . _____ I am not-OK
(male/female)   (male/female)

Men are OK . . . _____ Men are
not-OK

Women are OK _____ Women are
not-OK

My Sweatshirt messages _____
My Stamp collection _____
The ways I cash in my stamps _____
The basic manipulative role _____

(Persecutor, Rescuer, Victim)
Complementary roles of _____ played by my _____

Favorite games I play:

_____

    as Persecutor   with whom?

_____

    as Rescuer   with whom?

_____

    as Victim   with whom?

Kind of script _____

                 (constructive, destructive, nonproductive)

Script theme _____

Epitaph if curtain fell now _____

_____

Type of drama _____

              (farce, tragedy, melodrama, saga, comedy, etc.)

Audience response to my drama _____

              (applauded, bored, awed, tearful, hostile)

New script if desired _____

_____

New epitaph if wanted _____

Contracts with self for new script _____

9

The Adult Ego State

*Man's mind stretched to a new idea
never goes back to its original
dimensions.*
   Oliver Wendell Holmes

People often feel unable to get out of a distasteful or unhappy situation. They assume they are trapped in a job, in a community, in a marriage, family, or a way of life. They do not see the alternatives of looking for a new job or improving the one they have, of moving out of the community, of changing their marriage patterns, of breaking off a relationship, or of loving and disciplining their children more effectively. They limit their perception of the problem, not seeing possible options or an obvious solution. They use one narrow approach and repeat this approach over and over even though it obviously does not resolve or change the situation.

THE BASH TRAP PHENOMENON

Sometimes, people's reluctance or refusal to look at the total situation results in their avoiding the obvious—the obvious diagnosis, solution, escape route, etc. Berne refers to avoidance of the obvious as a "bash trap." When people are caught in a bash trap, they compulsively continue to bash themselves against the same situation. They are much like a goat butting its head against a rock wall, wanting something on the other side but not observing that there are ways of getting there other than head-bashing. They expect that if they just keep trying harder and harder, they will somehow break through the barrier and get what they want.

People caught in bash traps often express themselves verbally with statements such as:

"I push and push and never get anywhere."

"Day after day I feel as if I'm hitting my head against a brick wall."

"I've tried for years and can't get anywhere."

"I've told that kid over and over and can't get through to him."

A person who strengthens the Adult ego state can stop bash trapping long enough to see that he or she obviously doesn't *have* to. The person is then free to examine the situation from a more objective point of view, using the full capacity of the Adult to test reality, to seek alternative solutions, to estimate the consequences of each alternative, and to make a choice.

THE ADULT EGO STATE

Everyone has an Adult ego state; and unless the brain is severely damaged, everyone is capable of using Adult data-processing ability. The often argued question of maturity versus immaturity is irrelevant in structural analysis. What is called "immature" is childlike behavior expressed habitually and inappropriately.

The Adult ego state can be used to reason, to evaluate stimuli, to gather technical information, and to store this information for future reference. It also enables a person to survive independently and to be more selective in making responses. Berne says the Adult is

. . . an independent set of feelings, attitudes, and behavior patterns that are adapted to the current reality and are not affected by Parental prejudices or archaic attitudes left over from childhood. . . . The Adult is the ego state which makes survival possible. [1]

. . . principally concerned with transforming stimuli into pieces of information, and processing and filing that information on the basis of previous experience. [2]

. . . concerned with the autonomous collecting and processing of data and the estimating of probabilities as a basis for action. [3]

. . . organized, adaptable, and intelligent, and is experienced as an objective relationship with the external environment based on autonomous reality testing. [4]

Reality testing is the process of checking out what is real. It involves separating fact from fantasy, traditions, opinions, and archaic feelings. It includes perceiving and evaluating the current situation and relating the data to past knowledge and experience. Reality testing allows a person to figure out alternative solutions.

A person who has alternative solutions can then estimate the probable consequences of the various courses of action. The Adult ego state's functions of reality testing and probability estimating serve the purpose of minimizing the possibility of failure and regret and increasing the possibility of creative success.

A person dissatisfied with a job but programmed "to stick with it no matter what" can reality test this value and decide whether or not it is appropriate. A person who decides that "sticking to it no matter what" is not good can search out alternatives on the basis of his or her capacities, talents, interests, job opportunities, and so forth. To gather data the person can visit a vocational counselor, get job aptitude testing, seek interviews with personnel managers, study want-ads, send for and read material about career opportunities.

The person can carefully study what she or he really wants in a job—security, a flexible time schedule, an expense account, travel assignments, regular hours, an intellectual challenge, a chance to be with people, or whatever. The person can decide which satisfactions are the most meaningful and in what ways to compromise these satisfactions if necessary. The person can then select available alternatives, estimate the probable consequences, and adopt a course of action that will offer the maximum satisfaction.

The criterion for functioning from the Adult ego state is not based on the correctness of the decisions, but on the process of reality testing and probability estimating by which the decisions are made. Colloquially, "This is your Adult means: 'You have just made an autonomous, objective appraisal of the situation and are stating these thought-processes, or the problems you perceive, or the conclusions you have come to, in a non-prejudicial manner.' " [5]

The quality of decisions will depend on how well informed the Adult is and how well the Adult can select and use information from the Parent and Child. However, a person's decisions, even if based on computed facts, are not necessarily "right." Being human, we sometimes have to make decisions on incomplete data, and we may draw the wrong conclusions.

An old woman may look before she steps into a street but not be conscious of a rapidly approaching truck.

A young man may weigh all the facts he can obtain before he accepts a new job, only to find later that the boss has a lonesome and demanding wife.

A scientist may work years on a research project, then fail for lack of one piece of essential knowledge.

Some people know many facts in one area but few in others.

A competent banker may be a novice in solving problems involving human relations.

A competent homemaker may be inadequate in a discussion of turbine engines.

A competent mechanic may be unable to diagnose a child's illness.

EGO STATE BOUNDARIES

A person's sense of *real self* can be experienced in any of the ego states, depending on where the free psychic energy resides at that particular time. When the sense of real self is experienced in one ego state, the others may be inactive. However, the others are always there and have the potential to become active.

At the moment the person is expressing Parental anger, he feels "This is really me" even though this Self resides in a borrowed ego state. At another moment, when he is objectively adding his client's accounts, he again feels "It is 'really me' adding these figures." If he sulks just like the little boy he once actually was, he feels at that moment "It is 'really me' who is sulking." In these examples, the free energy, which gives rise to the experience of "really me," was residing in the Parent, Adult, and Child, respectively [6].

It is useful to think of each ego state as having boundaries. Berne suggests that ego boundaries can be thought of as semipermeable membranes through which psychic energy can flow from one ego state to another [7]. Ego boundaries must be semipermeable; otherwise, psychic energy would be bound up in one ego state and unable to move about spontaneously as situations change.

In some highly effective people the flow of energy may be quite rapid; in others it may be sluggish. The person whose free energy moves rapidly may be exciting and stimulating, but others may have difficulty keeping up with this fast-moving pace. The one whose energy moves more slowly is the person who is slow to start and slow to stop activities, including thinking. Other people may become impatient with such slowness, even though the person's responses are of high quality.

The physiology of the ego state boundaries is not yet understood, but the assumption that they exist is made by observing specific kinds of behavior defects. Some people continually act in unpredictable ways; others are so predictable they seem monotonous; some explode or go to pieces with the slightest provocation; the thinking of others is distorted with prejudices and delusions. These disorders are caused by ego state boundaries which are too lax or too rigid, have lesions, or overlap.

LAX EGO BOUNDARIES

Samuel Butler wrote, "An open mind is all very well in its way, but it ought not to be so open that there is no keeping anything in or out of it. It should be capable of shutting its doors sometimes, or it may be found a little drafty." A person with lax ego boundaries doesn't close the doors between ego states, but appears to lack identity and gives the impression of slipshod behavior [8]. The psychic energy slips continually from one ego state to another in response to very minor stimuli. This person may have great difficulty functioning in the real world and be in serious need of professional help.

One woman with this boundary problem was described by others in a counseling group: "You never know what's going on with her or what she's going to do next." A personality with lax boundaries can be diagrammed as in Fig. 9.1.

The person with lax ego boundaries has little Adult control and behaves differently from the person whose psychic energy moves rapidly from one ego state to another, yet with the Adult in control. In the latter case the person's behavior may be quite rational. In the former, it is unpredictable, often irrational.

RIGID EGO BOUNDARIES

Rigid ego state boundaries do not permit the free movement of psychic energy. It is as though a thick wall holds the psychic energy bound up in one ego state, excluding the other two. This phenomenon is called *exclusion*. The behavior of persons with this problem appears *rigid* because they tend to respond to most stimuli with only *one* of their ego states. The person always comes on Parent, always comes on Adult, or always comes on Child.*

A person who uses only the Parent ego state or the Child ego state and does not use the Adult is likely to be seriously disturbed. This person is not in touch with what is currently happening, is not reality testing in the here and now.

The Parent,
excluding the
Adult and Child

The Adult,
excluding the
Parent and Child

The Child,
excluding the
Parent and Adult

A person who excludes the Parent and Child and uses only the Adult may be a bore or a robot, without passion or compassion. Berne describes the excluding Adult as "devoid of the charm,

* A variation of this problem is found in the person who turns off only one ego state. In some cases, when a person has few redeeming qualities in the Parent, this may be in order. The person can learn to parent others from the Adult and put the inner Child under Adult control, or the person may be re-parented.

spontaneity, and fun which are characteristic of the healthy child, and. . . . unable to take sides with the conviction or indignation which is found in healthy parents" [9]. Rigidly responding from only one ego state is a serious enough personality problem to profit from professional help.

There are some people who have a problem similar to exclusion but to a less serious degree. They favor using one ego state fairly consistently over the other two, but the other two are not totally excluded. In the following examples we are referring to this less serious ego boundary problem as Constant Parent, Constant Adult, and Constant Child.

The Constant Parent

A person who operates primarily from the Parent ego state often treats others, even business associates, as if they were children. Such behavior can be found in the secretary who "takes care of" everyone's problems at the office or in a corporation boss who tries to run the personal lives of staff members, who cannot be approached reasonably, or who displays little or no sense of humor. Either knowingly or unknowingly, the Constant Parent collects people who are willing to be dependent or subordinate and often role plays with someone in the complementary role of Constant Child.

One type of Constant Parent is hardworking and has a strong sense of duty. This person may be judgmental, critical of others, moralistic, and may neither laugh nor cry from the Child, nor be objectively reasonable from the Adult. The Constant Parent "knows all the answers," manipulates others from the top-dog position, and is domineering, overpowering, and authoritarian.

Specific kinds of occupations which offer authority over others attract this domineering type of person. Some presidents of business firms, some homemakers, some officials in church or school hierarchies, some political or military figures, and indeed some dictators seek these positions because it fulfills their need to have parental power over others. Many multimillion dollar businesses were originally carved out by one strong, determined person of this nature whose employee/employer relationships were those of compliant Child and authoritarian Parent.

Another type of Constant Parent is the perpetual nurturer or rescuer who may play the role of benevolent dictator or may come on as a saintly person who is devoted to helping others. The following expressions may be associated with this type of Constant Parent.

The 100% available one: "Call me just anytime you need me."

The perpetual self-sacrificing one: "I can go without; it's better that you have it."

The perpetual rescuer: "Don't worry. I can always help you."

A constant nurturer is often drawn to one of the "helping" professions and may be very effective. Yet, by keeping others unnecessarily dependent, the constant nurturer is overindulging his or her nurturing capacities and does more harm than good.

The Constant Adult

The person who operates primarily as Constant Adult is consistently objective, uninvolved, and concerned primarily with facts and data processing. This person may appear unfeeling and unsympathetic, may not empathize with someone who has a headache, and may be a bore at a party.

People who exhibit the rigid boundary problem of the Constant Adult may seek jobs that are object-oriented rather than people-oriented. They may select vocations in which abstract thinking devoid of emotion is valued. They may be attracted, for example, to accounting, computer programming, engineering, chemistry, physics, or mathematics.

The Constant Adult often experiences trouble on a job if supervising others is required. With little caring Parent or fun-loving Child, this person's relationships are likely to be sterile. Subordinates may be unhappy because the Constant Adult gives them so little stroking. Many work situations suffer if there is no one acting as a nurturing Parent. A physician with this problem may make competent diagnoses, but patients may complain that the doctor lacks a "bedside manner," is cold, aloof, and doesn't care about them. A patient on the operating table may be emotionally better prepared for surgery if the doctor says parentally, "Now don't worry. We'll take good care of you," rather than factually, "You have a 50-50 chance of surviving this operation."

The Constant Child

The person who operates primarily as Constant Child is the one who is the perpetual little boy or girl who, like Peter Pan, doesn't want to grow up. People who act from their Constant Child don't think for themselves, make their own decisions, or take responsibility for their own behavior. These people may exhibit little conscience in their dealings with other people, attaching themselves to someone who will take care of them. A man or woman who wants to be "kept," babied, punished, rewarded, or applauded is likely to seek out a Constant Parent.

People with this ego boundary problem are often successful as performers on the stage or on the playing field. However, without adequate Adult functioning, the performer may spend her or his large salary impulsively, often ending up broke. Other types of jobs that may appeal to the Constant Child are those that are highly routine and require no decision-making, for example, assembly-line work.

CONTAMINATION OF THE ADULT

The clear thinking of the Adult is often spoiled by *contamination.* Contamination can be thought of as an intrusion of the Parent ego state and/or the Child ego state into the boundary of the Adult ego state.

Contamination occurs when the Adult accepts as *true* some unfounded Parent beliefs or Child distortions and rationalizes and

The Adult,
contaminated
by the Parent

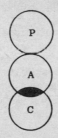

The Adult,
contaminated
by the Child

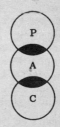

The Adult,
contaminated by the
Parent and Child

justifies these attitudes. These intrusions are problems of ego boundaries and can be diagrammed as in Fig. 9.3 on page 255.

Contamination from the Parent Ego State

In extreme cases, contamination from the Parent is experienced as hallucinations [10], the *sensory* perception of things that are not real. When a person sees something that is not there or imagines hearing accusing or commanding voices, i.e., "You're a monster," "Kill those bastards. They don't deserve to live," that person is hallucinating.

To a lesser degree, Parent contaminations are prejudices—tenaciously held opinions which have not been examined on the basis of objective data. Parental figures often express their prejudices to children with such conviction that they appear to be facts. The person who believes these Parental opinions without evaluating them has a contaminated Adult.

Butler observed, "The difference between a conviction and a prejudice is that you can explain a conviction without getting angry." Parental contaminations often involve considerable emotion and are likely to occur in relation to specific subjects, such as food, religion, politics, class, race, and sex.

One woman's contamination was in the area of female roles. Helen believed as her mother had that working mothers ruin their children. When her opinion was challenged, she conducted a survey in suburbia to prove her point. She first interviewed a sample of working and nonworking mothers. With parental permission she then discussed the children with their teachers, asking about the children's competency, independence, and emotional stability.

When her findings were tabulated, these particular qualities were slightly higher (though not significantly so) in children of working mothers than in those of nonworking mothers. Yet Helen would not believe her own research. Instead, she rationalized, "These teachers lied to me because most of them are working mothers and they don't want to look bad themselves."

Prejudicial statements are usually voiced as facts:

Blacks can't be trusted.
Men can't be trusted.
Republicans can't be trusted.
Children can't be trusted.

Whites can't be trusted.
Women can't be trusted.
Democrats can't be trusted.
People over thirty can't be trusted.

At times, large segments of society agree with prejudiced ideas. For example, most people in a city may come to believe that sturdy houses should be built of brick, even though the city is located on an earthquake fault.

Contamination often intrudes on the laws of society. Until recently, under Texas law a man who killed his wife for adultery was practicing justifiable homicide; however, if a wife killed her husband in a similar circumstance, it was first-degree murder. The same dynamic seemed to be at work when a Wyoming legislator introduced a bill early in 1969 asking that young people of nineteen be given the vote, with the exception, however, of young men with long hair. He admonished, "If they're going to be citizens, they should look like citizens."

Contamination from the Child Ego State

Severe contamination from the Child ego state often occurs because of some delusion. A common one is the delusion of grandeur. In its extreme form a person may believe that she or he is the savior of the world or the ruler of the world. Another common delusion is feeling persecuted—being poisoned, spied upon, or plotted against.

In its less severe forms a person whose Child contaminates the Adult has distorted perceptions of reality. This person may believe and say, for example,

"The world owes me a living."
"People are talking about me behind my back."
"No one could possibly: forgive/love/want/dislike me."
"Some day I'll be rescued."

A woman who holds the delusion that one day her prince will come may stay on a menial job, a Cinderella "waiting" for a rescuer. Her assumption is she's going to get married and is just marking time until "he" comes along.*

Children learn distortions many ways. Some are taught; some are conjured up. For example, a boy may have a nightmare in

---

* If this woman would reverse her assumption to, "I am never going to get married," she could reconsider her contamination and might re-examine her attitudes about her education, job, where she's living, and where she is going with her life.

which a monster under his bed is about to devour him. If his mother admonishes the monster, "Don't you dare eat my little boy, you bad thing! Now get out of here!" she reinforces the distortion. If she says instead, "I've looked under the bed and there's no monster there. You must have had a terrible dream that seemed very real," she helps her son separate reality and the figments of his imagination by giving him accurate information without putting down his ability to "dream things up."

Double contamination occurs when both Parent prejudices and Child delusions envelop the Adult ego state like layers. Instead of being objectively aware of the facts, the Adult attempts to rationalize the contaminations. If these distortions are removed, a person has a clearer perception of what is real.

When the ego state boundaries are realigned, the person understands the Child and Parent rather than being contaminated by these influences. One client expressed this decontamination process when he said, "I used to have this strange idea that no one could ever like me. Now I see that that's just the way I felt at home as a kid. Now I realize that not everybody likes me, but many people do." A realization such as this increases a person's possibility for being a winner.

BOUNDARY LESIONS

A person with ego boundary lesions is one who exhibits uncontrollable behavior when "sore points" are touched. This person's psyche has been seriously injured by one traumatic event or by a series of unhappy experiences during childhood. When something rubs the sore spot, the injury may "break open" with an outpouring of strong, irrational emotion. This was observed in a counseling group. A woman asked a man, "Will you please look at me when you speak to me?" At this simple request he turned on her, exploding in rage and yelling, "You really know how to push my button, damn you!"

A lesion is usually indicated when a person faints at the sight of a mouse, gets hysterical over a clap of thunder, panics and hides at the thought of performing, and so forth. Some people break into tears or sink into depression when even mildly criticized. A lesion is manifested by a gross overreaction to the reality of the stimulus. If it interferes with adequate functioning, professional help is needed.

THE ADULT AS EXECUTIVE OF THE PERSONALITY

Each person has the potential to put the Adult in executive control of the other ego states. If freed from negative or irrelevant influence from the Parent and Child, the person is emancipated to make autonomous decisions.

Unless a person has Adult self-awareness, most outside stimuli are likely to be first felt and responded to by either the Parent or Child ego states or both. When the Adult becomes the executive, a person learns to receive more and more stimuli through the Adult. The person stops, looks, and listens, perhaps counting to ten, and thinks. The person evaluates before acting, takes full responsibility for personal thoughts, feelings, and behavior, and assumes the task of determining which of the possible responses in his or her ego states are appropriate, using that which is OK from the Parent and Child ego states.

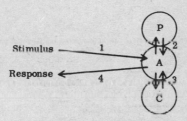

The Adult as Executive

In some instances the person may take a look at the situation and decide that what his or her mother or father would do is the appropriate thing to do. For example, the person may decide to adopt parental behavior by sympathetically comforting a crying, lost child in a large department store (Fig. 9.5a). At another time a person may reject this Parent response and withhold a critical remark learned from a parent figure (Fig. 9.5b).

In some instances a person can take a look at a situation and decide to make a response learned in childhood. For example, when driving past a reservoir on a hot, sultry day, the person may suddenly stop the car, check out if it's safe, and decide to take a running jump into the water to cool off. At another time the person may reject a Child impulse to "play around."

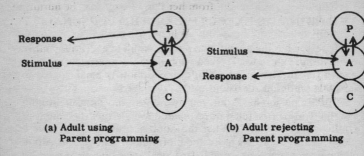

(a) Adult using
Parent programming

(b) Adult rejecting
Parent programming

According to Berne, a person who has Adult executive control "learns to exercise Adult insight and control so that these child-like qualities emerge only at appropriate times and in appropriate company. Along with these experiences of disciplined awareness and disciplined relationships goes disciplined creativity" [11].

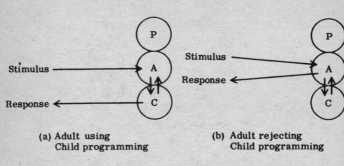

(a) Adult using
Child programming

(b) Adult rejecting
Child programming

Making a conscious choice involves controlling the psychic energy so that a person can actually shift from one ego state to another when it is appropriate. For example, by an act of free will, a person can shift from Parent disdain to Adult concern or from Child resentment to constructive Adult actions. This capacity is illustrated by an incident reported by two students.

June and Sally, both trained in TA, were studying together for a course they were taking. Their young children were playing quietly in the kitchen when suddenly there was a loud noise of something falling and cries of terror from the children. Immediately, June rushed to the kitchen to see what was wrong, as her own nurturing, responsive parents would have done. Her experience had taught her that she could, from her Parent ego state, be nurturing without thinking.

Sally responded differently. When she heard the noise, her initial response was similar to what her mother would have said when she did not want to be interrupted, "Those damn kids don't even give us five minutes of peace and quiet!" Sally had had inadequate parenting and was aware of it. Therefore, she had to activate her Adult by *concious decision*. She then responded in appropriate ways and, like June, went out to see what was wrong.

The Adult ego state as executive of the personality referees between the Parent ego state and the Child ego state, especially when the inner dialogue is hurtful or destructive. In such cases the Adult becomes a more rational Parent to the Child than the actual parents were—setting rational limits, giving rational permissions, seeking reasonable gratification for the Child. The following cases indicate how the Adult might referee or effect a compromise between Child and Parent dialogue.

Jim

(C) I'm going to play sick this week and not go to work.

(P) Mommie's boy should stay home if he doesn't feel good.

(A) I could get away with it, but I'd have to work twice as hard to make up for it. No point in staying home.

Mary

(C) If I make good money, the men might not like me.

(P) Women shouldn't make as much money as men.

(A) I'm capable, but I'll never get a raise here. I think I'll look for a new job.

Larry

(C) I'm *trapped* in this marriage. (P) You should count your
blessings, Larry. Besides,
there's never been a
divorce in our family.

(A) What are the pros and cons
of staying married? What are
the pros and cons of being
divorced? I'll get some
objective data before deciding.

Bill

(C) I want sex tonight. (P) A man's home is his castle.
What a man says, goes!

(A) My wife is just getting
over the flu. I can wait.

Susy

(C) Bill doesn't love me
or he wouldn't
be out tonight. (P) I told you you couldn't
trust men! They've only got
one thing on their minds.

(A) I know Bill had to work
tonight. I'll call Mabel, and
maybe we can take in a movie.

Tom

(C) I don't get that word the instructor just used but if I ask, I'll sound stupid.

(P) Never interrupt when someone is talking. You might make a fool of yourself.

(A) If I don't ask my question, I'll miss the whole point of the lecture. So here goes, even if I feel stupid.

PLACATING YOUR PARENT

Sometimes, the inner Child feels constantly under the pressure of the influence of a Parent ego state which is overly critical, brutal, threatening, punishing, or withholding approval or affection. With the Adult as executive, a person can learn to "throw a crumb" to the Parent. This helps allay the stressful discomfort experienced when the person goes against a parental permission or injunction.

"Throwing a crumb" implies placating the influencing Parent by doing one "little" thing that would please the Parent. People are often placating their Parent when they do such things as go to church at Christmas and Easter or to the synagogue on the Day of Atonement.

Case Illustration

One woman lived under the compulsion of saving all the family relics, collecting nearly a roomful of doilies, pictures, embroidered pillowcases, etc. While she needed this space, she could not bring herself to throw these things out. She claimed to feel guilty when she even thought about doing so, as it would be disloyal to her family. Later she reported, "It always pleased my mother to give to the needy. So I threw her two crumbs that really made me feel good. First, I saved one little box of mementos to keep my mother in my head happy.

Then, I gave a whole roomful of things away to some people who really needed them. What a relief."

PLEASING THE CHILD

Most people have occasions when they need to use their Adult for sustained periods of time. They may be facing crises—death, disease, deformity, or some other disaster. They may, for example, be under the pressure of taking an examination, getting an article finished, or starting a new business. In such cases the inner Child may be ignored and, like an actual child, becomes a nuisance or a "pain in the neck." The person in this situation may be disorganized, unable to think clearly, irritable, weepy, or feel as though something is acting as a restraint. These feelings often occur when a new baby in the family requires and gets most of the attention; and consequently, father feels left out and mother feels blue. Such feelings also occur when a person is automated out of a job, is a victim of recession, or is replaced by a younger person.

When the sheer burden of always being an adult or parent becomes too heavy, it is useful to deliberately do something special for the Child. The activity may be reassuring. Sometimes, it is refreshing or renewing.

Case Illustration

Donald had worked hard putting himself through law school while taking care of his family. Although he knew his subject well, he failed his bar examinations three times. Donald complained, "I couldn't think. I was so fearful of failing that even the pencil froze in my hand and I couldn't write."

When Donald was asked what pleased him most as a very young child, he immediately replied, "Hershey's chocolate bars with nuts, but they were forbidden because my teeth were so poor." He decided to try pleasing his Child. So the fourth time he took the exam he also took chocolate candy bars to eat during the breaks.

Donald passed with flying colors. Since then he has continued to use this technique on rare, but important occasions.

Many people have found specific ways to please their Child. Each person must find her or his own way by checking out the desires of the Child and deciding with the Adult on something appropriate.

One man relieved the tension caused by an irritable boss by playing a vigorous game of touch football with his kids.

Another man sustained himself while recuperating from severe burns by taking short trips to the mountains.

One woman soothed herself from the strain of caring for a handicapped child by taking warm, luxurious bubble baths while her child napped.

Another woman maintained a rigid diet for several months by allowing herself to indulge in one hot fudge sundae a month.

This technique of "taking five" for the Child enables a person to keep going when it's necessary. It involves indulging in something that was particularly pleasurable in childhood or fulfilling an unfulfilled desire. Each person needs to assess what pleases the Child and set rational limits on the frequency of such self-indulgence.

ACTIVATING AND STRENGTHENING THE ADULT EGO STATE

The Adult ego state is strengthened with use "in much the same light as a muscle, which increases in strength with exercise" [12]. The more people use it, the more they are able to use it.

Education

Education which strengthens a person's ability to gather, organize, and evaluate information contributes to more accurate Adult judgments. Everyone's Adult is affected by many types of learning experiences. Some learning hinders Adult functioning; some enhances it. Berne cautions, "In the individual case, due allowance must be left for past learning experiences" [13].

Education as "past learning experience" can be thought of in many ways. It can be academic or nonacademic, formal or informal. For example, most people receive their education about history, arithmetic, and English in a formal school setting with trained teachers. However, their education about sexuality is likely to occur in a less formal way—from their peers—in the locker room, at the street corner, behind the barn. Information acquired in this way may be accurate or inaccurate. Unless what is learned is accurate and unless it is evaluated, it is not useful to the Adult. The computer phrase "garbage in, garbage out" applies to the quality of input into the Adult or for that matter into any ego state.

In addition to gathering data through education, the Adult ego state also gathers data from experiences with reality. People hear, smell, feel, and see their environment and observe certain phenomena recurring at predictable intervals. They observe that the trees flower about the same time each year, that the seeds swell and the meat around them produces a distinct fruit. They learn how far they can go on a tank of gas, the best entrance to the freeway, how much time it takes to get to work, or where to buy the best fish. Their Adult ego state collects data constantly through everyday experiences.

Sometimes, information is evaluated inaccurately. Even what a person "sees" can be wrong. The earth may look flat, but it isn't. And what trial lawyer hasn't heard three "honest" but conflicting testimonies from three different witnesses of the same event.

A person who uses the Adult as executive and wants to improve the quality of his or her responses may need to strengthen the Adult by gathering data from many external sources as well as by gaining self-knowledge. Collecting and evaluating information enable a person to determine more accurately what response is appropriate to the reality of the here and now. A person with Adult executive control needs continual self-education and needs to sort out this inner world in order to use wisely what is OK from the Parent and what is OK from the Child.

Contracts

Making an Adult contract is a most important TA tool for strengthening the Adult. A contract is an Adult commitment to one's self and/or to someone else to make a change. Contracts can be established to change feelings, behavior, or psychosomatic problems. According to Berne:

. . . the contract may refer to symptoms characteristic of particular disorders, such as hysterical paralyses, phobias, obsessions, somatic symptoms, fatigue, and palpitation in the neuroses; forgery, excessive drinking, drug addiction, delinquency, and other such game-like behavior in the psychopathies; pessimism, pedantry, sexual impotence, or frigidity in the character disorders; hallucinations, elation, and depression in psychoses [14].

A contract must be clear, concise, and direct. It involves (1) a decision to do something about a specific problem, (2) a statement of a clear goal to be worked toward in language simple enough for the inner Child to understand, and (3) the possibility of the goal's being fulfilled.

In order to make a contract, a person must have enough awareness of his or her approach to life to know what is causing dissatisfaction or undue discomfort to self or to others. Dissatisfaction often motivates change.

It is important that a contract be made by the Adult ego state. The Parent ego state may make a promise to put off a Child, and the Child ego state may make a "New Year's resolution" with no honest intention of keeping it. The Adult plays it straight!

Although TA was originally designed as a contractual form of therapy, a person can make a contract with anyone—self, spouse, boss, co-worker, or friend—to

stop indulging in self-pity

stop self-degrading thoughts and acts

stop acting like a martyr

stop discounting others

stop destroying his or her body;

start listening to people

start being pleasant

start relaxing

start laughing

start using his or her head.

Learning to make contracts, seeing them through, changing them when appropriate, and moving on to the next problem and next contract are signs of autonomy, signs of a winner.

Raising the Right Question

After defining the problem and making a contract, the person can program the Adult ego state with a question appropriate to that particular problem. Then, at the crucial moment, whenever a behavior pattern the person has decided to change is about to be used, the person asks the question. The question activates the Adult ego state.

A person who is defensive, hurt, or easily depressed in the face of criticism may make the contract, "I will learn to evaluate criticism." The person can raise the question, "I wonder if by any chance that criticism could be true?" and may also raise the question, "I wonder if by any chance it could be wrong?"

A person who tends to withdraw may make the contract, "I will speak up." When the old behavior pattern is about to be used, the person can raise the question, "What responsibility am I avoiding?" or "What is wrong with what I have to say?" or "What is the worst thing that can happen to me if I speak up?"

A person who always wants to be the center of the stage may make the contract, "I will share the stage with others and let them have the stage to themselves sometimes." When the urge for the spotlight arises, the person can raise the question, "What do I have to do or say that everyone has to see or hear?" or "When is enough, enough?" or "What could I learn by watching and listening to someone else?"

A person whose Parent ego state is arbitrarily authoritarian and says "no" to most requests, especially those made by his or her own children, may make the Adult contract, "I will listen to all requests and respond reasonably."

When a request is made, this person can activate the Adult by asking, "Why not?" If the request would honestly be injurious to the health or safety of the child, the person can say "no" from the Adult, stating the reasons and remaining firm. If there are no good reasons, the individual can say "yes," stating the limitations and conditions. By following this procedure, the "yes" or "no" will come from the Adult ego state even though it is an act of parenting.

If a person's "no's" are too frequently self-imposed, the inner Child is still responding to too many Parent "don'ts." Expressions of pleasure and fun from the inner Child are disallowed, so he or she may make the contract, "I will allow myself to laugh, to love, to play." When a person with this contract has the impulse for playfulness, he or she can ask, "Why not?" If there are good reasons (not rationalizations), the person can postpone the pleasure for another time. If there are none, the person can let go and can have a good time.

If a person's Parent is overly permissive, saying an unthinking "yes" to most impulses (liquor, drugs, food, sleep, etc.) or to other people's demands, the person may make the Adult contract, "I will not say 'yes' to myself or to others if the behavior is destructive." The person can raise the questions, "Why should I do this to myself?" or "Why should I hurt other people or allow them to hurt themselves?"

When people use the contract-question technique to activate the Adult, they design their own unique question related to the contract to engage their intelligence so that they can evaluate the situation more rationally. They risk taking the responsibility for their actions.

Learning from Projections

People who are aware use their Adult to learn about some of their alienated personality fragments from their projections. Projection is a common phenomenon of human behavior. Perls writes:

A projection is a trait, attitude, feeling, or bit of behavior which actually belongs to your own personality but is not experienced as such; instead, it is attributed to objects or persons in the environment and then experienced as directed *toward* you by them instead of the other way around. . . .

The picture of being rejected—first by his parents and now by his friends—is one that the neurotic goes to great lengths to establish and maintain. While such claims may have substance, the opposite is also certainly true—that the neurotic rejects others for not living up to some fantastic ideal or standard which he imposes on them. Once he has projected his rejecting onto the other person, he can, without feeling any responsibility for the situation, regard himself as the passive object of all kinds of unwarranted hardship, unkind treatment, or even victimization [15].

People may project any positive or negative trait they have alienated from their awareness. In an unaware way they may accuse others of being angry, when actually it is they who are angry at them. They may perceive others as being tender and kind, when

PLATE XVIII

EVERYONE HAS AN ADULT EGO STATE

It can collect and
evaluate information,
reason, and solve
problems.

actually their cold-hearted exterior, like Scrooge's, hides a capacity for tenderness. They may claim that their spouse is not affectionate, when actually they do not feel affection toward their spouse.

Some games, such as *Blemish*, are played by projecting one's own traits onto another. Rather than admitting to personal feelings of inadequacy, the person who plays *Blemish* comes on as Parent and picks at the inadequacies attributed to others.

People who use their projections to gain self-knowledge, question their accusations and admirations of others. When they make an accusation or state an admiration, they learn to ask, "Could it possibly be true that that trait really belongs to me?" By using this question:

> A woman who complains, "Nobody appreciates me," may discover that she is the one who rarely shows appreciation of others.
>
> A friend who gushes, "You're so wonderful—no one could ever do what you do," may discover the capacity to do similar things.
>
> A teacher who says, "That stupid kid," may discover his or her own stupidity.
>
> A boy who says, "That door is always hitting me in the face," may discover that he is going out of his way to hit the door.
>
> A man who always complains, "Nobody ever listens to me," may discover that he is the one who never listens.
>
> A man in a counseling group who says, "You just won't open up to me," may discover that he is the one who is unwilling to be open.
>
> A sexually inhibited woman who complains, "Men are always making passes at me," may discover that she is the one who is desirous of men.

Learning from Dreams

Just as people can learn from their projections, they can also learn from their dreams. Perls describes dreams as "the most spontaneous expression of the existence of the human being" [16]. Dreams are like a stage production, but the direction and action are not under the same control as in waking life.

The Gestalt approach is to integrate dreams rather than to analyze them. Integrating can be accomplished by consciously reliving the dream, by taking responsibility for being the objects and people in the dream, by becoming aware of the messages the dream holds. To learn from dreams, it is not essential to work out an entire dream. Working with small bits of the dream are often fruitful.

To relive a dream the person first tells it or writes it down as a story that is happening *now*. Using the present tense, for example, "I am walking down a lonely road . . .," "I am sitting in an airplane . . .," the person includes everything experienced in the dream, but does not add anything that wasn't actually there.

In the next step the person begins a dialogue—speaking out loud. As a help in getting started, each person, object, or event is asked, "What are you doing in my dream?" Then becoming each person, object, or event the person answers, beginning with "*I*," again using the present tense. For example, "*I* am a jazzy red sports car . . .," "*I* am a rug stretched out on the floor . . .," "*I* am an old woman trying to climb some stairs. . . ."

Each part of the dream is likely to disguise a message about the person dreaming it. When the message comes through, the person is likely to feel "Ah, ha! So that's the way I am."

One woman, on being an unbending boss in her dream, discovered that she herself was unbending and unwilling to make a change. One man, speaking as the steam roller in his dream, discovered that he rolled over other people if they got in his way. In both cases the alienated personality fragment was "re-owned" and thus integrated into the whole personality. Perls cautions:

. . . if you work on dreams it is better if you do it with someone else who can point out where you avoid. Understanding the dream means realizing when you are avoiding the obvious. The only danger is that this other person might come too quickly to the rescue and tell you what is going on in you, instead of giving yourself the chance of discovering yourself [17].

DAYS OF DESPAIR

A person who activates the Adult begins to see life more realistically and may discover things that are hard to accept, for example, that the job is a dead end.

that a spouse is mentally disturbed.

that some people really hate each other.

that some people really hurt each other.

that the children are alienated.

that the piper must be paid.

that real friendships are scarce.

that many potentials are unrealized.

Furthermore, some people discover that the magic person or event they were waiting for to improve their lot in life is not going to come,

that their ship is never going to come in.

that opportunity is going to remain "around the corner."

that the mailman is not going to "ring twice."

that Beauty has no magic power.

that there is no fairy godmother or wizard.

that the frog is really a frog, not a prince.

Faced with such awareness, many people fall into despair, losing the hope that someone else will rescue them. For the first time, perhaps, they realize that if they are to be rescued, they must rely on themselves and strengthen their own resources, for much of life is a do-it-yourself project.

Although the feeling of despair is painful, it is a challenge to do something different. At this point a person can (1) withdraw from society by becoming a hermit in some isolated place, by being committed to a state institution, or by staying locked up in a hotel room; (2) try to eliminate personal problems by "tuning out" with alcohol or other drugs, or more decisively by committing suicide; (3) get rid of the people causing the pain—sending the children away, shedding a wife or husband, or murdering someone; (4) do nothing and wait; (5) get better and begin to live in the real world. Berne describes it in this manner:

In the long run, the patient must undertake the task of living in a world in which there is no Santa Claus. He is then faced with the existential problems of necessity, freedom of choice, and absurdity, all of which were previously evaded in some measure by living with the illusions of his script [18].

People who decide to live in the real world, who decide that they were born to win, agree with Disraeli that "Life is too short to be small."

SUMMARY

The Adult ego state deals objectively with reality. The Adult is not related to age, but is influenced by education and experience. When it is activated, a person can collect and organize information, predict possible consequences of various actions, and make conscious decisions. Even though a decision is made from the Adult, it is not necessarily accurate if information is lacking. However, using the Adult can help to minimize regrettable actions and can increase a person's potential for success.

When there is inner conflict or self-defeating interaction between the inner Child and Parent, the Adult ego state can interfere: it can referee, arbitrate, find compromises, and make new decisions for the expression of the inner Child. It can also accept or reject Parental assumptions on the basis of reality and appropriateness. To achieve this integration of personality, the Adult must gain knowledge about the Child and Parent ego states. This is part of self-awareness.

A person's spontaneous use of personality resources can be affected by ego boundary problems. If the ego boundaries are too lax, psychic energy slips erratically from one ego state to another, causing the person to be highly unpredictable. If the ego boundaries are too rigid, the psychic energy is "locked" in one ego state, excluding the others. This problem manifests itself by a continuous use of one ego state—the person chooses to act almost exclusively from the Parent, the Adult, or the Child. When trauma or a piling up of negative experiences occurs, the ego boundaries suffer lesions. The result is a flow of emotion which appears unreasonable in terms of the stimulus. The Adult's clear perception of current reality can also be contaminated by prejudiced beliefs and childhood delusions.

PLATE XIX

EVEN CHILDREN HAVE AN
ADULT EGO STATE

The Adult ego state is ageless.

When a person first gains Adult awareness, despair often results. The person can react to this uncomfortable feeling by hiding out, copping out, getting rid of others, doing nothing, or putting the Adult ego state in executive control of the personality and going about the business of running his or her own life.

The Adult ego state as executive does not mean that the person is always acting from the Adult. It means that the Adult allows appropriate expression of all ego states because each has its contribution to make to a total personality. The Adult is "tuned in" and knows when an impulse may be acted on with great pleasure and when it must be contained or modified to fit the reality of the moment.

For the Adult to gain executive control, this ego state must be activated and used. Everyone has this potential, even though for some it may not seem so. Berne makes the analogy: " . . . if no radio is heard in someone's house, that does not mean he lacks one; he may have a good one, but it needs to be turned on and warmed up before it can be heard clearly" [19].

When your Adult ego state is turned on and tuned in, it can help you set the course of your life much more intelligently. An old Polish proverb advises, "If there is no wind, row."

EXPERIMENTS AND EXERCISES

People who are aware know the urgency of life because they know the inevitable reality of death. They make their choices on the basis of what they want their life to mean.

1. Deathbed Scene (fantasy)

Find a quiet place where you can sit down and not be interrupted. Imagine yourself very old and on your deathbed. Your life is passing before you. Close your eyes. Project your life drama on an imaginary screen in front of you. Watch it from its beginning up to the present moment. Take your time. After your experience consider:

• What memories bring you the most pain? The most pleasure?

• What experiences, commitments, and accomplishments have given meaning to your life?

- Do you have any regrets? If so, what could you have done differently? What can you do differently now?

- Do you wish you had spent more time or less time with anyone in particular?

- Were there choices you weren't aware of? Or perhaps afraid of?

- Did you discover what you value? Are your values what you want them to be?

- Did you discover something you want to change now?

2. Your Last Hour (fantasy)

Now look at your life from another perspective. Imagine that you have one hour of life left and you can spend it with whomever you wish.

- Whom would you want to have with you?

- How and where would you like to spend the last hour together?

- Does the person(s) know you feel this way?

3. Breaking Out of Your Bash Trap

If you feel trapped in any area of your life or up against a wall, try the following fantasy excursion.

- Close your eyes and fantasize you are bashing your head against a high, brick wall, trying to get to something on the other side.

- Watch yourself beating your head.

- Now stop bashing and look around.

- Find some way to get over, under, or around the wall without bashing. If you need something to help you, invent it.

If you think of yourself as "boxed" in, take a fantasy trip into a box.

- Imagine yourself curled up inside. How does it feel? Does it protect you from something or someone?

- Imagine several ways of getting out of your box. Now, get out of it.

- After you have escaped from your box, see yourself sitting outside, under a tree.

- Look around. Look back at your box, then at the rest of the world.

If you feel up against a wall or boxed in, and if you're not listening to old tapes that say "grownups don't do those kind of things,"

- Build yourself a wall out of cardboard, newspapers, etc. Bash your head against it. Look behind you. Is there a simpler way out?

- Get a big cardboard box. Get inside and pull down the lid. Sit there awhile and get in touch with your feelings. Next, break out. Look at the box. Look at the rest of your world.

Then ask yourself the questions:

- Is it by any chance true that I build my own wall, climb into my own box?

- If so, what do I get out of it for myself?

- What does it do to others?

- What positions do I reinforce in myself?

- What stamps do I collect in doing this?

- How does it fit my script?

- Is this what I really want for myself?

Now, stop bashing and look around.

4. Examining Constant Parent, Constant Adult, and Constant Child

Consider: *Could it possibly be true that I operate too frequently and/or inappropriately from the Parent ego state?*

- Do others accuse you of doing their thinking for them, putting words in their mouths, never letting them stand on their own two feet, having all the answers, being unapproachable or unreachable?

- Do you evangelize, propagandize, or bulldoze others?

- Examine closely the groups with which you affiliate.

- Is there room for disagreement within each organization, or are most of the members of the same opinion?

- Would your parents have belonged (or liked to have belonged) to these groups?

- Is creative thinking appreciated or repressed in these groups?

- What common opinions do the groups you belong to hold?

- If you tend to belong to rescuing groups, question whether they really solve problems or just talk about them. Do they approach problems from one point of view or from many?

- Do your groups depend on you to make decisions for them?

- Do you tell them what to do? Encourage them to think and act for themselves?

- How often do you say "should," "ought," or "must" to others? Are these Adult "shoulds" or Parent "shoulds"?

- What subjects do you find yourself talking heatedly and repeatedly about?

- Could it possibly be true that you are expressing someone else's value judgments without applying your own thought and examination to the subject?

Consider: *Could it possibly be true that I operate too frequently and/or inappropriately from my Adult ego state?*

- Do you find yourself to be overly analytical, too rational, nonspontaneous, and machinelike most of the time?

- Do you consistently deal with data processing, rarely expressing parental concern or childlike playfulness?

- Are you always rational with money, never "splurging" impulsively or overindulging someone with a present they have always wanted?

- Do you have little time for recreation or just doing nothing?

- Do you belong only to professional groups—groups which gather primarily to exchange data?

- Now think of your close friends. Are they limited to business associates?

- When you go to a social gathering, do you always talk shop or find a corner and gather data from magazines?

- Are you accused of being "no fun" or of "not taking your share of responsibility for the children"?

- Do you tend to be a machine—a computer just grinding out information and decisions?

- Do you use your Adult to rationalize—to explain away faults and prejudices?

- Do you use it to "stick up for" and perpetuate Parent opinions that were once too threatening for you to examine intelligently?

- Do you use it to help the Child "con" others and to give your Child "good" reasons for playing games?

Consider: *Could it possibly be true that I operate too frequently and/or inappropriately from my Child ego state?*

- Do you give others authority over you in many ways?

- Do others do your thinking for you, put words in your mouth, smother you, give you the answers, often come to your rescue, or keep you in your place?

- Examine the groups to which you belong.

- Are they primarily for fun?

- For overthrowing or bugging authorities?

- For advising you how to run your life?

- Do you turn your back on, panic, or become weak in the face of problems and decisions?

- Do you look to others for constant approval, criticism, or support?

- Think of your ten closest friends. Do they have anything in common? Are they playmates? Do they serve as parent figures?

- Do you often say "I can't" when you really mean "I won't" or "I don't want to"?

5. Your Ego State Portrait

Using circles of different sizes, draw your ego state portrait as you *perceive yourself* most of the time. Your portrait might look something like Fig. 9.7 below.

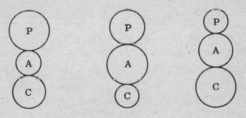

- Do you see yourself as having a favorite ego state?

- Does your portrait change when the situation changes? At work? At home? At school? At a party? Where else?

- Does it change with certain people? A boss? Subordinate? Spouse? Children? Friends? Who else?

- Now ask a child, spouse, friend, relative, and/or business associate to draw how he or she perceives you. Notice any differences?

After you have drawn your ego state portraits, both from your own perspective and that of others, ask yourself,

- Does this satisfy me? If not, what needs to be changed?

- What contracts do I need to make? What Adult questions do I need to raise?

6. Decontaminating Your Adult

One effective method for decontaminating your Adult from the
prejudices of your Parent and delusions of your Child is to reverse your assumptions.

For Parent Contaminations

• List four adjectives you use when talking about persons of a
  different race, sex, age, religion, education, class, back-
  ground, etc. For example:
  Men are _____, _____, _____, _____
  Women are _____, _____, _____, _____
  Jews are _____, _____, _____, _____
  Gentiles are _____, _____, _____, _____
  Blacks are _____, _____, _____, _____
  Whites are _____, _____, _____, _____
  _____ are _____, _____, _____, _____
  _____ are _____, _____, _____, _____

• Do you have sufficient and accurate data to verify your above
  beliefs, or by any chance have you taken the above position
  on the basis of one experience? On the basis of hearsay? On
  the basis of mass media programming?

• Now reverse your assumptions, using adjectives that are the
  reverse of the ones you used. What do you discover?

For Child Contaminations

• Do you often use words indicating that you are waiting for a
  magical person or event? Words such as
  When (if only) he/she changes. . . .
  When (if only) I get married. . . .
  When (if only) I get divorced. . . .
  When (if only) I get the right job. . . .
  When (if only) the kids grow up. . . .

• Do you often use words that indicate you think of yourself in
  one way and cannot change? Words such as

  I'm so helpless that. . . .

  I'm so stupid that. . . .

  I'm so depressed that. . . .

I'm so confused that. . . .

- What do you frequently state about yourself?
  I'm so . . . that. . . .

- Now reverse any of the above assumptions you have made,
  for example:
  He/she may never change so. . . .
  I'm so powerful that. . . .
  I'm so . . . that. . . .

After you have considered possible Parent and Child contaminations, ask yourself the following questions.

- Am I satisfied with what I've discovered?

- What do I need to re-evaluate?

- What do I need to change?

- What contracts do I need to make?

- What Adult questions do I need to raise?

7. Learning from Your Projections

Others often serve as mirrors. When you look, you see yourself! Learning from your projections is a useful tool in self-knowledge. Let us look at one way to begin.

Visualize someone whom you particularly dislike.

- What are the things you don't like about this person?

- Do you know others who are this way? Do you also dislike them?

- Now visualize yourself as having these same traits. See yourself in action.

- Do or be the very things that annoy you in others.

- Now raise the question: Could it possibly be true that I am the one who does or is these things?

Now visualize someone you particularly admire.

- What are the things you like about this person?

- Do you know others who possess similar traits? Do you also admire these people?

- Next, visualize yourself talking, walking, performing, doing, and being what you admire in them. See yourself as having their traits.

- Now raise the question: Could it possibly be true that I have the potential to actually do and be these things myself?

For one week keep two separate lists.

- On one list write down all the things you accuse others of (she rejects me, he's stupid, my husband/wife is fooling around, she's always angry, he hates me, etc.)

- On the other list keep track of all the statements of admiration you make (she's so affectionate, he's thoughtful, my wife/husband always knows the right thing to say, he's great with children, her style is very clear, etc.)

- At the end of the week, examine your lists. Do you see any patterns?

- Now raise the question: Could it possibly be true that I. . . .?

For example, "Could it possibly be true that I reject Mary for the very reasons I claim she rejects me?" "Could it possibly be true that I'd like to walk out of this marriage as I have accused Dick of wanting to do?"

8. Learning from Your Dreams

Many people claim to forget their dreams. If you are one of these, keep pencil and paper by your bed and write your dreams down immediately. Every dream has a message. To discover the message your dream holds for you, Perls suggests the following process.

Write the dream down and make a list of *all* the details in the dream. Get every person, every thing, every mood, and then work on these to *become* each one of them. Ham it up, and really transform into each of the different items. Really *become* that thing—whatever it is in a dream—*become* it. Use your magic. Turn into that ugly frog or whatever is there—the dead thing, the live thing, the demon—and stop thinking.

Next, take each one of these different items, characters, and parts, and let them have encounters between them. Write a script. By "write a script" I mean have a dialogue between the two opposing parts and you will find—especially if you get the correct opposites—that they always start out fighting each other [20].

- After you have worked through a dream or a dream fragment as Perls suggests, ask yourself, "Was I avoiding something in the dream? Was I running away? Hiding? Not able to use my legs or voice? What?"

- . . . If so, is it similar to my real-life avoidance patterns?

9. Problem-Solving Technique

If you have a problem that needs solving—such as how to get a job, how to change a behavior pattern, how to improve family relationships—activate your Adult by following specific steps. Some steps may not apply to all problems, but at least consider them as you move through the process.

1. Define the problem and write it down (you may find that what you thought was the problem isn't the basic one).

2. What are your Parents' opinions, information, and behavior concerning this problem?
    - List what each of your Parent figures would say or do about it.
    - Listen to your Parents speaking in your head. Write down their shoulds, oughts, etc. Now list what they avoided and their nonverbal messages.

3. Next, consider your Child's feelings, attitudes, and information about the problem.
    - List the feelings you have that are related to the problem. Are these stamps, or are they legitimate feelings?
    - Are any games being played in connection with the problem?
    - Does the problem fit into your constructive, destructive, or nonproductive script? Are any manipulative roles being played?

4. Evaluate the above Parent and Child data with your Adult.
    - What Parent attitudes hinder you in solving the problem?

What Parent attitudes aid you in solving the problem?
- What Child feelings and adaptations hinder you in solving the problem? What Child feelings and adaptations aid you in solving the problem?
- What solution would please your Parent? Would it be appropriate or destructive for you to do this?
- What solution would please your Child? Would it be appropriate or destructive?

5. Imagine alternative ways to solve the problem. Do not censor any ideas. Instead, use your Little Professor and "brainstorm." Come up with as many possibilities as you can—even if some seem ridiculous.

6. Then consider internal and external resources necessary for each brainstorming solution. Are the resources available? Are they appropriate?

7. Estimate the probabilities of success from each alternative. Weed out those that are not possible.

8. Select two or three that are the most possible. On the basis of the facts and your creative imagination, make your decision.

9. Be aware of the effects of your decision.

Decisions that make you "feel good" may be satisfying to all ego states. A decision that makes you feel uncomfortable may have your Parent and/or Child fighting against it, may actually be harmful to yourself or others, or may be simply the wrong decision.

10. Establish the contract you need to carry out the decision. Raise the appropriate Adult questions that fit your contract.

11. Implement your decision with action. If possible, test it first in a small way. Then move ahead with more power.

12. Evaluate the strengths and weaknesses of your plan as you go along. Make any necessary adjustments.

13. Enjoy your successes. Do not be overly cast down by your failures. Learn from them and start again. Consider John

Dewey's statement, "The person who really thinks, learns quite as much from his failures as from his successes."

When losers make decisions, they usually put the blame somewhere else if things go wrong. When winners make decisions, they usually take responsibility for them whether the decisions are right or wrong.

10
Autonomy and Adult Ethics

Man ultimately decides for himself!
And in the end, education must be
education toward the ability to decide.
  Viktor Frankl

Achieving autonomy is the ultimate goal in transactional analysis. Being autonomous means being self-governing, determining one's own destiny, taking responsibility for one's own actions and feelings, and throwing off patterns that are irrelevant and inappropriate to living in the here and now.

Everyone has the capacity to obtain a measure of autonomy. But in spite of the fact that autonomy is a human birthright, few actually achieve it. Berne writes:

Man is born free, but one of the first things he learns is to do as he is told, and he spends the rest of his life doing that. Thus his first enslavement is to his parents. He follows their instructions forevermore, retaining only in some cases the right to choose his own methods and consoling himself with an illusion of autonomy [1].

People suffer under the illusion of autonomy if they think they have changed their script, but in reality have changed only the setting, characters, costumes, etc., not the essence of the drama. For example, a person who is Parent programmed to be an evangelist may join the drug scene and then with religious zeal evangelize others into following. Choosing the setting for evangelizing may give the person the illusion of freedom when actually the enslavement to parental instructions has only been disguised.

Similarly, a woman with a script like Beauty and the Beast may believe she is freeing herself from a life of misery by divorcing a beast and remarrying when actually she may be only trading in one kind of beast for another.

A truly autonomous person, according to Berne, is one who demonstrates "the release or recovery of three capacities: awareness, spontaneity, and intimacy" [2].

AWARENESS

Awareness is knowing what is happening now. An autonomous person is aware. This person peels away the layers of contamination from the Adult and begins to hear, see, smell, touch, taste, study, and evaluate independently. Shedding old opinions that distort present perception, the aware person perceives the world through personal encounter rather than the way he or she was "taught" to see it.

Knowing that life is temporal, an aware person appreciates nature *now*. An aware person experiences that part of the universe known to the self, as well as the mystery of those universes yet to be discovered. An aware person can stand by a lake, study a buttercup, feel the wind, and experience a sense of awe. An aware person can look at a sunset and say, "Wow!"

An aware person listens to the messages of the body, knowing when he or she is becoming tense or relaxed, is being open or withdrawn. An aware person knows the inner world of feelings and fantasies and is not afraid or ashamed of them.

An aware person also hears other people, listening and giving active feedback when they talk. An aware person's psychic energy isn't used to form a question, create a diversion, or plan a mental counterattack. Instead, he or she attempts to make genuine contact with the other person by learning the skills of both talking and listening.

An aware person is all there and fully aware. His or her mind and body respond in unison to the here and now; the body is not doing one thing while the mind focuses on something else. This person

doesn't use angry words while smiling.

doesn't frown or scowl when the situation calls for laughter.

doesn't rush through a picnic to get back to something that "really matters."

doesn't mentally write an important business letter while making love.

doesn't rehash what happened last night while writing that important letter at the office.

doesn't wear rose-colored glasses to avoid the hard facts of life.

doesn't fiddle while Rome burns.

People who are aware know where they are, what they're doing, and how they feel about it. As Abraham Lincoln observed, "If we could first know where we are and whither we are tending, we could better judge what to do and how to do it."

The first step to integration is awareness, with the Adult as executive. A person who becomes aware of acting like a tyrant or a sulk can decide what to do about this behavior—whether to knowingly keep it, own it, and be it, or whether to throw it in the pail along with the rest of the garbage, if that is what he or she decides it is. Perls claims, "Everything is grounded in *awareness*" [3].

SPONTANEITY

Spontaneity is the freedom to choose from the full spectrum of Parent behavior and feelings, Adult behavior and feelings, and Child behavior and feelings [4]. An autonomous person is spontaneous and flexible—not foolishly impulsive. This person sees the many options available and uses what behavior seems to be appropriate to the situation and to her or his goals.

A spontaneous person is liberated, making and accepting responsibility for personal choices. This person gets rid of the compulsion to live a predetermined life style and instead learns to face new situations and to explore new ways of thinking, feeling, and responding. This person constantly increases and re-evaluates a repertoire of possible behavior.

The spontaneous person uses or recaptures the ability to decide independently. This person accepts the Parent and Child as personal history but makes new decisions rather than remaining at the mercy of "fate." Unless a person makes decisions, even though they are not always right, personal power remains undirected and the ethic unclear or unstable. Decisionlessness, according to Martin Buber, is evil—"evil is the aimless whirl of human potentialities without which nothing can be achieved and by which, if they take no direction but remain trapped in themselves, everything goes awry" [5]. In this sense the autonomous person is one who makes decisions which give purposeful direction to his or her own potentialities. Within realistic limitations, the person knowingly takes responsibility for a self-imposed destiny.

To consciously decide for oneself from the Adult ego state is to be free—free in spite of basic instincts or drives, free in spite of inherited characteristics and environmental influences. Viktor Frankl writes:

Certainly man has instincts, but these instincts do not have him. We have nothing against instincts, nor against a man's accepting them. But we hold that such acceptance must also presuppose the possibility of rejection. In other words, there must have been freedom of decision. . . .

. . . As for inheritance, research on heredity has shown how high is the degree of human freedom in the face of predisposition. For example, twins may build different lives on the basis of identical predispositions. Of a pair of identical twins, one became a cunning criminal, while his brother became an equally cunning criminologist. . . .

. . . As for environment, we know that it does not make man, but that everything depends on what man makes of it, on his attitude toward it [6].

A person must do more, however, than make a decision. Unless the person acts on that decision, it is meaningless. Only when one's inner ethic and outward behavior match is a person congruent and whole. A spontaneous person is free to "do his own thing," but not at the expense of others through exploitation and/or indifference.

INTIMACY

Intimacy is expressing the Natural Child feelings of warmth, tenderness, and closeness to others. Many people suffer from an inability to express such closeness. Maslow sees this as particularly true of Americans:

. . . Americans need so many more therapists than the rest of the world needs because they just don't know how to be intimate—that they have no intimate friendships, by comparison with the Europeans and that, therefore, they really have no deep friends to unburden themselves to [7].

Autonomous persons risk friendships and intimacy when they decide it is appropriate. This does not come easily to people who

PLATE XX

WINNERS ENJOY INTIMACY

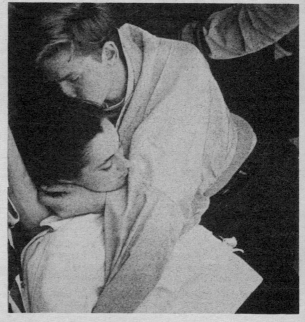

Intimacy is expressing feelings of warmth, tenderness, and closeness toward others.

have restricted their affectionate feelings and are not in the habit of expressing them. In fact, they may feel awkward, even phony, when they first try to go against old programming. Nevertheless, they try.

In the process of developing this capacity for intimacy, a person becomes more open—learns to "let go," becomes more self-revealing by dropping some of the masks—but always with the awareness of the Adult. The person refrains from transacting with others in ways that prevent closeness, avoids using discounts, crossed transactions, or playing games. The person plays games only if it is a conscious decision—perhaps not wishing to invest time or energy in a particular person or situation. The person does not force others to play Persecutor, Rescuer, or Victim roles or to remain Constant Child, Constant Parent, or Constant Adult. Instead, the person attempts to be open and authentic, existing with others in the here and now, and also attempts to see others in their own uniqueness, not through distortions of past experiences. The person doesn't use accusations such as

"You're just as sloppy as your mother!"

"My father could fix anything. Why can't you even fix the water faucet?"

"You're just like my brother, always whining for what you want!"

"You're just like my sister—everything had to be her way!"

People who reject awareness, spontaneity, and intimacy also reject the responsibility for shaping their own lives. They think of themselves as either lucky or unlucky, assuming without question that

it's meant to be and can't be changed.

it's meant to be and shouldn't be changed.

it's meant to be and only _____ can change it.

In contrast, autonomous persons are concerned with "being." They allow their own capacities to unfold and encourage others to do the same. They project their own possibilities into the future as realistic goals which give aim and purpose to their lives. They sacrifice only when they are sacrificing a lesser value for a greater value according to their own value system. They are not concerned with getting more, but with *being* more.

THE INTEGRATED ADULT

People moving toward autonomy expand their personal capacities for awareness, spontaneity, and intimacy. As this occurs they develop integrated Adult ego states. Filtering more and more Parent and Child material through their Adult and learning new behavior patterns are parts of the integrating process. Berne describes the integrated Adult [8]:

. . . it appears that in many cases certain child-like qualities become integrated into the Adult ego state in a manner different from the contamination process. The mechanism of this "integration" remains to be elucidated, but it can be observed that certain people when functioning *qua* Adult have a charm and openness of nature which is reminiscent of that exhibited by children. Along with these go certain responsible feelings toward the rest of humanity which may be subsumed under the classical term "pathos." On the other hand, there are moral qualities which are universally expected of people who undertake grown-up responsibilities, such attri-

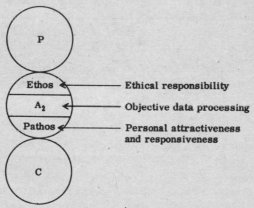

Second Order
Structural Analysis of the Adult [9]

butes as courage, sincerity, loyalty, and reliability, and which meet not
mere local prejudices, but a world-wide ethos. In this sense the Adult can
be said to have child-like and ethical aspects, but this remains the most ob-
scure area in structural analysis, so that it is not possible at present to clarify
it clinically. For academic purposes and in order to explain certain clinical
phenomena, however, it would be defensible to subdivide the Adult into
three areas.

. . . Transactionally, this means that anyone functioning as an Adult
should ideally exhibit three kinds of tendencies: personal attractiveness
and responsiveness, objective data-processing, and ethical responsibility
. . . This "integrated" person *is* charming, etc., and courageous, etc., in his
Adult state, whatever qualities he has or does not have in his Child and Parent ego states. The "unintegrated" person may *revert* to being charming,
and may feel that he *should* be courageous [10].

The person in the *process* of integration takes responsibility for
everything he or she feels, thinks, and believes and also either has
or develops an ethical system for life—ethos. The person also gathers information and computes objectively—technics [11]. In addition, the person develops social graciousness and experiences the
emotions of passion, tenderness, and suffering—pathos.
During this process the ego states go through a series of changes,
which are illustrated in Fig. 10.2.

  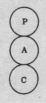 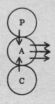 

| Unaware and Contaminated Adult | Adult Awareness of Parent and Child | Adult Re-alignment and De-contamination | Adult Filtering of Behavior | Integration Process |

A person whose Adult is integrated may revert at times to archaic behavior from the Parent or Child. Perls claims that there is

no such thing as total integration. However, in the ongoing process of integration, a person becomes more and more responsible for her or his own life.

The integrated Adult appears to be similar to what Erich Fromm calls the *fully developed person* [12], and to what Abraham Maslow calls the *self-actualizing person*. In addition to using their own talents and intellects, Maslow claims, self-actualizing people take responsibility for others as well as for themselves and have a childlike capacity for awareness and pleasure.

These individuals customarily have some mission in life, some task to fulfill, some problem outside themselves which enlists much of their energies. . . . In general, these tasks are nonpersonal or unselfish, concerned rather with the good of mankind in general, or of a nation in general. . . . Ordinarily concerned with basic issues and eternal questions, such people live customarily in the widest possible frame of reference. . . . They work within a framework of values that are broad and not petty, universal and not local, and in terms of a century rather than a moment . . . have the wonderful capacity to appreciate again and again, freshly and naively, the basic goods of life with awe, pleasure, wonder, and even ecstasy, however stale these experiences may have become to others [13].

It appears that the person who is most fully in touch with his or her own human potential is in the process of integrating the Adult. This person has the honest concern and a commitment toward others that are characteristic of a good parent, the intelligence to solve problems that is characteristic of an adult, and the ability to create, express awe, and show affection that are characteristic of a happy and healthy child.

ADULT FEELINGS

At the time of this writing, research workers are still conducting further studies in an effort to better understand feelings in the Adult and the integrated Adult. We believe that unless integrated, the Adult functions only as a data-processing machine.

An unfeeling machine as the executive of the personality would create an inadequate personality. A machine has no ethical value system, no emotional capacity. It cannot change or program itself. Therefore, we think it is the integrated Adult that contains Adult feelings and ethics as well as technical skills and ability.

Feelings that are *copied,* usually as attitudes or beliefs, are likely to be in the Parent. Feelings *experienced* in infancy and childhood are likely to be in the Child. Feelings that are a *genuine response to an actual situation happening now* are likely to have some Adult involvement. Either the Adult informs the Child of the situation so that the response is authentic or certain feelings have been integrated into the Adult.

For example, angry temper tantrums are rackets of the Child, but legitimate indignation or outrage that is based on observing an actual injustice indicate Adult responsibility.

Trust and admiration are feelings of the Child who believes that people are OK. But genuine respect of others based on objective observations of them is Adult.

Depression is an indulgence of the Child, whereas despair implies Adult awareness of a tragic reality.

Guilt feelings can be a stamp added to the Child's collection or can be an authentic response to an actual wrongdoing.

Sympathy is likely to be copied from a parent; understanding involves Adult information.

ADULT ETHICS

The process of integrating serves as a catalyst motivating the person to re-evaluate a present value system and to design a personal ethical code.

If a person does something "good" because of a *should* feeling from Parent programming, this is an act of obedience rather than one based on an ethical principle. Although a Parent-programmed act may be wholesome, it is not necessarily based on the person's autonomous ethical decision. History is filled with human tragedies of unaware obedience, tragedies brought about because people blindly conformed to an authority whose purpose was to keep others dependent, unable to change, or to destroy them.

To establish an Adult code of ethics, both Parent and Child opinions and feelings need to be scrutinized objectively with the Adult. This scrutiny does not imply that past teachings are necessarily thrown out by the rebellious Child, for many parents transmit a rational ethical system. Rather, both Parent and Child values are examined. What is found to be arbitrary, irrelevant, or destructive is discarded. What is found to be conducive to growth is integrated. This process brings into question many treasured opinions—opinions which may have been carefully handed down from generation to generation through the Parent ego state and perhaps obeyed by a compliant Child.

A person does not have to be enslaved by the past, but can transcend past influences and respond in freedom. Using the Adult ego state, a person can *re-decide* what is right and what is wrong based on actions that, when examined in their reality, preserve the health and dignity of the person and of the human race.

An Adult ethical system is based on an Adult I'm OK and You're OK. This Adult position is different from an unexamined Child position of I'm OK and You're OK which is basic to mental health, but which can remain either as a naive, exaggerated sense of OKness or as a manic refusal to recognize anything negative [14]. An ethical position, evaluated by the Adult, reflects a basic respect for oneself and for others until reality indicates otherwise. It is a position that discriminates and recognizes the negative as well as the positive.

The protection, enhancement, and well-being of people and the protection, enhancement, and well-being of the inanimate and animate natural world are fundamentals on which Adult ethics are based. Adult ethics are supportive of human life—supportive of winners.

A decision is ethical if it enhances self-respect, develops personal integrity and integrity in relationships, dissolves unreal barriers between people, builds a core of genuine confidence in self and others, and facilitates the actualizing of human potentials without bringing harm to others.

A decision is not ethical if as a result a person is exploited and used as an inhuman object, if human life is threatened for ulterior purposes, if barriers are built between people, if human potentials are belittled, squelched, or ignored, and if there is no possibility of free choice.

One's value system can be judged by the way in which a person relates to all things. The ethical person establishes a practical, workable, concerned, and enhancing relationship with the *total* environment.

Human survival and continuing development depend not only on how we transact with our fellow humans but also on how we relate to the rest of our environment. The inanimate world, which includes rocks, sunsets, water, and air, and the animate world of living plants and animals are at our mercy. We have the power to enjoy them, to enhance them, or to destroy them. When we misuse them by polluting air and waterways, by rendering land barren, by causing the extinction of a species, or by upsetting the ecological balance, it is our own existence and continuance as a race which are, in the long run, threatened. Our own exploitation of our environment unnecessarily can doom us to a tragic ending.

An ethical person does not discount problems or their significance, but instead assumes that people can work together to solve them. An ethical person works on personal problems, community problems, and such worldwide problems as those caused by rats and disease that eat away at babies, and overpopulation and wars that bring death and hopelessness to millions of people. An ethical person can crusade, as Berne suggests, [15] against the Four Horsemen—War, Pestilence, Famine, and Death—whose innocent victims are the infants of nations, and the resulting bleakness when aesthetic values are ignored and give way to ugliness. An ethical person recognizes that apathy is consent in matters such as infant mortality, child beatings, urban deterioration, and unfair employment, education, and housing practices. An ethical person is indignant over the injuries and injustices suffered by humanity and tries to change them. An ethical person is aware of and responsive to all creation.

An ethical person works for an environment in which people can become winners, cherishes and actualizes personal potentials, and becomes the winner he or she was born to be.

EPILOGUE

It takes courage to be a real winner—not a winner in the sense of beating out someone else by always insisting on coming out on top—but a winner at responding to life. It takes courage to experience the freedom that comes with autonomy, courage to accept intimacy and directly encounter other persons, courage to take a stand in an unpopular cause, courage to choose authenticity over approval and to choose it again and again, courage to accept the responsibility for your own choices, and, indeed, courage to be the very unique person you really are. New ways are often uncertain ways and, as Robert Frost expressed it, "courage is the human virtue that counts most—courage to act on limited knowledge and insufficient evidence. That's all any of us have."

The path of an ethical person who is autonomously aware, spontaneous, and able to be intimate is not always easy; however,

PLATE XXI

*To be nobody-but-yourself in a world which is
doing its best, night and day, to make you
everybody else—means to fight the hardest
battle which any human being can fight; and
never stop fighting.*

e. e. cummings [16]

if such people recognize their "losing streaks" and decide against them, they are likely to discover that they were born with what it takes to win.

EXPERIMENTS AND EXERCISES

1. Your Adult Ethics

In developing your own code of Adult ethics, examine all those areas where your life touches the lives of others—where your opinions affect people who may be living a great distance from you and/or who may be extremely different from you.

Also examine your behavior and attitudes toward your total environment, including the inanimate as well as the animate world.

From your Adult ask:

• Who and what do *I* value?

• Who and what do *I* live for?

• Who and what would *I* die for?

• What does my life mean to me now?

• What could it mean?

• What does my life mean to others now? Others to come?

• Do I act in such a way as to preserve and enhance creation?

• What is *really* important?

List the five things you value most in life.

1. _____
2. _____
3. _____
4. _____
5. _____

Now rate your values in their priority.

1. _____
2. _____
3. _____
4. _____
5. _____

Study your priority list. Ask yourself:

• How do my values relate to my home life, my social life, my job?

• How do they relate to my Parent and Child ego states?

• Does the way I am living my life now reflect what I say I value?

2. Adult Questions on Your Life

If you are beginning to think at a deep level about who you really are, why you are, what you are really doing with your life, and where your present patterns will lead you, let your Adult become more aware by asking:

• Who do I feel I am? (from my Child experience)

• Who do I believe I am? (from my Parent opinions)

• Who do I believe I am? (from my Adult data-processing)

• Do other people treat me like a parent, adult, or child? (spouse, children, friends, business associates)

• Who do I want to be? (today, in 5 years, 10 years, 20 years)

• What potentials do I have for becoming that person?

• What are the barriers?

• What am I going to do about the potentials and barriers?

• Do I value that which enhances my potentials?

• Do I value that which helps others develop their potentials?

• How can I become more of the winner I was born to be?

Footnotes and References

CHAPTER ONE "Winners and Losers"

1. Martin Buber, *Hasidism and Modern Man* (New York: Harper & Row, 1958), pp. 138-144.
2. Karen Horney, *Self Analysis* (New York: W. W. Norton, 1942), p. 23.
3. Muriel James, *What Do You Do With Them Now That You've Got Them? Transactional Analysis for Moms and Dads* (Reading, Mass.: Addison-Wesley, 1974), pp. 4-5, 12.
4. Frederick S. Perls, *Gestalt Therapy Verbatim* (Lafayette, Calif.: Real People Press, 1969), p. 29.
5. Frederick S. Perls, *In and Out the Garbage Pail* (Lafayette, Calif.: Real People Press, 1969), n.p.
6. Abraham Levitsky and Frederick S. Perls, "The Rules and Games of Gestalt Therapy." Joen Fagan and Irma Lee Shepherd, Eds., *Gestalt Therapy Now* (Palo Alto: Science and Behavior Books, 1970), pp. 140-149.
7. J.L. Moreno, "The Viennese Origins of the Encounter Movement, Paving the Way for Existentialism, Group Psychotherapy, and Psychodrama," *Group Psychotherapy,* Vol. XXII, No. 1-2, 1969, pp. 7-16.
8. Perls, *Gestalt Therapy Verbatim,* p. 121.
9. *Ibid.,* p. 66.
10. *Ibid.,* p. 67.
11. *Ibid.,* p. 236.
12. Eric Berne, *Games People Play* (New York: Grove Press, 1964; André Deutsch, Ltd.).
13. Eric Berne, *Principles of Group Treatment* (New York: Oxford University Press, 1964).
14. *Ibid.,* p. 216.

CHAPTER TWO "An Overview of Transactional Analysis"

1. Perls, *Gestalt Therapy Verbatim,* p. 40.
2. *See* Dorothy Jongeward, *Transactional Analysis Overview* (Reading, Mass.: Addison-Wesley, 1973). A cassette.
3. Eric Berne, *Transactional Analysis in Psychotherapy* (New York: Grove Press, 1961; Souvenir Press of London), pp. 17-43.
   Cf. Paul McCormick and Leonard Campos, *Introduce Yourself to Transactional Analysis: A TA Handbook* (Stockton, Calif.: San Joaquin TA Study Group, distributed by Transactional Pub., 3155 College Ave., Berkeley, Calif., 94705, 1969).
   Also see John M. Dusay, "Transactional Analysis," in *A Layman's Guide to Psychiatry and Psychoanalysis* by Eric Berne (New York: Simon and Schuster, 3rd ed., 1968), pp. 277-306.
4. Berne, *Principles of Group Treatment,* p. 364
5. *Ibid.,* p. 281.
6. Berne, *Transactional Analysis in Psychotherapy,* p. 32.
7. Berne, *Games People Play,* pp. 29-64.
8. *Ibid.,* p. 29.
9. *See* Eric Berne, *The Structure and Dynamics of Organizations and Groups* (Philadelphia: J. B. Lippincott, 1963).
10. *See* Claude M. Steiner, *Games Alcoholics Play: The Analysis of Life Scripts* (New York: Grove Press, 1971).
    Cf. David Steere, "Freud on the 'Gallows Transaction,'" *Transactional Analysis Bulletin,* Vol. 9, No. 1 (Jan. 1970), pp. 3-5.
11. Eric Berne, "Transactional Analysis," in *Active Psychotherapy,* Harold Greenwald, Ed. (New York: Atherton Press, 1967), p. 125.
12. Berne, *Games People Play,* p. 64.
13. Berne, *Principles of Group Treatment,* pp. 269-278.
14. *See* Thomas A. Harris, *I'm OK—You're OK* (New York: Harper & Row, 1969).
15. Eric Berne, "Standard Nomenclature, Transactional Nomenclature," *Transactional Analysis Bulletin,* Vol. 8, No. 32 (Oct. 1969), p. 112.
    Cf. Zelig Selinger, "The Parental Second Position in Treatment," *Transactional Analysis Bulletin,* Vol. 6, No. 21 (Jan. 1967), p. 29.
16. Muriel James, "The Downscripting of Women for 115 Generations: A Historical Kaleidoscope," *Transactional Analysis Journal,* Vol. 3, No. 2 (Jan. 1973), pp. 15-22.
17. Greenwald, *op. cit.,* p. 128.

CHAPTER THREE "The Human Hunger for Strokes and Time Structuring"

1. Berne, *Games People Play,* p. 15
   For a focus on stroking in families, see James, *What Do You Do With Them Now That You've Got Them?* pp. 16-17.

2. R. Spitz, "Hospitalism: Genesis of Psychiatric Conditions in Early Childhood," *Psychoanalytic Study of the Child,* 1945, **1**: 53-74. *See also* "Hospitalism: A Follow-Up Report" and "Anaclitic Depression," *Ibid.,* **2**: 113-117 and 312-342.

3. Berne, *The Structure and Dynamics of Organizations and Groups,* p. 157.

4. Film, *Second Chance,* American Medical Association, 6644 Sierra Lane, Dublin, California 94566.

5. *See* Dorothy Jongeward and Contributors, *Everybody Wins: Transactional Analysis Applied to Organizations* (Reading, Mass.: Addison-Wesley, 1973) pp. 76-78.

6. Jacqui Lee Schiff with Beth Day, *All My Children* (New York: M. Evans, distributed in association with J. B. Lippincott, 1971), pp. 210-211.

7. *Planned Parenthood Report,* published by Planned Parenthood World Population, 810 Seventh Ave., New York, 10019, Vol. 1, No. 5 (June-July 1970), p. 3.

8. Virginia M. Axline, *Dibs in Search of Self* (New York: Ballantine Books, 1964), pp. 85-86.

9. George R. Bach and Peter Wyden, *The Intimate Enemy* (New York: William Morrow, 1969), p. 302.

10. Berne, *Principles of Group Treatment,* pp. 314-315.

11. *See* Dorothy Jongeward and Contributors, pp. 72-78.

12. For information, write Thomas Gordon, Ph.D., Effectiveness Training Associates, Inc., 110 Euclid Ave., Pasadena, Calif., 91101.

13. Sidney M. Jourard, *Disclosing Man to Himself* (New York: Van Nostrand Reinhold, 1968), pp. 136-151.

14. Bernard Gunther, *Sense Relaxation* (New York: Macmillan, 1968), p. 13.

15. *Cf.* Eric Berne, "Social Dynamics: The Intimacy Equipment," *Transactional Analysis Bulletin,* Vol. 3, No. 9 (January, 1964), p. 113. *Also,* Vol. 3, No. 10 (April, 1964), p. 125.

CHAPTER FOUR "The Drama of Life Scripts"

1. Perls, *Gestalt Therapy Verbatim,* p. 47.

2. Berne, *Principles of Group Treatment,* p. 368.

3. *See* Dorothy Jongeward and Contributors, Chapter 1, "Organizations Have Scripts."

4. *See* Dorothy Jongeward and Dru Scott, *Affirmative Action for Women: A Practical Guide* (Reading, Mass.: Addison-Wesley, 1973), Chapter 2, "Women's Lack of Achievement: Then and Now."

5. *See* Dorothy Jongeward and Dru Scott, Chapters 1 and 2, "The Organization Woman: Then and Now" and "Women's Lack of Achievement: Then and Now."

6. Herbert Hendin, *Suicide and Scandinavia* (New York: Doubleday, Anchor Books Edition, 1965), p. 5.
7. *Oakland Tribune,* Oakland, Calif., Feb. 13, 1970, p. 10.
8. Eleanor Flexner, *Century of Struggle* (Cambridge: Belknap Press, Harvard University, 1959), pp. 9-12.
   See also Muriel James and Dorothy Jongeward, *The People Book: Transactional Analysis for Students* (Reading, Mass.: Addison-Wesley, 1975), Chapter 1.
9. *See* Dorothy Jongeward and Dru Scott, Chapter 2, "Women's Lack of Achievement: Then and Now."
10. Matina Horner, "Woman's Will to Fail," *Psychology Today,* Vol. 3, No. 6 (November 1969), pp. 36 ff.
    Cf. Dorothy Jongeward, "New Directions: Changing Family Patterns," *California State Marriage Counseling Quarterly,* **I,** No. 4 (May 1967).
11. Thomas Szasz, *The Myth of Mental Illness* (New York: Dell Publishing, 1961), p. 230.
12. Muriel James, "Ego States and Social Issues: Two Case Studies from the 1960s," *Transactional Analysis Journal,* Vol. 5, No. 1, (Jan. 1975). *Cf.* Muriel James, *Born to Love,* pp. 119-151.
13. Berne, *Principles of Group Treatment,* p. 310.
14. *Cf.* Leonard P. Campos, "Transactional Analysis of Witch Messages," *Transactional Analysis Bulletin,* Vol. 9, No. 34 (April 1970), p. 51. *See also* Claude M. Steiner, "The Treatment of Alcoholism," *Transactional Analysis Bulletin,* Vol. 6, No. 23 (July 1967), pp. 69-71.
15. Perls, *Gestalt Therapy Verbatim,* p. 42.
16. Claude Steiner, *Games Alcoholics Play* (New York: Grove Press, 1971), p. 49.
17. Perls, *Gestalt Theory Verbatim,* p. 42.
18. *Cf.* Stephen B. Karpman, "Fairy Tales and Script Drama Analysis," *Transactional Analysis Bulletin,* VII, No. 26 (April 1968), pp. 39-43.
19. Thomas Bullfinch, *The Age of the Fable* (New York: Heritage Press, 1958), p. 11.
20. *See* Dorothy Jongeward, "What Do You Do When Your Script Runs Out?" *Transactional Analysis Journal,* **2,** No. 2 (April 1972), pp. 78-81.
21. *Ibid.*
22. *Cf. also* William Bridges, "How Does a Narrative Mean?" (unpublished paper), Mills College, Oakland, Calif.
23. W. R. Poindexter, "Hippies and the Little Lame Prince," *Transactional Analysis Bulletin,* VII, No. 25 (Jan. 1968), p. 18.
24. James Aggrey, "The Parable of the Eagle," in *Darkness and Light* (Leighton Buzzard, Bedfordshire, England: The Faith Press Ltd., n.d.).

CHAPTER FIVE "Parenting and The Parent Ego State"

1. *Dictionary of Quotations,* "Notebook of a Printer" (Reader's Digest Assoc., 1966), p. 114.
   Cf. Muriel James, *What Do You Do With Them Now That You've Got Them?*

2. Harry Harlow, "The Nature of Love," *The American Psychologist,* 13 (12): 673-685, 1958.
   Also see H.F. Harlow and M.K. Harlow, "Social Deprivation in Monkeys," *Scientific American,* 207:136-46 (Nov. 1962).

3. Source unknown.

4. Selma Fraiberg, *The Magic Years* (New York: Scribner's, 1959), p. 135.

5. Erik H. Erikson, "Identity and the Life Cycle," *Psychological Issues* (monograph), Vol. I, No. 1, (New York: International Univ. Press), p. 68.

6. Karen Horney, *Neurosis and Human Growth* (New York: W. W. Norton, 1950), p. 65.

7. Frederick S. Perls, "Four Lectures." Joen Fagan and Irma Lee Shepherd, Eds., *Gestalt Theory Now* (Palo Alto: Science and Behavior Books, 1970), p. 15.

8. Carl R. Rogers and Barry Stevens, *Person to Person: The Problem of Being* (Walnut Creek, Calif.: Real People Press, 1967), pp. 9-10.

9. Eleanor Roosevelt, *This Is My Story* (New York: Harper, 1937), p. 21.

10. Urie Bronfenbrenner, "The Changing American Child," *Journal of Social Issues,* XVII, No. 1 (1961) pp. 6-18.

11. Urie Bronfenbrenner, *Two Worlds of Childhood, U.S. and U.S.S.R.* (New York: Russell Sage Foundation, 1970), p. 104.

12. Evan S. Connell, Jr., *Mrs. Bridge* (New York: Viking Press, 1958), p. 13.

13. *Cf.* Jacqui Lee Schiff with Beth Day, *op. cit.,* n.p.

14. *See* Muriel James, *What Do You Do With Them Now That You've Got Them?* (Reading, Mass.: Addison-Wesley, 1974).
    See also Muriel James, "Self Reparenting: Theory and Process," *Transactional Analysis Journal,* Vol. 4, No. 3 (July 1974), pp. 32-39.

15. Muriel James, "The Use of Structural Analyses in Pastoral Counseling," *Pastoral Psychology,* Vol. 19, 187 (Oct. 1968), pp. 8-15.
    See also Muriel James, *Born to Love: Transactional Analysis in the Church* (Reading, Mass.: Addison-Wesley, 1973).
    Cf. Muriel James and Louis Savary, *The Power at the Bottom of the Will: Transactional Analysis and the Religious Experience* (New York: Harper & Row, 1974).

16. *Psychologia—An International Journal of Psychology in the Orient,* Ed., Koji Sato, Kyoto Univ., Vol. 8, No. 1-2, 1965.

CHAPTER SIX "Childhood and The Child Ego State"

1. A. A. Milne, *Winnie the Pooh* (London: Methuen, 1965), pp. 1-18.
2. Fraiberg, *op. cit.,* p. 109.
3. Compiled by Lee Parr McGrath and Joan Scobey, *What Is a Mother* (New York: Simon & Schuster, 1968), n.p.
4. Berne, *Principles of Group Treatment,* p. 283.
5. Fraiberg, *op. cit.,* p. 109.
6. Berne, *Games People Play,* p. 173.
7. Berne, *Principles of Group Treatment,* p. 305.
8. *Oakland Tribune,* Oct. 15, 1967.
9. *See* Muriel James, *What Do You Do With Them Now That You've Got Them?,* pp. 33-34.
10. Perls, *Gestalt Therapy Verbatim,* p. 236.

CHAPTER SEVEN "Personal and Sexual Identity"

1. Billie T. Chandler, *Japanese Family Life with Doll-and-Flower Arrangements* (Rutland, Vt.: Charles Tuttle, 1963), pp. 29-30.
2. Caroline Bird, *Born Female* (New York: Simon & Schuster, 1969), p. 183.
3. Erich Fromm, *The Art of Loving* (New York: Harper & Row, 1956), pp. 18-19.
4. Anthony Storr, *The Integrity of the Personality* (Maryland: Penguin Books, 1966), p. 43.
5. Virginia Satir, *Conjoint Family Therapy* (Palo Alto: Science and Behavior Books, 1964), pp. 29, 48-53.
6. Merle Miller, "What It Means to Be a Homosexual" (New York Times Service, *San Francisco Chronicle,* Jan. 25, 1971).
7. Peter and Barbara Wyden, *Growing Up Straight* (New York: Stein and Day, 1968).
8. *Cf.* Dorothy Jongeward, "Sex, Roles, and Identity: The Emergence of Women," *Calif. State Marriage Counseling Quarterly,* I, No. 4 (May, 1967).
9. Sidney Jourard, *The Transparent Self* (Princeton, N.J.: D. Van Nostrand, 1964), p. 46.
   Cf. Muriel James, *Born to Love,* pp. 119-122.
10. *See* Dorothy Jongeward and Contributors, *op. cit.*
    For Seminars about Career Women, see pp. 106-109, 152-182.
11. *See* Dorothy Jongeward and Dru Scott, *op. cit.,* pp. 203-250.
12. Erikson, *op. cit.,* p. 68.
13. The Child Study Association of America, *What to Tell Your Children About Sex* (New York: Pocket Books, 1964), p. 22.
14. *See* Renatus Hartogs, *Four-Letter Word Games* (New York: Dell Publishing, 1968).

15. *See* Alexander Lowen, *The Betrayal of the Body* (London: Macmillan, 1969).
16. Muriel James, "Curing Impotency with Transactional Analysis," *Transactional Analysis Journal*, Vol. 1, No. 1 (Jan. 1971), pp. 88-93.

CHAPTER EIGHT "Stamp Collecting and Game Playing"

 1. Berne, *Principles of Group Treatment*, pp. 286-288.
    Cf. Muriel James, *What Do You Do With Them Now That You've Got Them?*, pp. 45-57.
 2. *Ibid.*, p. 308.
 3. Haim G. Ginott, *Between Parent and Child* (New York: Macmillan, 1967), pp. 29-30.
    For techniques for recognizing family games, see John James, "The Game Plan," *Transactional Analysis Journal*, Vol. 3, No. 4 (Oct. 1973), pp. 194-197.
 4. *See* Berne, *Principles of Group Treatment*, pp. 278-311. *See also* Berne, *Games People Play*, p. 53.
    For games commonly played in the church, see Muriel James, *Born to Love*, pp. 95-110.
 5. Berne, *Games People Play*, p. 102.
 6. Dorothy Jongeward, "Games People Play—In the Office, *P.S. For Private Secretaries*," Vol. 13, No. 12 (June 1970), Roterford, Conn.: Bureau of Business Practices, Section II, pp. 1-8.
 7. Berne, *Games People Play*, p. 95.
 8. Perls, *Gestalt Therapy Verbatim*, p. 53.
 9. For a detailed description of how games are adapted, see Dorothy Jongeward and Contributors, *op. cit.*, Chapter 2, "Games Cost Organizations Money," pp. 23-49.
10. *Ibid.*, Chapter 3, "Games Can Be Stopped Many Ways," pp. 51-59.
11. *See* Dorothy Jongeward and Muriel James, *Winning With People: Group Exercises in Transactional Analysis* (Reading, Mass.: Addison-Wesley, 1973), pp. 80-81.
12. Stephen Karpman, "Options," *Transactional Analysis Journal*, Vol. 1, No. 1 (Jan. 1971), pp. 79-87. *Cf.* John James, "The Game Plan," p. 195.
13. Franklin Ernst, *Activity of Listening* (monograph, 1st ed., Mar. 1968, available through Golden Gate Foundation for Group Treatment, Inc., P.O. Box 1141, Vallejo, Calif.) pp. 13-14.
14. Taken from *Gestalt Therapy*, by Frederick Perls, M.D., Ph.D., Ralph F. Hefferline, Ph.D., and Paul Goodman, Ph.D. Copyright © 1951 by Frederick Perls, M.D., Ph.D., Ralph F. Hefferline, Ph.D., and Paul Goodman, Ph.D. Used by permission of The Julian Press, a division of Crown Publishers, Inc.

15. *Ibid.,* p. 168.
16. *See* Alexander Lowen, *op. cit.,* pp. 237-250.
17. Perls, *Gestalt Therapy Verbatim,* p. 127. *Cf.* Muriel James, *What Do You Do With Them Now That You've Got Them?,* pp. 61-71.
18. *Cf.* Muriel Schiffman, *Self Therapy: Techniques for Personal Growth* (Self Therapy Press, Menlo Park, California, 1967), n.p.
19. *Cf.* William C. Schutz, *Joy* (New York: Grove Press, 1967), p. 66.
20. *Cf.* W. Cheney, "Hamlet: His Script Checklist," *Transactional Analysis Bulletin,* Vol. 7, No. 27 (July 1968), pp. 66-68.
    Cf. also Claude Steiner, "A Script Checklist," *Transactional Analysis Bulletin,* Vol. 6, No. 22 (April 1967), pp. 38-39, 56.

CHAPTER NINE "The Adult Ego State"

1. Berne, *The Structure and Dynamics of Organizations and Groups,* p. 137.
2. Berne, *Transactional Analysis in Psychotherapy,* p. 37.
3. Berne, *Principles of Group Treatment,* p. 220.
4. Berne, *Transactional Analysis in Psychotherapy,* p. 77.
5. Berne, *Games People Play,* p. 24.
6. Berne, *Principles of Group Treatment,* pp. 306-307. For clarification on energy and the sense of self as it is cathected, see Muriel James and Louis Savary, *The Power at the Bottom of the Will,* pp. 145-146.
7. Berne, *Transactional Analysis in Psychotherapy,* pp. 39-40.
   Cf. Muriel James, *Born to Love,* pp. 48-52.
8. *Ibid.,* p. 31.
9. *Ibid.,* p. 46.
10. *Ibid.,* p. 62.
11. Berne, *Principles of Group Treatment,* p. 306.
12. Berne, *Transactional Analysis in Psychotherapy,* p. 146.
13. Berne, *The Structure and Dynamics of Organizations and Groups,* p. 137.
14. Berne, *Principles of Group Treatment,* p. 90.
    See also Muriel James, *What Do You Do With Them Now That You've Got Them?* pp. 23-43.
15. Perls, *Gestalt Therapy Verbatim,* pp. 211-212.
16. *Ibid.,* p. 66.
17. *Ibid.,* p. 70.
18. Berne, *Principles of Group Treatment,* p. 311.
19. *Ibid.,* p. 221.
20. Perls, *Gestalt Therapy Verbatim,* p. 69.

CHAPTER TEN "Autonomy and Adult Ethics"

1. Eric Berne, *Sex in Human Loving* (New York: Simon & Schuster, 1970), p. 194.
2. Berne, *Games People Play*, p. 178.
3. Perls, *Gestalt Therapy Verbatim*, p. 44.
4. Berne, *Games People Play*, p. 180.
5. Martin Buber, *Between Man and Man* (New York: Macmillan, 1968), p. 78.
6. Viktor E. Frankl, *The Doctor and the Soul* (New York: Alfred Knopf, 1957), pp. xviii, xix.
7. Abraham H. Maslow, *Eupsychian Management* (Homewood, Ill.: Richard D. Irwin and The Dorsey Press, 1965), p. 161.
8. Berne, *Transactional Analysis in Psychotherapy*, pp. 194-195.
9. *Ibid.*, p. 193.
10. *Ibid.*, p. 195.
11. Drs. Roberto Kertesz and Jorge A. Savorgnan of the University of Buenos Aires, Faculty of Medicine, first used "technics" as a term to describe the Adult in the Adult.
12. Erich Fromm, *The Revolution of Hope* (New York: Bantam, 1968), p. 16.
13. Abraham H. Maslow, *Motivation and Personality* (New York: Harper & Row, 1954), pp. 211-214.
14. Kertesz *et al.*, claim the Adult's "I'm OK/You're OK" position is quite different from the manic Child's "I'm OK/You're OK" position.
15. Eric Berne, "Editor's Page," *Transactional Analysis Bulletin*, Vol. 8, No. 29 (Jan. 1969), pp. 7-8.
16. Copyright, 1955, by E. E. Cummings. Reprinted from E. E. Cummings: *A Miscellany* edited by George J. Firmage by permission of Harcourt Brace Jovanovich, Inc.

Index

game, in childhood, 189
theme and purpose of, 221
When, waiting for the magical
rescue, 5
*Why Does This Always Happen to
Me?* game, 98
Winnie-the-Pooh as prototype of
Little Professor, 149
Winner/loser checklist
(experiment), 13-14
Winner/loser rating (experiment),
14
Winners, 1-3
and Adult contract, 267
and Adult ethics, 302
and authenticity, 1
avoiding contamination, 258
avoiding stamps and games,
232
and decisions, 289
and family scripts, 84-85
and feelings, 210
giving up games, 232
and gold stamps, 216
vs. losers, and Child ego state,
169

Withdrawal, description of, 59-60
a pattern of adaptation, 159,
161
questioning from the Adult,
268-69
Wooden Leg game, and
childhood games, 189
and parental absence, 122-23
theme and purpose of, 222
Work, or activities, 61-64
and your parents (experiment),
132-33
Working environment and
positive strokes, 49
World problems, winner's
response to, 3, 301-2
Worry and the Child ego state,
167

Yes, But game, description of,
223
stopping of, 231

Zeus script, 99

There's an epidemic with 27 million victims. And no visible symptoms.

It's an epidemic of people who can't read.

Believe it or not, 27 million Americans are functionally illiterate, about one adult in five.

The solution to this problem is you... when you join the fight against illiteracy. So call the Coalition for Literacy at toll-free **1-800-228-8813** and volunteer.

Volunteer Against Illiteracy. The only degree you need is a degree of caring.